Social Change and Development

Modernization, Dependency, and World-System Theories

Alvin Y. So

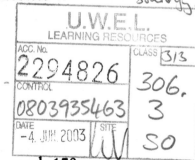

Sage Library of Social Research 178

SAGE PUBLICATIONS
The International Professional Publishers
Newbury Park   London   New Delhi

For information address:

 SAGE Publications, Inc.
2455 Teller Road
Newbury Park, California 91320
E-mail: order@sagepub.com

SAGE Publications Ltd.
6 Bonhill Street
London EC2A 4PU
United Kingdom

SAGE Publications India Pvt. Ltd.
M-32 Market
Greater Kailash I
New Delhi 110 048 India

Printed in the United States of America

Library of Congress Cataloging-in-Publication Data

So, Alvin Y., 1953-
    Social change and development : modernization, dependency, and
  world-system theories / Alvin Y. So.
       p.   cm. — (Sage library of social research : v. 178)
    Includes bibliographical references.
    ISBN 0-8039-3546-3. — ISBN 0-8039-3547-1 (pbk.)
       1. Economic development. 2. Economic development—Social aspects.
    3. Dependency. 4. Capitalism. I. Title. II. Series.
    HD75.S617   1990
    306.3—dc20   89-28110
                                                               CIP

01 18

Contents

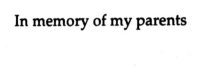
In memory of my parents

Preface

I have been teaching a course on development for the past five years, and I have never been able to find a truly suitable textbook for my classes. Those currently available on this subject are mostly old and fail to include new theories, such as the world-system perspective. Those that articulate a sophisticated theoretical analysis often fail to provide an objective review of other development theories. While there is no lack of good empirical studies, they are too specialized to provide a comprehensive review of the critical issues in this field. Often I have ended up simply adopting a collection of readings on theories and empirical studies, but these have often proven to be too difficult for undergraduates, and even for beginning graduate students, to understand.

However, it was not just these problems, but my arguments with my colleagues that finally prompted me to write a book on development. A year ago I attended a presentation by Andre Gunder Frank, where I heard him say that "the modernization school is dead; nothing new has come out of this school during the last two decades." On another occasion, one of my colleagues on a dissertation committee remarked that "the world-system perspective is just another variant of the dependency perspective. Since both have run their course in the 1980s, we should not pay any more attention to them." But is it true that the modernization school, the dependency school, and the world-system school have nothing new to offer the field of development in the 1980s? I believe the real problem is that, after reading a few classics from these three schools, many scholars have failed to follow up on new publications. Consequently, they have missed the exciting research carried out by the three schools during the last two decades.

7

The goal of this book is to show that these three schools are still very much alive in the 1980s. They have been revitalized by researchers who have listened to the strong points made by their critics and have incorporated suggested changes in their recent studies. In this respect, social scientists should judge the merits of these three schools by their recent publications (which I call the "new" modernization studies, the "new" dependency studies, and the world-system studies at "global" and "national" levels) rather than by their "classical" empirical studies, published before the early 1970s.

The most gratifying part of writing this book is to be able to acknowledge the many debts I have incurred. I first began to be interested in development when I took an exciting undergraduate course from Professor Ambrose King at the Chinese University of Hong Kong. I became more and more interested in this field after I took a number of stimulating seminars from Professors Lucie Cheng, John Horton, Bill Roy, Sam Surace, and Maurice Zeitlin at the University of California, Los Angeles. Since I started my teaching career at the University of Hawaii, I have benefited greatly from sharing my ideas on development theories with Professors Hagen Koo, Ravi Palat, Walter Goldfrank, Bob Stauffer, Pat Steinhoff, and Steven Yeh, and members of the Political Economy Study Group. I am also grateful for the support of Professor Don Topping, the director of the Social Science Research Institute at the University of Hawaii, for reducing my teaching load while I was preparing this book for publication.

In addition, I want to thank several graduate students at the University of Hawaii. Suwarsono and Macrina Abenoja provided very helpful comments on an earlier draft of the manuscript. Although Sungnam Cho did not have the time to coauthor this volume with me, I am still deeply appreciative of her contributions in helping me to prepare for the book proposal. And, of course, the stimulating questions of my undergraduate students in Sociology 316 over the past five years have greatly helped me to clarify my arguments on theories of development.

Furthermore, I want to thank Professors Herbert Barringer and Joe Leon for offering their expertise on how to look for a good publisher. The critical remarks made by two anonymous reviewers for Sage Publications have been very helpful to me in my work on revising the manuscript. I am also grateful to Blaise Donnelly, an associate editor at Sage, for his sympathetic understanding about the slow progress of my writing. My thanks go also to Professor Everett Wingert for his help in the preparation of the camera-ready artwork for the three figures in Chapter 4. Finally, I want to express my gratitude to my wife, Judy Chan So, who sustained me unfalteringly in the completion of this book while she was carrying twins.

Since my parents passed away while I was working on this project, I want to take this opportunity to dedicate this book to them. My parents lived through the joys and agonies of development in this century, and much of what I know about Third World development is reinforced for me through my fond memories of them.

Alvin Y. So

CHAPTER 1

Introduction:
The Power of Development Theories

Without theories, social scientists would find it difficult to carry out empirical research. Scientists use theories to help them define what needs to be studied, and to guide them in sharpening research questions and in deciding what evidence is necessary to support their arguments. In this respect, theories are very powerful research tools. Theories shape researchers' thinking processes, lay the foundation for their analytical frameworks, guide their research theses, and set their research agendas. In addition, theories lead researchers to adopt certain methodologies, attract them to examine certain data sets, and influence them to draw certain conclusions and policy implications.

For these reasons, theories demand social scientists' loyalty. When researchers have immersed themselves in a particular theoretical perspective, they tend to develop an "ethnocentric" outlook, thinking that their own theoretical perspective is the very best in the field. Consequently, they often look at other theoretical perspectives with contempt, and sometimes engage in attacks on those perspectives. This leads to heated academic debates as well as to "theory wars" in the literature.

At the height of such theory wars, academic debates are frequently turned into ideological debates, into struggles between *our* scientific theories and *their* ideological doctrines. During this period of ideological polarization, researchers often totally dismiss the other camp's theoretical perspectives, as if there could be nothing good in the other side's work. Only after the emotional debates have subsided can social scientists from different camps approach one another and begin to take the arguments of their critics seriously. Learning from their past mistakes, social scientists can gradually incorporate the strong points of their critics into their own theoretical perspectives. This incorporation may seem to amount to nothing more than putting new wine into old bottles, but the attempt to synthesize can help to revitalize old perspectives and to stimulate new directions in empirical studies.

Theories are not static entities. They attack other theories, and they defend their own arguments. After engaging in heated theoretical debates, they can transform themselves into better research tools than they were before. The field of development offers a perfect example of the dynamics of change in theoretical perspectives.

THE THREE DOMINANT SCHOOLS
IN THE FIELD OF DEVELOPMENT

In the late 1950s, the field of development was dominated by the modernization school. In the late 1960s, this school was challenged by the radical dependency school. In the late 1970s, the world-system school rose up to offer an alternative perspective from which to examine the issue of development. And in the late 1980s, it seems that these three schools are moving toward a convergence.

Focusing on the modernization, dependency, and world-system schools of development, this book is an attempt to examine the following five sets of questions:

(1) What explains the emergence of these three schools of development? In what historical context and through what theoretical heritage did these three schools emerge?

(2) In what ways are the three schools different from one another? What are their unique theoretical assumptions, key theories, and policy implications?

(3) What are the "classical" empirical studies for which these three schools are well known? To what extent were these studies informed by the theories of development?

(4) Why did critics attack these three schools of development? What was wrong with their theories and their "classical" empirical studies?

(5) How did these three schools respond to their critics? To what extent have they incorporated their critics' strong points into their theories? And to what extent are their "new" empirical studies different from their "classical" ones?

Through the above questions, this book will review the emergence, development, and transformation of each of the three dominant schools of development. First, the dynamic nature of the modernization school, the dependency school, and the world-system school over the past three decades will be illustrated—how they attacked other schools, how they defended themselves, and how they were transformed in the process of participating in the theoretical debates. Second, the power of each of these development theories in empirical studies will be addressed; the discussion will show how changing theoretical perspectives are accompanied by changing research questions, research agendas, research methodologies, and research findings. The final aim of this book is to show the distinctiveness of the world-system perspective. Although the literature often mixes the world-system school with the dependency school, it will be argued here that the two schools are quite different in terms of their theoretical frameworks, research foci, methodologies, and empirical studies. The world-system school has started a chain of innovative studies on the cyclical rhythms of the capitalist world-economy that go beyond the confines of dependency studies.

PLAN OF STUDY

This book is divided into three parts: Part I is on the modernization school; Part II, the dependency school; and Part III, the world-system school. Each part consists of three chapters, and in all parts the organization of the chapters is the same. The first chapter presents the historical context, theoretical heritage, key theories, basic assumptions, and policy implications of the school being discussed. The second chapter deals with the "classical" empirical studies of the school, and discusses the strengths and the criticisms of the classical theories. The third chapter examines responses to the critics, "new" empirical studies, and the strengths of the new theories of that school.

In presenting these three schools, I have adopted an approach that can be called a "generous interpretation." For example, in reviewing the key theories of the modernization school, I take on the perspective of a modernization researcher. I take the position of an advocate, presenting modernization theories in as strong a light as possible, trying to convince the reader of the merits of the modernization school. However, to be fair to the other two schools, I also interpret their theories and research "generously." In other words, I bring out the best of their arguments and do not address their weaknesses. Only in the sections on criticism do I assume the role of a critic; in that role, I try to convince the reader that there are indeed serious problems in the theories and research of the school under discussion. Since this book is intended for use as a textbook, it is my hope that this mode of presentation will force students to think through the critical issues of development. They will have to form their own independent judgments as to whether they believe in the strengths of a particular school or in the arguments of its critics.

It should be noted that the focus of this book is on theories, not on theorists. Consequently, theorists' names are included in the discussion only if their theories and empirical studies provide useful examples of the typical approach of the modernization, dependency, or world-system school. Obviously, this book cannot review all of the good theories and empirical studies in the field of development. Accordingly, rather than touch upon a large number of them in a casual manner, the strategy of this book is to concentrate on about a dozen key theories and two dozen empirical studies, to discuss these works in detail, and to spell out their implications for the literature of development.

Part I

THE MODERNIZATION SCHOOL

CHAPTER 2

The Modernization Perspective

THE HISTORICAL CONTEXT

The modernization school was a historical product of three crucial events in the post-World War II era. First, there was the rise of the United States as a superpower. While other Western nations (like Great Britain, France, and Germany) were weakened by World War II, the United States emerged from the war strengthened, and became a world leader with the implementation of the Marshall Plan to reconstruct war-torn Western Europe. In the 1950s, the United States practically took over the responsibility of managing the affairs of the whole world. Second, there was the spread of a united world communist movement. The Soviet Union extended its influence not only to Eastern Europe, but also to China and Korea in Asia. Third, there was the disintegration of the European colonial empires in Asia, Africa, and Latin America, giving birth to many new nation-states in the Third World. These nascent nation-states were in search of a model of development to promote their economy and to enhance their political independence. In such historical context, it was natural that American political elites encouraged their social scientists to study the Third World nation-states, to promote economic development and political stability in the Third World, so as to avoid losing the new states to the Soviet communist bloc (Chirot 1981, p. 261-262).

With generous support from the U.S. government and private foundations, a new generation of young political scientists, economists, sociologists, psychologists, anthropologists, and demographers published dissertations and monographs on the previously little-researched Third World states. An interdisciplinary modernization school was in the making in the 1950s. In Almond's (1987, p. 437) words, modernization studies were "growth industries" until the mid-1960s.

It is appropriate to characterize modernization studies as belonging to a school because their researchers formed an energetic "social movement with its own sources of funds, close interpersonal links and rivalries, its own journals and publication series, a sense of shared mission and camaraderie, and, of course, its hangers on, peripheral allies, and even its acceptable heretics" (Chirot 1981, p. 261). For example, the Social Science Research Council generously funded the Committee on Comparative Politics to embark on a program of conferences and publications by Princeton University Press to study the communications media (Pye 1963), bureaucracy (LaPalombara 1963), education (Coleman 1965), political culture (Pye and Verba 1965), political parties (LaPalombara and Weiner 1966), and crises in Third World modernization (Binder et al. 1971). The journal *Economic Development and Cultural Change* published the findings of the modernization studies.

THE THEORETICAL HERITAGE

From the very beginning, the modernization school was in search of a theory. It adopted both an evolutionary theory and a functionalist theory in its effort to illuminate the modernization of Third World countries. Since the evolutionary theory helped to explain the transition from traditional to modern society in Western Europe in the nineteenth century, many modernization researchers thought that it would shed some light on the modernization of Third World countries. As Portes (1980) and Rhodes (1968) point out, the evolutionary theory was highly influential in the shaping of the modernization school. Furthermore, since many prominent members of the modernization school—such as Daniel Lerner, Marion Levy, Neil Smelser, Samuel Eisenstadt, and Gabriel Almond—were schooled in the functionalist theory, their modernization studies are inevitably stamped with the functionalist trademark as well. Accordingly, it is worthwhile to review the evolutionary and the functionalist heritage that informed the modernization school.

Evolutionary Theory

Evolutionary theory was born in the early nineteenth century—in the aftermath of the Industrial Revolution and the French Revolution. These two revolutions not only shattered the old social order but also laid the foundation for a new one. The Industrial Revolution, with its application of science and technology, led to rising productivity, a new factory production system, and the conquest of the world market. The French Revolution created a whole new political order based on equality, liberty, freedom, and parliamentary democracy. In observing this changing social, economic, and political order, evolutionary theorists have used different labels to characterize the old and the new societies, such as Tonnies's *gemeinschaft* (community) and *gesellschaft* (society), Durkheim's mechanical and organic solidarity, Spencer's military and industrial society, and Comte's theological, metaphysical, and positive stages.

The classical evolutionary theory had the following features (see Comte 1964). First, it assumed that social change is unidirectional; that is, human society invariably moves along one direction from a primitive to an advanced state, thus the fate of human evolution is predetermined. Second, it imposed a value judgment on the evolutionary process—the movement toward the final phase is good because it represents progress, humanity, and civilization. Third, it assumed that the rate of social change is slow, gradual, and piecemeal—evolutionary, not revolutionary. The evolution from a simple, primitive society to a complex, modern society will take centuries to complete. Another part of the theoretical heritage of the modernization school is the functionalist theory of Talcott Parsons (1951; Parsons and Shils 1951), whose concepts—such as system, functional imperative, homeostatic equilibrium, and pattern variables—have entered into the works of many modernization theorists.

Functionalist Theory

Parsons was originally trained as a biologist, and his early training greatly influenced his formulation of a functionalist theory. For Parsons, human society is like a biological organism and can be studied as such. The organism metaphor provides the key to understanding Parsons's work.

First of all, the different parts of a biological organism can be said to correspond to the different institutions that make up a society. Just as the parts that make up a biological organism (such as the eye and the hand) are interrelated and interdependent in their interaction with one another, so the institutions in a society (such as the economy and the government) are closely related to one another. Parsons uses the concept of "system" to denote the harmonious coordination among institutions.

Second, just as each part of a biological organism performs a specific function for the good of the whole, so each institution performs a certain function for the stability and growth of the society. Parsons formulates the concept of "functional imperatives," arguing that there are four crucial functions that every society must perform, otherwise the society will die:

- adaptation to the environment—performed by the economy
- goal attainment—performed by the government
- integration (linking the institutions together)—performed by the legal institutions and religion
- latency (pattern maintenance of values from generation to generation)—performed by the family and education

These four functions constitute the scheme known as AGIL (for adaptation, goal attainment, integration, latency).

Third, the organism analogy also led Parsons to formulate the concept of "homeostatic equilibrium." A biological organism is always in a uniform state. If one of the parts changes, then the other parts will change accordingly in order to restore equilibrium and reduce tension. For example, if an organism needs to maintain a normal body temperature of 98.6 degrees, then the body will sweat in very hot temperatures and shiver in very cold temperatures in order to maintain the desired norm. According to Parsons, society also observes the rhythms needed for homeostasis; there are constant interactions among institutions to maintain homeostatic equilibrium. When one institution experiences social change, it causes a chain reaction of changes in other institutions so as to restore equilibrium. From this angle, Parsons's social system is not a static, stationary, unchanging entity; rather, the institutions that constitute the system are always changing and adjusting.

It has often been pointed out that Parsons's scheme has a conservative bias, because of the assumption that society is striving for harmony, stability, equilibrium, and the status quo. This conservative bias may be a result of the influence of the organism analogy on Parsons's thinking. As the left hand of the human body will not fight with the right hand, so Parsons assumes that institutions will generally be in harmony, rather than in conflict, with one another. Furthermore, as a biological organism will not kill itself, so Parsons assumes that society will not destroy its existing institutions.

Finally, Parsons has formulated the concept of "pattern variables" to distinguish traditional societies from modern societies. Pattern variables are the key social relations that are enduring, recurring, and embedded in the cultural system—the highest and the most important system in Parsons's theoretical framework. For Parsons, there are five sets of pattern variables.

The first set is the *affective* versus *affective-neutral* relationship. In traditional societies, social relationships tend to have an affective component—personal, emotional, and face-to-face. Even the employer-employee relationship is affective in traditional societies. Employers treat employees as household members, and will not discharge them even when their companies are losing money. In modern societies, social relationships tend to have an affective-neutral component—impersonal, detached, and indirect. In modern societies, employers must treat employees in an affective-neutral manner; they fire employees when necessary, otherwise economic productivity suffers and companies lose their profitability.

The second set of pattern variables is the *particularistic* versus *universalistic* relationship. In traditional societies, people tend to associate with members of the same social circle; for example, they work for a relative's firm or buy from a neighborhood store. Since they know one another very well, they treat each other particularly. They trust one another and feel an obligation to fulfill social promises. Usually an oral agreement is all that is necessary to carry out a business transaction. In modern societies, where there is a high density of population, people are forced to interact with strangers frequently, and they tend to interact using universalistic norms. For example, bank tellers routinely ask for identification in cashing a check, and will not cash any check unless all of the proper documents have been presented. In modern societies there are written rules that spell out the rights and responsibilities of the parties in each business transaction.

The third set of pattern variables is *collective orientation* versus *self-orientation*. In traditional societies, loyalty is often owed to the collectivity, such as the family, the community, or the tribal state. People are asked to sacrifice their own interests for the sake of fulfilling collective obligations. This stress on a collective orientation is a means of avoiding social instability caused by individual innovation, creativity, and imagination. In modern societies, self-orientation is stressed—encouragement to be yourself, to develop your own talent, to try your best, and to build up your own career is everywhere. This stress on self-orientation serves to energize the individual, leading to technological innovation and rising economic productivity.

The fourth set of pattern variables is *ascription* versus *achievement*. In traditional societies, a person is evaluated by his or her ascribed status. During a job interview, for example, the employer would ask for the names of the applicant's parents and other relatives. Hiring is frequently based on whether the employer is a good friend or a relative of the applicant. In modern societies, a person is evaluated by his or her achieved status. During job recruiting, the employer cares most about the technical qualifications and past job experience of the applicant. In modern societies, evaluation has to be carried out on an achievement basis because of keen market competition. Employers cannot afford to hire incompetent people, because if they do their firms will be easily squeezed out of business.

The fifth and the final set of pattern variables is *functionally diffused* versus *functionally specific* relationships. In traditional societies, roles tend to be functionally diffused. For example, the employer's role is not just to hire employees; frequently it involves the training of the employee through apprenticeship, the responsibility of being the employee's guardian, the provision of living arrangements, and more. This functionally diffused role is, of course, highly inefficient. Employees take years to learn technical skills, and training is individualistic and nonsystematic. In modern societies, roles tend to be functionally specific. The employer's role, for example, is very narrowly defined. The employer has limited obligations to the employee, and their relationship seldom extends beyond the work sphere. Because they are able to avoid other obligations to each other, the employer and employee can pay more attention to increasing efficiency and productivity.

In the following section, the influence of evolutionary and functionalist theories on the formulation of the theories of modernization will be examined. It should be pointed out that the modernization school does not lend itself easily to simple characterization. Different disciplines raise different research questions, and different area specialists highlight different aspects of the modernization process. In what follows, therefore, only four modernization theories have been selected to illustrate the viewpoints of sociologists, economists, and political scientists concerning the issues of Third World development.

THE SOCIOLOGICAL APPROACH: LEVY'S RELATIVELY MODERNIZED SOCIETIES

How is modernization defined? Why does modernization occur? How do relatively modernized societies differ from relatively nonmodernized societies? And what are the prospects for the modernization of Third World countries? These are the central questions that run through Levy's (1967) work.

First, how is modernization defined? For Levy, modernization is defined by the extent to which tools and inanimate sources of power are utilized. Obviously, there is no society totally lacking in tools and inanimate sources of power, so modernization is only a matter of degree. Based on this premise, Levy distinguishes relatively modernized societies and relatively nonmodernized societies as two locations at the opposite ends of a continuum. Levy considers Great Britain, modern Japan, and the United States to represent relatively modernized societies, and China, India, and the Trobriand Islands to be examples of relatively nonmodernized societies. Levy further argues that all relatively nonmodernized societies have more in common with each other, as regards social structure, than with any relatively modernized societies. For example, thirteenth-century English society would have had more in common with the society of the present-day Trobriand Islands than it would with modern England. Of course, Levy makes clear that he is talking about "extremely general levels" of comparison.

Second, why does modernization occur? One factor that Levy points out is contact between relatively modernized societies and relatively nonmodernized societies. Levy treats modernization as a universal social solvent:

> The patterns of the relatively modernized societies, once developed, have shown a universal tendency to penetrate any social context whose participants have come in contact with them. . . . The patterns always penetrate; once the penetration has begun, the previous indigenous patterns always change; and they always change in the direction of some of the patterns of the relatively modernized society. (p. 190)

To illustrate this concept with a commonplace example: Once the members of a relatively nonmodernized society taste American Coke and Pepsi, they will not want to go back to tasteless tap water.

Third, how do relatively modernized societies differ from relatively nonmodernized societies? According to Levy, relatively

Table 2.1 Levy's Foci of Differences Between Relatively Modernized and Relatively Nonmodernized Societies

	Relatively Nonmodernized Societies	*Relatively Modernized Societies*
Specialization of organization	low compartmentalization of life	high
Interdependency of organization	low (high level of self-sufficiency)	high
Relationship emphasis	tradition, particularism, functional diffuseness	rationality, universalism, functional specificity
Degree of centralization	low	high
Generalized media of exchange and market	less emphasis	more emphasis
Bureaucracy and family consideration	precedence of family norm (nepotism as a virtue)	insulate bureaucracy from other contacts
Town-village interdependence	one-way flow of goods and services from rural to urban contexts	mutual flow of goods and services between towns and villages

SOURCE: Levy (1967, pp. 196-201).

nonmodernized societies are characterized by the following: low degree of specialization; high level of self-sufficiency; cultural norms of tradition, particularism, and functional diffuseness; relatively little emphasis on money circulation and market; family norms such as nepotism; and one-way flow of goods and services from rural to urban areas. In contrast, the characteristics of relatively modernized societies include the following: high degree of specialization and interdependency of organizations; cultural norms of rationality, universalism, and functional specificity; high degree of centralization; relatively great emphasis on money circulation and market; the need to insulate bureaucracy from other contexts; and two-way flow of goods and services between towns and villages (see Table 2.1).

Finally, what are the prospects for the Third World latecomers in their modernization efforts? Levy points out that there are both advantages and disadvantages for these countries. On the one hand, they possess the advantages of knowing where they are going; of being able to borrow initial expertise in planning, capital accumulation, skills, and patterns of organization without the cost of invention; and of skipping some of the nonessential stages associated with the process. Furthermore, Levy asserts that "those who have previously achieved in these respects are likely to offer or insist on assistance." On the other hand, the latecomers face problems of scale (that they must do certain things from the very outset on a fairly large scale); problems of conversion of resources, materials, skills, and so on from one use to another; and problems of disappointment (such as the frustration of trying harder and harder only to fall further and further behind). Levy points out that many people always get hurt in the process of a society's movement toward relatively modernized patterns.

THE SOCIOLOGICAL APPROACH: SMELSER'S STRUCTURAL DIFFERENTIATION

Another sociological approach is that of Smelser (1964), who applies the concept of structural differentiation to the study of Third World countries. For Smelser, modernization generally involves structural differentiation because, through the modernization process, a complicated structure that performed multiple functions is divided into many specialized structures that perform just one function each. The new collection of specialized structures, as a whole, performs the same functions as the original structure, but the functions are performed more efficiently in the new context than they were in the old.

The classic example of structural differentiation is the family institution. In the past, the traditional family had a complicated structure—it was large and multigenerational, with relatives living together under one roof. In addition, it was multifunctional. It was responsible not only for reproduction and emotional support, but for production (the family farm), for education (informal parental socialization), for welfare (care of the elderly), and for religion (ancestral worship). In the modern society, the family institution has undergone structural differentiation. It now has a much simpler structure—it is small and nuclear. The modern family has lost a lot of its old functions as well. The corporate institution has taken over the employment function, the formal education institution now provides schooling for the young, the government has taken over the welfare responsibilities, and so on. Each institution specializes in just one function, and the new institutions collectively perform better than did the old family structure. Modern society is more productive, children are better educated, and the needy receive more welfare than before.

Smelser's analysis, however, goes beyond the concept of structural differentiation. Smelser has raised an important follow-up question: What happens after a complicated institution has differentiated into many simpler ones? Smelser argues that although structural differentiation has increased the functional capacity of institutions, it has also created the problem of *integration*, that is, of coordinating the activities of the various new institutions. The traditional family institution, for instance, was largely spared the problem of integration. Many functions, such as economic production and protection, were carried out within the family. The children worked on the family farm and were dependent upon the family for protection. However, after the family underwent structural differentiation, integration problems arose in the modern society. Now there is the problem of coordinating the family institution and the economic institution, for the children need to go outside the family to find jobs. There is also the problem of coordinating the family institution and the protection institution, for the family can no longer protect family members from injustice in the workplace. In these respects, structural differentiation has created problems of integration.

According to Smelser, new institutions and roles have to be created to coordinate the newly differentiated structures. For instance, to facilitate job hunting, new institutions such as college placement offices and newspaper advertisements needed to be created to bring the family institution and the economic institution together. And in order to protect employees from the abuse of employers, new organizations such as labor unions and the Department of Labor have been created to perform the protection function.

Nevertheless, the problem of integration may still not have been solved satisfactorily. First, there is the issue of values conflict. A new structure may have a set of values that are different from and in conflict with those of the old structure. New agencies such as the college job placement office, for example, stress affective-neutral social relationships, while the family emphasizes affective relationships. Children raised in the family context may find it difficult to adjust to the different values systems of the placement office and the workplace. Second, there is the issue of uneven development. Since institutions develop at different rates, there may be some that are not yet available although they are badly needed. For example, even though there is employer abuse, there may not be a trade union available to protect the interests of employees.

According to Smelser, social disturbances are the result of lack of integration among differentiated structures. These disturbances can take the form of peaceful agitation, political violence, nationalism, revolution, or guerrilla warfare. Those who are displaced by structural differentiation are most likely to participate in these social disturbances. For example, in the rural areas of the Third World, production for the world market tends to create groups of poverty-stricken peasants, displaced from their local communities. These groups often provide ready recruits for the Communist party.

Using this framework of structural differentiation, problems of integration, and social disturbances, Smelser shows that modernization is not necessarily a smooth and harmonious process. This framework serves to draw attention to the examination of the problems of integration and social disturbances that are so common in Third World countries.

THE ECONOMIC APPROACH:
ROSTOW'S STAGES OF ECONOMIC GROWTH

Rostow has written a classic work concerning the stages of economic growth; in a representative chapter, "The Take-Off into Self-Sustained Growth" (1964), he states that there are five major stages of economic development, beginning with traditional society and ending with high mass-consumption society. In the middle, between these two poles of development, there is what Rostow calls the "takeoff stage."

It is most likely that Rostow acquired insight concerning the takeoff stage from sitting on an airplane. At first, the airplane is stationary, then it begins to move slowly on the ground, and finally it takes off into the sky. Rostow sees Third World countries as exhibiting a similar pattern in their move toward development. At first, a Third World country is at the traditional stage, with little social change. Then it begins to change—the rise of new entrepreneurs, the expansion of markets, the development of new industries, and so on. Rostow calls this stage the "precondition for takeoff growth." This is only a precondition stage because, even though economic growth has begun to take place, there is also a decrease in death rate and an expansion of population size. There is little momentum for self-sustained economic growth because the larger population size has, to a certain extent, consumed all of the economic surplus.

Thus Rostow argues that a stimulus is needed in order to propel Third World countries beyond the precondition stage. The stimulus can be a political revolution that restructures major institutions, a technological innovation such as the invention of the steam machine in the Industrial Revolution, or a favorable international environment with rising export demands and prices. Then, according to Rostow, after moving beyond the precondition stage, a country that wants to have self-sustained economic growth must have the following structure for takeoff: Capital and resources must be mobilized so as to raise the rate of productive investment to 10% of the national income, otherwise economic growth cannot overtake the rate of population growth.

How then can a nation obtain the needed capital and resources for productive investment? According to Rostow, they can be obtained by the following means. First, productive investment can come from income detained through confiscatory and taxation devices. For example, in Meiji Japan, productive investment was obtained through very heavy taxation of the peasantry in order to transfer economic resources from the countryside to the city. In socialist Russia, also, productive investment was obtained by confiscating the landlords' property and channeling it into urban investment. Second, productive investment can come from such institutions as banks, capital markets, government bonds, and the stock market, which serve to channel the nation's resources into the economy. Third, productive investment can be obtained through foreign trade. Foreign earnings from exports can be used to finance the importation of foreign technology and equipment. Fourth, direct foreign capital investment such as building subways and opening mines can also provide productive investment for Third World countries.

The critical factor, therefore, is to have 10% or more of the national income to be plowed back continuously into the economy. Productive investment can start first in a leading manufacturing sector, and then can quickly spread to other sectors of the economy. Once economic growth has become an automatic process, the fourth stage—the drive to maturity—is reached. This stage is soon followed by growth in employment opportunities, increase in national income, rise of consumer demands, and formation of a strong domestic market. Rostow labels this final stage the "high mass-consumption society."

Based on his five-stage model of growth (traditional society, precondition for takeoff, takeoff, the drive to maturity, and high mass-consumption society), Rostow has found a possible solution for the promotion of Third World modernization. If the problem facing Third World countries lies in their lack of productive investment, then the solution lies in the provision of aid to these countries—in the forms of capital, technology, and expertise. Concurring with Rostow, U.S. policymakers therefore view American aid as the best way to help Third World countries to modernize.

Thus millions and millions of U.S. dollars are given each year to Third World countries to build up their infrastructures and manufacturing sectors, and hundreds of thousands of U.S. technicians are sent to help them reach the takeoff stage.

THE POLITICAL APPROACH: COLEMAN'S DIFFERENTIATION-EQUALITY-CAPACITY MODEL

To a certain extent, Coleman's political approach is similar to Smelser's sociological analysis, because both theorists start their discussions with the process of differentiation. Political modernization, in Coleman's (1968) formulation, refers to the process of (1) differentiation of political structure and (2) secularization of political culture (with the ethos of equality), which (3) enhance the capacity of a society's political system.

First, Coleman stresses that political differentiation is the dominant empirical trend in the historical evolution of modern political systems. Like Smelser, Coleman refers to differentiation as the process of progressive separation and specialization of roles and institutional spheres in the political system. For example, political differentiation includes the separation of universalistic legal norms from religion, the separation of religion and ideology, and the separation between administrative structure and public political competition. Greater functional specialization, more structural complexity, and a higher degree of interdependence of political institutions are the products of the differentiation process.

Second, Coleman argues that equality is the ethos of modernity. The politics of modernization is the quest for and the realization of equality. What then are the issues concerning equality? For Coleman, they include the notion of universal adult citizenship (distributive equality), the prevalence of universalistic legal norms in the government's relations with the citizenry (legal equality), the predominance of achievement criteria in the recruitment and allocation of political and administrative roles (equality of opportunity), and popular involvement in the political system (equality of participation).

Third, Coleman asserts that the quest for differentiation and equality may lead to the growth of political capacity of the system. In fact, modernization is seen as the progressive acquisition of political capacity for the system. Political capacity is manifested in an increase in scope of the following political functions:

- scale of political community
- efficacy of the implementation of political decisions
- penetrative power of central governmental institutions
- comprehensiveness of the aggregation of interests by political associations
- institutionalization of political organization and procedure
- problem-solving capabilities
- ability to sustain new political demands and organization

Finally, Coleman cautions that differentiation and demands for egalitarianism may also create tension and divisiveness within the political system. Like Smelser, Coleman ends his discussion of political modernization by pointing out the critical "system development problems" or "crises" that a Third World nation-state must cope with and surmount if it is to continue to modernize. In reviewing the literature on political modernization, Coleman mentions the following six crises of modernization:

(1) the crisis of national identity during the transfer of loyalty from primordial groups to the nation
(2) the crisis of political legitimacy for the new state
(3) the crisis of penetration (the difficulty in effecting policies throughout the society through the central government)
(4) the crisis of participation when there is a lack of participatory institutions to channel rising mass demands to the state
(5) the crisis of integration of various divisive political groups
(6) the crisis of distribution that arises when the state is unable to bring about economic growth and distribute enough goods, services, and values to satisfy mass expectations

For Coleman, the modernization of a political system is measured by the extent to which it has successfully developed the capacities to cope with these generic system-development problems.

THEORETICAL ASSUMPTIONS AND METHODOLOGY

As shown in the previous discussion, the modernization school represents a multidisciplinary effort to examine the prospects for Third World development. Each discipline contributes in its own way to identifying key issues concerning modernization. Thus sociologists focus upon the change of pattern variables and structural differentiation, economists stress the importance of speeding up productive investments, and political scientists highlight the need to enhance the capacity of the political system.

Despite the school's multidisciplinary nature, however, researchers in the modernization school do share two sets of assumptions and methodology in their study of Third World development. Since many modernization theorists fail to spell out their assumptions and methodology explicitly, it may be fruitful to review them.

The first set of assumptions shared by modernization researchers are certain concepts drawn from European evolutionary theory. According to the evolutionary theory, social change is unidirectional, progressive, and gradual, irreversibly moving societies from a primitive stage to an advanced stage, and making societies more like one another as they proceed along the path of evolution. Building upon such a premise, modernization researchers have implicitly formulated their theories with the following traits (see Huntington 1976, p. 30-31).

(1) Modernization is a *phased* process. Rostow's theory, for instance, distinguishes different phases of modernization through which all societies will travel. Societies obviously begin with the primitive, simple, undifferentiated traditional stage and end with the advanced, complex, differentiated modern stage. In this respect, Levy argues that societies can be compared in terms of the extent to which they have moved down the road from tradition to modernity.

(2) Modernization is a *homogenizing* process. Modernization produces tendencies toward convergence among societies. As Levy (1967, p. 207) contends, "As time goes on, they and we will increasingly resemble one another . . . because the patterns of modernization are such that the more highly modernized societies become, the more they resemble one another."

(3) Modernization is a *Europeanization* (or *Americanization*) process. In the modernization literature, there is an attitude of complacency toward Western Europe and the United States. These nations are viewed as having unmatched economic prosperity and democratic stability (Tipps 1976). And since they are the most advanced nations in the world, they have become the models the latecomers would like to emulate. In this respect, modernization is simply a process of Europeanization or Americanization, and is often defined as such. For example, since Western Europe and the United States are highly industrialized and democratic, industrialization and democracy have become the trademarks of the modernization perspective.

(4) Modernization is an *irreversible* process. Once started, modernization cannot be stopped. In other words, once Third World countries come into contact with the West, they will not be able to resist the impetus toward modernization. Although the rate of change will vary from one country to another, the direction of change will not. Thus Levy calls modernization a "universal social solvent" that dissolves the traditional traits of the Third World countries.

(5) Modernization is a *progressive* process. The agonies of modernization are many, but in the long run modernization is not only inevitable, but desirable. For Coleman, the modernized political system has a much better capacity to handle the functions of national identity, legitimacy, penetration, participation, and distribution than the traditional political system.

(6) Finally, modernization is a *lengthy* process. It is an evolutionary change, not a revolutionary change. It will take generations, or even centuries, to complete, and its profound impact will be felt only through time.

The other set of assumptions shared by modernization researchers are drawn from functionalist theory, which emphasizes the interdependence of social institutions, the importance of pattern variables at the cultural level, and the built-in process of change through homeostatic equilibrium. Influenced by these Parsonian ideas, modernization researchers have implicitly formulated the concept of modernization with the following traits.

(1) Modernization is a *systematic* process. The attributes of modernity form a consistent whole, thus appearing in clusters rather than in isolation (Hermassi 1978). Modernity involves changes in virtually all aspects of social behavior, including industrialization, urbanization, mobilization, differentiation, secularization, participation, and centralization.

(2) Modernization is a *transformative* process. In order for a society to move into modernity, its traditional structures and values must be totally replaced by a set of modern values. As Huntington (1976) points out, the modernization school considers "modernity" and "tradition" to be essentially asymmetrical concepts. Although the traits of modernity are clearly laid down, those of tradition are not. For the sake of convenience, everything that is not modern is labeled traditional. Consequently, tradition has a small role to play and has to be replaced (or completely transformed) in the process of modernization.

(3) Modernization is an *immanent* process. Due to its systematic and transformative nature, modernization has built change into the social system. Once a change has started in one sphere of activity, it will necessarily produce comparative changes in other spheres (Hermassi 1978). For example, once the family has begun the process of differentiation, other institutions—the economy, the mass media, the police, and so on—have to undergo the process of differentiation and integration too. Due to this assumption of immanence, the modernization school tends to focus upon the internal sources of change in the Third World countries.

In addition to sharing evolutionary and functionalist assumptions, members of the modernization school also adopt a similar methodological approach for their research. First, modernization researchers tend to anchor their discussions at a highly general and abstract level. Since their aim is to explain general patterns, universal trends, and common prospects for Third World development, they do not want to be preoccupied with unique cases and historically specific events. In order to draw high-level generalizations, modernization researchers rely upon Parsons's ideal-type construction (such as traditional societies versus modern societies) to summarize their key arguments. After that, the indexing of the features of dichotomous ideal types becomes a major effort of students of the modernization school (see Table 2.1).

With regard to units of analysis, Tipps (1976) points out that it is the national territorial state that is of critical theoretical significance to the modernization theorist, even if this does remain largely implicit. However it may be conceptualized, whether as industrialization or structural differentiation, each component of the modernization process is viewed as a source of change operated at the national level. Thus modernization theories are basically theories of transformation of nation-states.

POLICY IMPLICATIONS

Modernization theories are not just academic exercises, however. They were originally formulated in response to the new world leadership role that the United States took on after World War II, and, as such, they have important policy implications. First, modernization theories help to provide an implicit justification for the asymmetrical power relationship between "traditional" and "modern" societies (Tipps 1976). Since the United States is modern and advanced and the Third World is traditional and backward, the latter should look to the former for guidance.

Second, modernization theories identify the threat of communism in the Third World as a modernization problem. If Third World countries are to modernize, they should be moving along the path that the United States has traveled, and thus should move away from communism. To help accomplish this goal, modernization theories suggest economic development, the replacement of traditional values, and the institutionalization of democratic procedures.

Third, modernization theories help to legitimate the "meliorative foreign aid policy" of the United States (Chirot 1981, p. 269; Apter 1987, p. 23). If what is needed is more exposure to modern values and more productive investment, then the United States can help by sending advisers, by encouraging American business to invest abroad, by making loans, and by rendering other kinds of aid to Third World countries. Although not all modernization theorists are necessarily apologists for American expansionism, as Tipps (1976, p. 72) remarks, there is "little in the modernization literature that would seriously disturb the White House, Pentagon, or State Department policy makers."

As will be discussed in the next chapter, these policy implications, as well as the school's theoretical assumptions and methodology, have shaped the contour of the empirical studies of the modernization school.

CHAPTER 3

The Classical Modernization Studies

This chapter will discuss four classical modernization studies: McClelland's study on achievement motivation, Inkeless's study on modern men, Bellah's study on the Tokugawa religion in Japan, and Lipset's study on the relationship between economic development and democracy. These studies are "classical" in the sense that they have become exemplars of modernization research, starting a chain of empirical investigations on entrepreneurial achievements, on modern attitudes and behaviors, on Japanese religion, and on the social and economic correlations of democracy. In addition, these studies represent the modernization approach to development because they are informed by the basic evolutionary and functionalist assumptions of the modernization school.

McCLELLAND: ACHIEVEMENT MOTIVATION

Which group is ultimately responsible for the economic modernization of the Third World countries? According to McClelland (1964), domestic entrepreneurs, not politicians or Western advisers, play the critical role. Thus McClelland argues that researchers need to go beyond the study of economic indicators to study the entrepreneur. He also argues that policymakers need to invest in human beings, not just in economic infrastructures.

McClelland asserts that the goal of entrepreneurial activities is not the pursuit of profit. While profit is an important aspect, it is merely an indicator of other goals. What entrepreneurs really possess is a strong desire for achievement, for doing a good job, for thinking of a new way to improve present performance—a desire that McClelland calls "achievement motivation," or the need for achievement.

Each of us has a lot of free time. If a person spends that free time in enjoying life—in activities such as sleeping, swimming, and drinking—then that person has a very low achievement motivation. If a person spends his or her free time thinking about friends, family, social gatherings, beach parties, and so on, then that person also has a low achievement motivation. Only when a person thinks about how to improve the present situation or how to perform an existing task in a better way can it be said that he or she has a strong achievement motivation.

How can achievement motivation be measured? Questionnaires do not represent a good method for gathering information on achievement motivation at the individual level, because people can and do lie about their motives, interests, and attitudes. So McClelland adopted the projection method to measure individual achievement motivation. After showing a picture to his research subjects, McClelland asked them to write a story. Content analysis of each story was then used to assess the achievement motivation of the storyteller. It is assumed that the storytellers are not just telling a story, but are actually revealing their own motivations through the medium of story telling. For example, after having been shown a picture of a man looking at a photograph on the top of a worktable, one research subject told a story about a man who was daydreaming, thinking about the vacation he had spent the weekend before with his family, and planning on how to spend the coming weekend in a more exciting way. Another research subject told a story about a man who was an engineer working at a drafting table, thinking about the important engineering problem of how to build a bridge that can withstand the stress of high wind. Obviously, the research subject who told the second story received a higher score on achievement motivation than the first subject.

If individual achievement motivation can be measured by the projection method, how can national achievement motivation be measured? McClelland, again, used an innovative method to measure achievement motivation at the national level. He first collected popular literature—such as folk songs, comic books, poems, plays, and children's stories used in public textbooks—and then coded the degree of achievement motivation displayed in each of them. For example, on the topic of boat building, the popular literature of one nation emphasized the fun children have in constructing a boat together, while the popular literature of another nation stressed that it is necessary to have a bright leader to organize and plan boat-building activities. Clearly, the literature of the second nation has a higher achievement motivation score than that of the first nation. It is McClelland's assumption that folk stories are reflections of the minds of the people in a nation, otherwise they would not have become folk stories.

After collecting information on national achievement motivation, McClelland raised an interesting question: To what extent is achievement motivation related to national economic development (as measured by the consumption of electricity)? His cross-national research revealed that countries with high scores on achievement motivation have high economic development. In addition, he reports that the timing of development is significant. The rise and fall of achievement motivation are also associated with the rise and fall of national economic development. For example, although Great Britain was very high on the scale of achievement motivation in the nineteenth century, British achievement motivation scores fell below average in 1950. On the other hand, although France, Russia, and Germany were all quite low on the achievement motivation scale at the turn of the twentieth century, all three countries' achievement motivation scores rose sharply by the 1950s. The United States had approximately the same level of achievement motivation as the Soviet Union in the 1950s, but the Soviet Union's score was on the way up, whereas that of the United States was on the way down. According to McClelland, it takes about 50 years for a nation's economic development to match its trend of rising achievement motivation.

Finally, what are the sources of achievement motivation? Where does it come from? As a psychologist, McClelland tends to locate it in the family, especially in the process of parental socialization. First, parents need to set high standards of achievement for their children, such as expecting their children to excel in education, to get good jobs, and to be well known and respected in the community. Second, parents need to use the methods of encouragement and warmth in socialization. They need to give their children encouragement and affection, and to reward them if the children actually accomplish the tasks assigned. Third, parents should not be authoritarian. They should not do everything for the children, but should let the children develop their own initiatives and create their own ways to handle different situations. In addition, McClelland points out that Western-style education and cultural diffusion are helpful for Western nations in injecting achievement motivation into Third World countries.

The policy implication of this line of research is as follows. In order to promote economic development in Third World countries, it is necessary to promote achievement motivation among Third World entrepreneurs. It is not sufficient for the United States to provide financial aid, technology, and advice to Third World countries; the Third World must have a group of high-achieving entrepreneurs who know how to turn foreign aid into productive investment. McClelland further assumes that the more contacts Third World countries have with Western countries (such as educational exchange and cultural diffusion), the easier it will be for Third World people to adopt the traits of high achievement motivation.

INKELESS: MODERN MEN

Another classic modernization research project was conducted by Inkeless (1964), who has written many books and articles on the subject of "modern men." Inkeless is concerned with the following research questions: What is the impact of modernization on the individual's attitudes, values, and ways of living? When Third

World people are exposed to Western, modern influence, will they adopt more modern attitudes than before?

In researching these questions, Inkeless, like McClelland, carried out cross-national studies. His research included Argentina, Chile, India, Israel, Nigeria, and Pakistan; these countries were chosen because they were situated at different positions on the scale of modernization, ranging from nonindustrialized to industrialized countries and from nondemocratic to democratic countries. Inkeless interviewed 6,000 young men, chosen from various categories such as peasantry, migrants, urban nonindustrial workers, urban industrial workers, and students. He developed a lengthy questionnaire that included over 300 items and took an average of three hours to complete. He received funding from the Rockefeller Foundation, the Ford Foundation, the National Science Foundation, the Department of Health, the U.S. Air Force, and Harvard University in carrying out this large-scale project.

Inkeless discovered a stable pattern of "modern men" across countries. In other words, the criteria used to define men as modern in one nation can be used to define men as modern in other countries as well. Inkeless constructed a scale of modernity ranging from 0 to 100 in order to measure this stable pattern of personality among modern men. The following are some of the traits shared by modern men, according to Inkeless:

- *Openness to new experience:* Modern men are willing to try new activities or to develop new ways of doing things.
- *Increasing independence from authority figures:* Modern men are not under the control of such figures as parents, tribal heads, and emperors.
- *Belief in science:* Modern men believe that human beings can conquer nature.
- *Mobility orientation:* Modern men are highly ambitious; they want to climb up the occupational ladder.
- *Use of long-term planning:* Modern men always plan ahead and know what they will accomplish in the next five years.
- *Activity in civil politics:* Modern men join voluntary associations and participate in local community affairs.

After describing the characteristics of the modern men, Inkeless raises another question: What makes men modern? What are the crucial factors that have led Third World men to adopt modern values? According to Inkeless, education is the most important indicator of modern values. One year of education increases modern values by 2 to 3 points on a modernization scale of 0 to 100. Inkeless further points out that it is not the technical curriculum—such as the study of mathematics, chemistry, and biology—that matters, but the informal curriculum—exposure to the pro-Western values of teachers, the use of Western textbooks, the watching of Western movies—that facilitates the acquisition of modern values. Occupation, as measured by factory work, also has an independent effect on modern values. There is a late socialization effect in the sense that if an individual has missed a good formal education, he or she could still have a chance of becoming modern by working in a large-scale factory.

The final question that Inkeless raises is whether modernization produces psychological stress among Third World people. According to Inkeless, the literature on Third World modernization has tended to stress the negative impacts of modernization—social disorganization, personal demoralization, deviance, and alienation. This is especially true of the work of the Parsonian functionalists, who favor slow, gradual social change instead of rapid, sudden social change in Third World countries. But, Inkeless argues, in using his Psychosomatic Symptoms Test on Third World people he has revealed no difference between modern men and nonmodern men on stress scores. Consequently, he concludes that modernization does not necessarily produce psychological stress among Third World people; modern men exhibit no more stress than do nonmodern men.

BELLAH: TOKUGAWA RELIGION

The research problem. Bellah's (1957) study examines how the Tokugawa religion has contributed to the rapid economic development of Japan. Bellah focuses on Japan not only because it was the only non-Western nation to undergo industrialization at the turn of the twentieth century, but also because it exhibited a peculiar pattern of industrialization. Japan's initial wave of industrializa-

tion in the late nineteenth century was promoted not by industrialists, craftsmen, or merchants, but by a samurai class. It was the
samurai class who restored the emperor, supplied a large number
of vigorous entrepreneurs, and lay the foundation for Japanese
modernization. In following the path of the research of Weber,
Bellah wonders "whether religious factor might also be involved
in the Japanese case." In other words, "was there a functional
analogue to the protestant ethics in Japanese religion" that gave
rise to modern Japanese industrial society?

Theoretical background. As a student of Parsons, Bellah borrows
many functionalist concepts to study the connections between
religion and modern industrial society in Japan. For Bellah, the
term *modern industrial society* refers to a society centered upon
economic values such as rationalization of means, universalism,
and achievement in the value system. Without such modern economic values, Bellah argues, it would be impossible to liberate the
economy from traditionalist restrictions to rational dynamism.
The term *religion* in Bellah's work refers to an individual's attitudes
and actions with respect to his or her ultimate values. Bellah
argues that it is one of the social functions of religion to provide a
meaningful set of ultimate values upon which the morality and
central values of a society can be based.

When the great world religions emerged out of primitive or
magical religion, they provided an impetus for redefinition of the
central values of a society from traditionalism to rationalism. For
Weber, Protestantism in Europe provided such a redefinition and
institutionalized the values of universalism and achievement. Bellah undertook the study of traits in the Japanese religion that might
have provided such a critical shift of central values.

Japanese religion. Bellah makes two basic observations concerning the study of Japanese religion. First, despite the fact that there
are many religions in Japan (including Confucianism, Buddhism,
and Shinto), it is possible to speak of Japanese religion as a single
entity. This is because the various religious traditions have inter-
penetrated and are inseparably fused together. Thus "Confucianism and Shinto had borrowed Buddhist metaphysics and
psychology; Buddhism and Shinto had borrowed much of Con-

fucian ethics, and Confucianism and Buddhism had been rather thoroughly Japanized." As a result, Japanese Confucianism is quite different from Chinese Confucianism, and Japanese Buddhism differs from Indian Buddhism.

The other observation that Bellah makes is that Japanese religion constituted the central value system of the society. Japanese religion historically began as the ethics of the samurai warrior class; it then became so popularized through the influence of Confucianism and Buddhism that it became the ethics of the entire Japanese population, including the backward peasantry living in remote villages.

With these two observations, how does Bellah explain the linkages between religion and economic development? Specifically, he points to three kinds of correlations: (1) Religion directly affected the economic ethics; (2) the influence of religion on the economy was mediated through the political institution; and (3) the influence of religion was mediated through the family institution.

Direct influence of religion. Bellah examines the Buddhist sect of Shinshu. In the early period, Shinshu stressed salvation by faith alone and paid little attention to ethical demands, so anyone could be saved, no matter how wicked. By middle Tokugawa (1600-1868), however, as a result of the promotion of Rennyo Shonin, the so-called second founder of the sect, salvation and ethical action became indissolubly linked. Nothing more was heard about the wicked being saved. There was a shift of religious values in that ethical action was emphasized as the very sign of salvation.

Bellah notes three characteristics of this new ethical requirement. First, diligent work in this world, especially in one's occupation, occupied the central place among the ethical duties. Second, an ascetic attitude toward consumption was also present, as can be seen from the following maxims:

- Always think of divine protection.
- Cheerfully do not neglect diligent activity, morning and evening.
- Work hard at the family occupation.
- Be temperate in unprofitable luxury.
- Do not gamble.
- Rather than take a lot, take a little.

Third, although dishonest profit was prohibited, normal business profit was legitimated in religious terms through the doctrine of Bodhisattva spirit. In Bellah's (1957, p. 120) account, the businesses of merchants and artisans were allowed because these activities were considered to be beneficial to consumers. By bringing benefits to other members of the community, merchants and craftsmen received the right to profit themselves. This was the virtue of the harmony of *jiri-rita.*

To document the impact of the Shinshu religion on the actual behavior of Japanese merchants, Bellah cites the concentration of Shin temples in the Omi merchant towns, the large number of merchants in the temple registers, and the pious statements frequently made in the biographies of these merchants.

Indirect influence of religion via the political system. In China, Confucianism stressed that production should be aimed at sufficiency, harmony, and integration among different parts of the society. But in Japan, as Bellah points out, Confucianism took on a new meaning after being integrated with Buddhism. Instead of stressing harmony among the parts, Japanese Confucianism advocated the selfless subordination of all the parts to a single collective whole.

This principle of subordination is reflected in the economic ethics of the Japanese samurai. The duties and tasks of the samurai's occupation were seen as fulfilling his limitless obligation to his lord. The samurai had to fulfill his obligation with utmost devotion and without any consideration for himself. According to Bellah, however, this samurai work ethic spread to the rest of the society in the Tokugawa period, and all classes of citizens were expected to be loyal and to make returns for the lord or for the blessings of the nation. Through this calling of limitless obligation, Japanese society was said to be moving in a unified direction of fulfillment of obligations to superiors.

This calling of limitless obligation explains why the samurai class started the Meiji Restoration. The aims of the Restoration were to revere the emperor, to expel the barbarians, and to increase national power. According to Bellah, the motivation of the samurai in leading the Meiji Restoration was primarily political rather than economic. The samurai were concerned with increasing national power; the increase in wealth was only a means to an end. Thus the samurai turned themselves into vigorous entrepreneurs on a massive scale, not because they wanted to get rich, but because they wanted to save the nation through economic development. As an illustration of the adaptation of samurai ethics to modern entrepreneurship, Bellah (1957, p. 187) cites the house rules of Iwasaki, the samurai founder of Mitsubishi:

- Operate all enterprises with the national interest in mind.
- Never forget the pure spirit of public service.
- Be hardworking, frugal, and thoughtful to others.
- Utilize proper personnel.
- Treat your employees well.
- Be bold in starting an enterprise but meticulous in its prosecution.

In observing the continuation of the Tokugawa central values in the modern Meiji period, Bellah remarks that the modern industrial economy is permeated by the political values of an earlier period.

Indirect influence of religion via the family. The notion of limitless obligation was used not only to govern the nation, but also to manage the merchant houses. The merchant house was considered a sacred entity that symbolized ancestral worship. In a manner similar to the expectation of filial service of children to parents and the loyal service of clerks to their superiors, it demanded the gratitude of all its members. The standards of filial service to the merchant house were set very high, rivaling in strictness those of the samurai. In order to promote family honor and to fulfill one's sacred obligation to the family, lazy, extravagant, or dishonest behavior was condemned. To injure the reputation of the merchant house or to let the business decline would bring shame on one's ancestors. Thus the merchant class's economic motivation was not self-interest, but "family profitism." Bellah argues that this ethics of family obligation reinforced high standards of honesty, quality, and credit; reinforced universalistic norms in the business world; and provided a powerful impetus toward economic rationalization in modern Japan.

If familism promoted modernization in Japan, why did it fail to do the same in China? According to Bellah, China had too much familism. In China, the family system was the central institution in the society, and filial piety formed the basis of Chinese moral principles. With the dominance of familism, loyalty to the lord (or the emperor) had a very restricted focus. Even the Chinese gentry entered government service not to build up national power, but to gain immunity and wealth for their families. In Bellah's functionalist terms, Chinese society was therefore characterized by the primacy of integrative values such as family solidarity and harmony. These values stressed system maintenance and lacked the dynamics to overcome the traditionalism of the masses.

In Japan, however, due to the fusion of Confucianism and Buddhism, the ethic of warrior loyalty persisted, and loyalty to the nation was therefore valued much more highly than filial piety to the family. Bellah characterizes Japan as being dominated by political or goal-attainment values, and this set of values provided the dynamism to pull the Japanese society together to pursue the collective goal of strengthening national power. Thus Bellah argues that the primacy of goal attainment explains the modernization of Japan and China.

In sum, Bellah's study of the Tokugawa religion shows that it directly or indirectly, through the polity and the family, exerted a favorable influence on the economic rationalization of Japan.

LIPSET: ECONOMIC DEVELOPMENT AND DEMOCRACY

The research problem. Lipset's (1963) work is concerned with examining how political democracy is related to economic development. He points out that from Aristotle to the present, the literature tends to assert that "the more well-to-do a nation, the greater the chances that it will sustain democracy" (p. 31). Lipset addresses the question of whether only wealthy societies can give rise to democracy, and whether poor societies with a large impoverished mass lead to oligarchy (government by a small upper stratum, such as traditionalist dictatorships found in Latin America) or to tyranny (popular-based dictatorship, such as communism or Peronism).

The variables. To carry out his research, Lipset needed to define and operationalize the concepts of democracy and economic development. *Democracy,* in Lipset's work, refers to a political system that supplies regular constitutional opportunities for changing the governing officials, and that permits the population to influence major decisions by choosing the holders of political office. Lipset distinguishes four types of political systems in Europe and Latin America:

- *European stable democracies* (e.g., United Kingdom): countries with an uninterrupted continuation of political democracy since World War I and the absence of a major political movement opposed to the democratic "rule of the game"
- *European unstable democracies and dictatorships* (e.g., Spain): countries in Europe that do not meet the above criteria
- *Latin American democracies and unstable dictatorships* (e.g., Brazil): countries with a history of more or less free elections since World War I
- *Latin America stable dictatorships* (e.g., Cuba): countries in Latin America that do not meet the above criteria

As Lipset explains, and as this list shows, the criteria for Latin American countries are less stringent. In Europe we look for stable democracies, while in South America we look for unstable dictatorships.

With respect to the concept of economic development, Lipset uses various indices, including the following:

- *wealth,* as measured by per capita income, number of persons per motor vehicle, and the number of physicians, radios, telephones, and newspapers per 1,000 persons
- *industrialization,* as measured by the percentage of employed labor in agriculture and per capita energy consumed
- *urbanization,* as measured by the percentage of population in cities over 20,000, in cities over 100,000, and in metropolitan areas
- *education,* as measured by primary education enrollment, post-primary enrollment, and higher education enrollment per 1,000 persons

The findings. Using data published by the United Nations, Lipset found that no matter what index is used for economic development, it is always higher for democratic countries than for dictatorships. Thus more democratic countries have higher average wealth, a higher degree of industrialization and urbanization, and a higher level of education than do less democratic nations. To illustrate, Lipset reports that the per capita income for European stable democracies is $695; for European dictatorships it is $308; for Latin American democracies it is $171; and for Latin American dictatorships it is $119.

Furthermore, Lipset notes that all the indices of economic development—wealth, industrialization, urbanization, and education—are so closely interrelated that they form one major factor that has high correlation with the variable of democracy. Citing Lerner, Lipset entertains the idea that this high correlation may be a result of the different phases of modernization: starting with urbanization, followed by the development of literacy and the mass media, and, finally, leading to the birth of the democratic institution of participation.

The explanation. What explains the strong relationship between economic development and democracy? Lipset (1963, p. 45) basically provides a social class explanation: "Economic development, producing increased income, greater economic security, and widespread higher education, largely determines the form of the 'class struggle' " that lays the foundation of democracy.

First, the lower class in poor countries experiences more status inferiority than its counterpart in wealthy countries. When a country is poor, the sharing of goods, services, and resources must inevitably be less equitable than in a country in which there is relative abundance. Consequently, when the lower class in the poor countries is exposed to a better way of life by modern means of communication and transportation, sufficient discontent is aroused to provide the social basis for political extremism. Thus the political parties in poorer countries are more extremist and radical than those in wealthier countries. On the other hand, economic development, with its accompanying increase in wealth and consumer goods, serves to reduce the social distance between the lower and upper classes. Thus the lower class in wealthy countries tends to develop longer time perspectives and more complex and reformist views of politics. Lipset points out that a belief in secular reformism can be the ideology of only a relatively well-to-do lower class in wealthy countries.

Second, increased wealth also affects the middle class. There is a diamond-shaped social stratification in wealthy countries, with an expanded middle class. Since middle-class members are the ones most likely to join voluntary political organizations, they provide a countervailing force to check the power of the state, form a source of new opinion for the mass media, and help to train citizens in political skills and to arouse political participation. Lipset asserts that a large middle class also tempers conflict by rewarding moderate and democratic parties and by penalizing extremist groups.

Third, the politics of the upper class is also related to national wealth. In poor countries, the upper class tends to treat the lower class as vulgar and innately inferior, as a lower caste beyond the pale of human society. Naturally, in poor countries, the upper class resists granting political rights to the lower class—which often intensifies the latter's extremist reactions. On the other hand, in wealthy countries, where there are enough resources for some redistribution to take place, it is easier for the upper class to extend some rights to the lower class.

In sum, Lipset has documented and explained the strong relationship between economic development and democracy. However, as a shrewd political sociologist, he also makes an important qualification. He disagrees with political commentators' interpretation of his findings that "if only the underdeveloped nations can be successfully started on the road to high productivity, . . . we can defeat the major threat to newly established democracies, their domestic Communists" (p. 54). Lipset disagrees with this interpretation because lower-class political extremism is found not only in low-income countries, but also in newly industrializing countries. Consequently, Lipset qualifies his findings by adding a new factor of the rate of industrialization. In Lipset's words, "Wherever industrialization occurred *rapidly*, introducing sharp *discontinuities* between pre-industrial and industrial situation, more rather than less extremist working-class movements emerged" (p. 54). This is because under slow industrialization, workers have been employed in an industry for a long time, and those newcomers who have been pulled from the rural areas and who might have supplied the basis for an extremist party are always in the minority. But if industrialization is rapid, it results in a sudden growth in the number of unskilled workers from the rural areas, thereby providing the fuel for extremist politics.

POWERS OF THE
CLASSICAL MODERNIZATION PERSPECTIVE

This chapter has reviewed four classical modernization studies: McClelland on achievement motivation, Inkeless on modern men, Bellah on Tokugawa religion, and Lipset on political democracy. These four studies show how the basic assumptions of the modernization perspective shape the research focus, the analytical framework, and the methodology of modernization research.

The research focus. Despite the fact that the above studies were carried out by a psychologist, a social psychologist, a sociologist of religion, and a political sociologist, respectively, they all share a similar research focus on modernization. They are interested in the examination of the following key research questions: What are the factors that have promoted the modernization of Third World countries? What are the consequences of the modernization process on Third World societies? For example, McClelland highlights the strong correlation between achievement motivation and economic development. Bellah examines the role of the Tokugawa religion on Japanese economic development. Lipset addresses the possible role of economic development in the democratization of Third World countries. And Inkeless discusses the consequences of the modernization process for individual attitudes and behavior.

The analytical framework. The four studies also share a similar modernization framework. The authors all assume that Third World countries are traditional and that Western countries are modern. In order for Third World countries to follow the Western path of modernization, the four studies explicitly or implicitly propose that Third World countries must drop their traditional traits and acquire Western traits. Thus McClelland advocates the injection of Western achievement values into Third World countries as a means of promoting entrepreneurship and modernization. Inkeless points out that modern men in Third World countries tend to possess Western traits, such as mobility orientation, the use of long-term planning, and participation in civil affairs. Bellah assumes that Western values such as universalism and achievement are necessary to liberate Third World economies from traditionalistic restrictions to rational dynamism. And Lipset implies that Third World countries need to attain a Western style of economic development (such as industrialization, urbanization, and education) before they can sustain a Western style of democracy (including elections and the change of government administrators).

The methodology. Except for Bellah's study, the empirical works discussed above tend to anchor their discussions at a highly general level. For example, achievement motivation and modern men are taken as universals that can be applied to any Third World country, irrespective of whether it is India, Chile, or Nigeria. Lipset combines Latin American countries into just two categories (democracies and unstable dictatorships versus stable dictatorships), without investigating the historically specific political developments of the different Latin American countries.

The modernization school was very popular in the post-World War II era. Students of development, therefore, tended to share the research focus, the analytical framework, and the methodology of the modernization school in the 1950s. However, by the late 1960s, the modernization school came under increasing attack.

CRITICISMS OF THE MODERNIZATION SCHOOL

Before presenting a discussion of the radical critiques of the Marxists, I will first present academic critiques of the modernization school from mainstream social scientists (Bendix 1967; Eisenstadt 1974; Gusfield 1967; Huntington 1976; Lauer 1971; Nisbet 1969; Tipps 1976). These academicians have reservations about the evolutionary and functionalist assumptions of the modernization school.

Unidirectional Development

First, the critics have challenged the evolutionary assumptions of unidirectional development. Why do Third World countries need to move in the direction of Western countries? According to the critics, this element of modernization theory is simply the result of the fact that most modernization researchers are Americans and Europeans. Born and raised in Western countries, modernization researchers believe that their own cultural values are the most natural and the best in the world. Thinking that their Western countries represent the future of the Third World countries, they assume that the Third World countries will move toward the Western model of development. According to the critics, this belief in Western superiority is "ethnocentric." For example, why are Western countries placed at the higher end of the evolutionary path and labeled "advanced" or "modern" societies? And why are Third World countries placed near the lower end of the evolutionary path and called "primitive" or "traditional" societies? The critics argue that concepts such as "advanced," "modern," "traditional," and "primitive" are merely ideological labels used to justify Western superiority.

Second, the critics assert that belief in unidirectional development has resulted in modernization researchers' overlooking alternative paths of development for Third World countries. Since modernization researchers assume that Third World countries must follow the Western model, they have practically defined away the possibility that these countries may select different models of development. For example, since the United States has democratic institutions, modernization researchers assume that democracy is a major component of modernization. But is democracy necessary for economic development? Do Third World countries have other choices? For instance, can they follow the authoritarian development of Taiwan and South Korea? Can they create their own models of development?

Third, the critics argue that modernization researchers are overly optimistic. They have mistakenly assumed that since Western countries have achieved development, Third World countries can also. Researchers have not fully explored the possibility of non-development. Many critics assert that the future of Third World development is uncertain. There is a real possibility of modernization breakdown such as that in Ethiopia, where the people have faced starvation and the nation has faced extinction. The critics point out that many Third World countries have in fact gotten worse over the past century. It seems that the modernization process can be stopped or even reversed, contrary to the claims of the modernization school.

The Need to Eliminate Traditional Values

Critics of the modernization school also attack the functionalist assumption of incompatibility between tradition and modernity. First, the critics ask: What is really tradition? Is it true that Third World countries have a set of homogeneous and harmonious traditional values? According to the critics, Third World countries have heterogeneous values systems. For example, Redfield (1965) has distinguished the "great tradition" (the values of the elites) from the "little tradition" (the values of the masses). The elites may value poetry, painting, dancing, hunting, leisure, and philosophy, while the masses may value working in the fields, diligence, thrift, and earning one's own living. Furthermore, not only are Third World countries culturally diverse, but their cultural systems are full of conflicts. The functionalists generally hold the misleading conception that societies in the past were peaceful and stable. But throughout history, there have always been conflict and instability in the form of peasant protests, national movements, and religious wars.

Second, the critics ask: Are traditional values and modern values mutually exclusive? The critics assert that in traditional societies, modern values have always been present. For example, in traditional Chinese society, which emphasized particularistic ascription, there was an impersonal examination system that stressed universalistic achievement. On the other hand, in the modern society, traditional values have always been present. For example, particularistic values (such as ethnicity, gender, and age) can never be eliminated in the recruitment and promotion of personnel in a modern bureaucracy. Consequently, it seems that traditional and modern values have always coexisted.

Third, the critics ask: Are traditional values always obstacles to modernization? Do we need to eliminate traditional values in order to promote modernization? As some critics point out, traditional values may sometimes be very helpful in promoting modernization. For example, in the modernization of Japan, the value of "loyalty to the emperor" was easily transformed to "loyalty to the firm," which helped to enhance workers' productivity and to cut down the turnover rate.

Finally, the critics ask: Can modernization totally displace traditional values? They point out that traditional values will always be present in the process of modernization. As the cultural lag theory points out, traditional values will persist for a very long time even though the original conditions that gave rise to them have disappeared. Not only is there never a simple, one-sided displacement of traditional values, but traditional values are bound to remain and affect the development of modern values. For example, strong beliefs about Chinese medicine have altered the manner in which the Chinese have accepted Western medicine in China—a Chinese person may drink a cup of herbal soup in the evening after taking an aspirin in the morning. Moreover, even when traditional values seem to be declining, they may come back at a later time to affect Third World development. Traditional values are usually revitalized at a crucial turning point in the modernization process. During national independence movements, for instance, traditional values such as folk religion, folk songs, and native language are often emphasized in the effort to unite the whole nation. As such, traditional values never die.

Methodological Problems

According to their critics, modernization researchers tend to formulate their arguments at such a high level of abstraction that it is hard to know what country and what historical period that they are discussing. For example, in discussing pattern variables such as particularistic, ascribed, collective, diffused, and affective values, it is not clear which nation (Japan, Egypt, or Peru?) the modernization school is talking about. It is also not clear which historical period the modernization school is describing. Is it the seventeenth, the eighteenth, the nineteenth, or the twentieth century? Modernization researchers anchor their arguments at such a high level of generalization that their propositions are beyond time and space limitations.

In addition, the critics argue that there is a lack of before-and-after historical research undertaken by modernization social scientists. They simply take cross-national research at a given period to be historical research over time. For example, to study why China has failed to modernize in the post-World War II era, critics of modernization researchers argue that the correct research method is to examine what China was like in the eighteenth century, what has happened to China since then, and how these historical factors have affected the Chinese path of development in the twentieth century. But, instead of pursuing a historical research method, modernization researchers simply adopt a cross-national method. They assume that twentieth-century China is like eighteenth-century Great Britain. If eighteenth-century Great Britain needed to invest 10% or more of its national income in the economy, then twentieth-century China needs to do the same in order to arrive at the takeoff stage of economic growth.

Aside from the above academic criticisms, the modernization school has been the subject of political criticisms from neo-Marxists (Bodenheimer 1970b; Cardoso and Faletto 1979; Chilcote and Edelstein 1974; Frank 1969; Portes 1976; Pratt 1973; Rhodes 1968). Since the neo-Marxist approach to development will be discussed in depth in Chapter 5, only a brief review of two aspects of neo-Marxist criticism are presented here—the ideological critique and a critique based on the neglect among modernization researchers of the issue of foreign domination.

The Ideological Critique

From the neo-Marxist viewpoint, the modernization perspective is a cold war ideology that is used to justify the intervention of the United States in Third World affairs. Thus in a well-known article titled "The Sociology of Development and Underdevelopment of Sociology," Frank (1969, p. xi) claims to examine "the North American emperor's social scientific clothes and exposes the scientific nakedness behind his ideological sham."

Along the same line of criticism, Bodenheimer (1970b) points to the "ideology of developmentalism" that has suffused the literature of comparative politics and sociological theory. According to Bodenheimer, the literature of development has suffered from the following four epistemological sins: (1) belief in the possibility of an objective social science free of ideology, (2) belief in the cumulative quality of knowledge, (3) belief in universal laws of social science, and (4) export of these three beliefs to Third World countries. "These epistemological sins led to the theoretical errors of belief in incremental and continuous development, the possibility of stable and orderly change, the diffusion of development from the West to the third-world areas, and the decline of revolutionary ideology and the spread of pragmatic and scientific thinking" (see Almond 1987, p. 445).

Neglect of the Issue of Foreign Domination

The modernization school is also criticized for ignoring the crucial element of foreign domination. While focusing on internal traits such as traditional values and lack of productive investment, modernization researchers have paid little attention to external dynamics such as the history of colonialism, the control of multinational corporations over Third World economies, the unequal pattern of trade between Western and Third World countries, and the nature of the international system. Although modernization researchers simply assume that Third World countries have attained political autonomy at the termination of formal colonial domination, the neo-Marxists argue that these countries are still politically, economically, and culturally dominated by Western countries. Consequently, the neo-Marxists criticize modernization researchers' neglect of such a crucial factor as foreign domination in the shaping of Third World development.

In sum, the academic and political critics of the modernization school have pointed to its misleading evolutionary and function-alist assumptions, methodological problems, and ideological biases. The issue facing modernization researchers, then, is how to address their critics. How seriously should they deal with these criticisms? Is it true that there is nothing good about the modernization school and that it therefore should be disbanded? Or is it possible for the modernization school to incorporate the strong points made by its critics into its theory and research?

In the heat of theoretical debate in the late 1960s, modernization researchers generally became defensive and paid little attention to their critics. However, after the dust has settled in the late 1970s, they began to take these criticisms seriously. The modernization school modified some of its basic tenets and embarked upon a series of original studies—the "new modernization studies" discussed in the next chapter.

CHAPTER 4

The New Modernization Studies

RESPONSES TO THE CRITICS

By the late 1970s, when the heat of criticism of the modernization school had subsided, there was a revival of modernization research. Like the classical modernization studies, these new modernization studies focus on Third World development. The analyses in these studies are conducted at the national level, and they aim to explain that development occurs mainly through internal factors, such as cultural values and social institutions. The new studies use terms similar to those found in the classical studies, terms like *tradition* and *modernity*, and they basically share the same assumption that modernization (and contact with Western countries) is generally beneficial to Third World countries.

However, there are also striking differences between the classical and the new modernization studies. Members of the new modernization school are now on the offensive. On the one hand, they have fought back and labeled their Marxist critics as propagandists who have misread their arguments (Almond 1987, p. 450-468; Moore 1979, p. 154). On the other hand, they have candidly reexamined the basic assumptions of the modernization school. They voice their own in-house criticisms, and they are not hesitant to eliminate some of the dubious assumptions of the classical modernization studies. As such, this new wave of modernization studies is different from classical modernization studies on the following grounds.

First, the new modernization studies avoid treating tradition and modernity as a set of mutually exclusive concepts. In new modernization research, tradition and modernity not only can coexist, but can penetrate and intermingle with each another. In addition, instead of arguing that tradition is an obstacle to development, the new modernization studies attempt to show the beneficial role of tradition. This new conception of tradition has opened up new research agendas, as new modernization researchers have placed much more emphasis on traditional traits (such as familism and folk religion) than they did before.

Second, there is a change in methodology. Instead of drawing typologies and anchoring their discussions at a high level of abstraction, the new modernization studies tend to focus upon concrete cases. History is often brought back in to show the specific pattern of development in a particular country. Often in-depth case studies are supplemented by comparative perspectives, such as research into why the same institution has played different roles in different countries.

Third, as a result of paying more attention to history and concrete case studies, the new modernization studies do not assume a unidirectional path of development toward the Western model. Instead, these studies take it for granted that Third World countries can pursue their own paths of development.

Finally, the new modernization studies lay more emphasis on external (international) factors than before. Although their focus is still on internal factors, they do not neglect the role played by external factors in shaping the development of Third World countries. In addition, they place more emphasis on the phenomenon of conflict. They often incorporate the factors of class conflict, ideological domination, and religious revolution into their analyses.

(See Table 4.1 for a summary of the differences and similarities between the new modernization studies and the classical studies.)

Table 4.1 Comparison of Classical Modernization Studies
and New Modernization Studies

	Classical Modernization Studies	New Modernization Studies
Similarities		
research focus	Third World development	same
level of analysis	national level	same
key variables	internal factors: cultural values and social institutions	same
key concepts	tradition and modernity	same
policy implications	modernization generally beneficial	same
Differences		
on tradition	tradition an obstacle to development	tradition an additive factor of development
on methodology	typology construction high-level abstraction	concrete case studies historical analysis
on direction of development	unidirectional path toward the U.S. model	multidirectional paths of development
on external factors and conflict	relative neglect of external factors and conflict	greater attention to external factors and conflict

By revising some of the basic assumptions of the modernization
school, the new modernization studies have opened up a whole
new set of research agendas. In the following sections, some research problems addressed by the new modernization studies will
be discussed, such as how familism has promoted entrepreneurship in Hong Kong, how folk religion has shaped the modernization of Japan, how the Islamic religion was related to the Iranian
Revolution, and how the international environment has influenced democratic development in Third World countries.

WONG: ENTREPRENEURIAL FAMILISM

Wong's (1988) study starts with a critique of the classical modernization theorists' interpretation of the traditional Chinese family. In the classical modernization literature, Chinese families are seen as a strong force of traditionalism that has promoted nepotism, weakened work discipline, thwarted the free market selection of labor, diluted individual incentives to invest, blocked rationalization, and inhibited the emergence of universalistic business norms. As a result, classical modernization researchers advocated discarding traditional Chinese family values in order to promote economic growth in China. However, Wong argues that this negative economic effect of traditional Chinese values has been exaggerated. Tracing the influence of the family on the internal organization of Chinese enterprises in Hong Kong—especially through paternalistic managerial ideology and practice, nepotistic employment, and family ownership—Wong demonstrates that the family does have a positive impact on economic development.

First, he addresses the practice of *paternalistic management* in Hong Kong enterprises. Wong's (1988, p. 137) research on the cotton spinners shows that there were "industrial patriarchs who exercised tight control, shunned the delegation of power, conferred welfare benefits on their employees as favors, acted as moral custodians of their subordinates, opposed protective labor legislation, and disapproved of trade union activities." Wong points out that the metaphor of the family provides ready-made cultural rhetoric to legitimate a patron-client relationship between employer and employee. The economic foundation of this benevolent paternalism is that it helps the entrepreneur to attract and retain workers in industries of highly fluctuating production. The political consequence of paternalism is that it retards the growth of class consciousness among workers. Wong asserts that when paternalism is working, labor discontent is expressed more in the form of individual acts, such as absenteeism and resignations, than in the collective acts of bargaining and strikes.

Second, *nepotism*—the preferred employment of one's relatives—may also contribute to the success of Hong Kong firms. Wong notes that most Chinese will ask relatives for jobs only as a last resort, and relatives generally make up just a tiny fraction of the personnel in nepotistic companies. On the other hand, for small firms, family members provide a reliable and cheap labor force. In fact, kin are expected to work harder for less pay, which helps to enhance the competitiveness of the firm during recession. If family members are in managerial positions, Chinese entrepreneurs are generally careful to equip them with formal education as well as on-the-job training. Therefore, Wong argues that the kin managers are seldom substandard employees with poor ability.

Third, Wong addresses the family mode of ownership; in 1978, nearly 60% of small factories in Hong Kong were owned by individual proprietors and their families. Wong points out that the principle of patrilineal descent has resulted in a discrete and enduring corporate kinship unit that is conducive to the management of economic resources. Even if family division were to take place, it would take the form of dividing profits rather than physical fragmentation of the family estate. With these family traits, Wong (1988, p. 142) asserts that the competitive strengths of the Chinese family firms are considerable:

> There exists a much stronger measure of trust among *jia* [family] members than among unrelated business partners; consensus is easier to attain; the need for mutual accountability is reduced. These factors enable family firms to be more adaptable in their operations. They can make quick decisions during rapidly changing circumstances and maintain greater secrecy by committing less to written records. As a result, they are particularly well-suited to survive and flourish in situations where a high level of risk is involved.

Therefore, instead of treating family as antithetical to economic development, Wong argues for an economically dynamic ethos of "entrepreneurial familism." This ethos involves the family as the basic unit of economic competition, providing the impetus toward innovation and risk taking. Furthermore, Wong argues that this ethos exists not only among the entrepreneurs, but throughout all of Hong Kong society.

Entrepreneurial familism has three distinguishing characteristics. The first is a high degree of centralization in decision making, but with a low degree of formalization of organizational structure. Second, autonomy is highly valued, and self-employment is preferred. The common ideal, for managers and workers alike, is to become one's own boss. Since managerial loyalty cannot be assumed, employers rely on paternalistic practice, tight supervision, and minimal delegation of authority as a means of coping with the situation. Third, family firms seldom endure, and they are constantly in flux. In addition, enterprises are unlikely to join in collusion since entrepreneurial autonomy is jealously guarded.

If the family plays such a positive role in Hong Kong, why did it fail to realize its potential in the past on the Chinese mainland? For Wong, the explanation lies in the external sociopolitical milieu of the family. Although the family is and was an economically active force, in the past it was probably checked by a state preoccupied with the task of integration and a peculiar ecological and economic environment that constituted a "high-level equilibrium trap." In Hong Kong, these external constraints of the state and environment are removed, as Hong Kong is governed by a colonial state that does not compete with the family for talent. Consequently, the family in Hong Kong has realized potential as the motor of economic development.

In sum, Wong criticizes classical modernization theorists for overlooking the dynamic role of the Chinese family in promoting economic development. Their tendency to see only the sharp dichotomy between European universalism and Chinese particularism resulted in their inability to understand the family's role. Wong believes that the European experience of capitalist development is not likely to be replicated in China; China's different patterns of social structure will necessarily result in divergent patterns of modernization. Wong further cautions that Chinese familism, too, may be different from its Korean and Japanese counterparts because of differences in social structures. As such, the roles of Korean and Japanese families in economic development might be distinctive enough to warrant individual treatment.

DAVIS: JAPANESE RELIGION REVISITED

Following Wong's line of argument in criticizing the classical modernization studies, Davis (1987) reexamined the intricate relationship between religion and development in general and the role of Japanese religion in Japanese modernization in particular.

A Theory of Hurdles

According to Davis, Weber (1958) has offered a theory of hurdles—treating development as though it were an extended obstacle course stretching between the starting line (traditional societies) and the finishing line (modern societies). In this race, runners (i.e., developing nations) who succeed in surmounting all of the hurdles of the course are rewarded with the trophies of "rationality" and modern civilization.

What, then, are these hurdles of development? First, developers must overcome economic hurdles to attain the basic characteristics of the capitalist system itself: rationality, asceticism, continuity in production and markets, and formally free labor markets. Second, there are social-political hurdles—replacement of patrimonialism and kinship economy with rational administrative organizations and legal institutions, separation of places of business and residence, distinctions between corporate and private property. Third, there are psychological hurdles—achievement of spiritual ethos (such as the duty to work according to one's "calling"), rejection of magic, and cultivation of an existential tension between the world as it is and the ethical demands of a transcendent deity. According to Weber, the Protestant ethic—especially the Puritan concern for the soul's salvation—provided Western Europe an impetus to leap these economic, social, political, and psychological hurdles in the race toward modern capitalism.

Weber's studies on religion started a trend of searching for analogues to the Protestant ethic in Japan, Korea, Singapore, and other Third World countries. In the 1950s, as discussed in Chapter 3, Bellah (1957) suggested that Tokugawa religion provided the source of a "central value system" to move Japan into modern capitalism. In the 1980s, Morishima (1982) has picked up Bellah's line of thinking, arguing that Japan's success can be attributed to its Confucian traits of loyalty, nationalism, and social collectivism. Morishima further asserts that due to its Confucian heritage, Japan failed to absorb the West's liberalism, internationalism, and individualism even though Japan imported the West's science, industry, and technology. As a result, the ex-samurai who founded and originally managed the large firms imparted to industry their own Confucian sense of loyalty, creating a loyalty market (permanent employment and seniority advancement) for its recruitment of employees. According to Davis, Morishima's account is a version of the popular "Japan theory" that has exaggerated the uniqueness of Japanese culture in order to provide an explanation for the economic success of Japan.

According to Davis, Weber and his followers in the modernization school have committed the following errors in explaining the relationship between religion and development. First, they assume a priori that religion is the source of some "spiritual ethos" or "central value system," which, in turn, influences all segments of society in the same way. Rather than one central value system, however, Davis sees the possible emergence of several different "spirits" in the rise of capitalism—buyers and vendors cultivate the spirit of "creditworthiness," entrepreneurs stand in need of an ethos that will promote risk taking, investors need a spirit that will inspire delayed gratification, and management needs a disciplinary spirit to impose on workers.

Second, Davis criticizes Weber and his followers for taking secularization or disenchantment for granted as part of the inevitable fate of modern civilization. Davis argues that if modern society consists of different "spirits," it need not be assumed that each one will be secularized in the same way. In fact, some "spirits" may not be secularized at all, while others, now and then, may even undergo "resanctification." Thus each modern society has to be studied anew with respect to its decline of religion.

Third, the followers of Weber, who tend to stress the uniqueness of Japanese culture in explaining its economic success, fail to deal with other social relations, such as the role of individual self-interest, competition, disloyalty, and conflict. Criticizing Morishima's loyalty theory, Davis points out that if ethos accounts for so much, how much weight should researchers put on the contribution of the government, banking system, tariffs, industrial planning, and wages and bonuses? Furthermore, Davis notes that loyalty cannot exist in a vacuum, but is always situated in a network of incentives, rewards, exchanges for patronage, coercion, and constraints. This material foundation must be considered in understanding the real dynamics at work in Japanese society.

A Theory of Barricades

After refuting Weber's theory of hurdles, Davis offers a new theory of barricades. The theory of hurdles looks at religion primarily from the point of view of aggressive modernizers and developers, and assumes that hurdles in the way of development can simply be leapt over in the race course. Davis offers another view of the same situation from the standpoint of traditionalism— how traditional societies set up barricades to protect themselves from the disruptive advance of capitalist values. What traditional societies fear is not progress, but the social turbulence and moral turpitude caused by unrestrained trade and commerce.

In presenting his theory of traditional barricades, Davis portrays traditional society as consisting of three concentric rings (see Figure 4.1):

- an inner ring representing the economy and its values (e.g., achievement and universalism)
- a middle ring representing the "immunological barricade" that traditional societies erect against the economy (made up of taboos, magic, traditional religion, morality, law, philosophy, folk religion, and the like)
- an outer ring representing the society and its values, status, and power relations

Davis conceptualizes the middle ring as made up of defensive institutions that would keep the economy in check. This middle ring operates in a way similar to Polanyi's (1944) "embedded

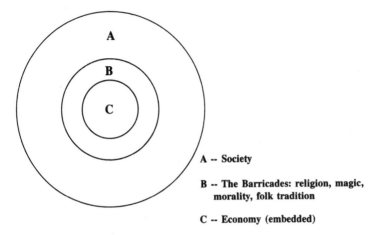

A -- Society

B -- The Barricades: religion, magic, morality, folk tradition

C -- Economy (embedded)

Figure 4.1. Davis's Model of Traditional Society
SOURCE: Davis (1987). Reprinted by permission of the author.

economy," which restricts the scope of the market by traditional rituals and ceremonies, ensuring that the market will function within existing narrow limits.

In Davis's (1987, p. 232) barricades model, "economic development takes place not just when an 'enemy' (i.e., a modernizer or developer) scales the ramparts and invades the citadel of society, but when the barriers themselves grow old and weak, and finally begin to crumble, or when their defenders lose heart and surrender."

In Figure 4.2, the porousness of the religious barricades (represented by a dotted line) has allowed the economy and its values to expand and penetrate the domain of society. Through the barricades metaphor, Davis reinterprets the rise of capitalism in the West. A rational economy came into being not only because "hot Protestants" filled the market with the "zeal of the Lord," but because lukewarm Christians offered so little resistance to exploitation. In England, the church had virtually nothing to say about the misery (such as enclosures, poorhouses, and sweatshops) produced by the Protestant modernizers. This barricades

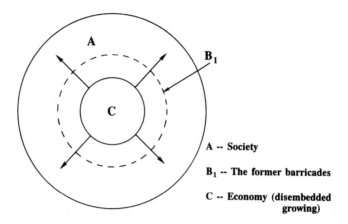

Figure 4.2. Davis's Model of Development and Secularization
SOURCE: Davis (1987). Reprinted by permission of the author.

model, therefore, offers a new approach to the examination of the
relationship between religion and development. Instead of focusing on the ways that modernizers leap over hurdles, Davis's new
approach calls for an analysis of the activities of the defenders of
traditional religion. Davis (1987, p. 247-248) says that we must be
careful to attribute to the new defending actors the same capacities
we ascribe to the advancing modernizers:

> We must endow them with the ability to dodge, huddle, feint,
> fall back, regroup, conspire, collaborate, betray, compromise,
> and even surrender to the foe, . . . how they grew as proud of
> development as the developers themselves, and how their
> rhetoric and strategies were co-opted by the victors and
> made part of the master plan of development itself.

Rewriting the Religious History of Japan

Using his barricades model, Davis attempts to reinterpret the
relationship between Japanese religion and development. He

focuses on two aspects: (1) the negative enablements of religion (Why did Japanese religion fail to obstruct change?) and (2) the positive enablements of religion (How did Japanese religion promote change?).

The negative enablements. Davis argues that Japanese religions have posed no obstruction to change for the following reasons. First, with respect to Buddhism, it had done nothing to prevent the rapid development of the Japanese countryside. Unlike Islam, Buddhism sought to impose no sacred law upon society that ultimately would obstruct change. For example, Buddhism imposes no restrictions on a person's occupation. Most Buddhist priests just limit their services to funerals and the routine performance of ancestral rites.

Second, since Shinto had no universal prelates to enforce its claims, it gave in even more easily to the modernizing forces. Davis (1987, p. 251) illustrates this point: "If a festival interfered with new work schedules, it was postponed, curtailed, or simply dropped from the calendar. Ancient taboos limiting intercourse with outsiders were prudently overlooked or forgotten."

Third, because of the coexistence of Confucianism, Buddhism, and Shinto, there is a high degree of religious tolerance in Japan. Furthermore, the Japanese even develop the practical value of multiple religious affiliations. Davis argues that this pattern of religious tolerance enabled the Japanese to borrow from the science, technology, and cultures of the Western world at minimal psychological cost.

Fourth, Japanese urbanization has promoted a secularization of religion, leading to a this-worldly spirit among urban merchants and Confucian scholars. Davis cites a Confucian scholar's remark that "in this world there are no gods, Buddhas, or ghosts, nor are there strange or miraculous things" (p. 253). This secular attitude also would not obstruct development.

Fifth, Davis observes the postwar boom in new religions, with huge mass movements founded by charismatic (or shamanistic) leaders who whipped up new confections in the old pantries of Shinto, Buddhism, Christianity, and Confucianism (p. 253). The new religions promoted ancestor worship, prewar ethnocentrism, and other traditional values. Their members were recruited from the segments of the population hurt by the rapid process of Japanese industrialization. Unprotected by large industries or labor unions, the oppressed turned to the new religions for miracles. The preachers' remedies were always religious or magical nostrums, such as a spell that would take care of everything or a vague promise of the coming of a "future Buddha" who would set everything right. New religions of this sort helped believers cope with a fallen world, enabled them to accept the unequal burdens of a rapidly developing society, and thus seldom got in the way of development.

Finally, observing the revival of folk religion, Davis asserts that magic and miracles are perfectly compatible with the "rationality" of industrial society. Magic could adapt itself to the modern economy once that economy was in place. Thus workers could be faithful to their industrial "callings" by tending their "gardens of magic" on weekends or on their days off. Davis argues that so long as magic is situational and functional, it poses no serious threat to modern institutions.

The positive enablements. According to Davis, religion is often used to enhance economic production. Even in premodern society, religion and magic were used to increase the productivity of the embedded economy. Thus the common man turned to religion when he wanted his cow to calve, his wife to bear, the plague to pass by, or the drought to end.

In early modern Japan, Davis (1987, p. 260) argues that the folk religion had developed a set of work ethics for the common people. The Fuji sect, for instance, promoted virtues of "benevolence, self-restraint, frugality, and diligence. . . . One should labor, they say, not merely to enrich oneself, but in order to support one's family and indigent neighbors." In the twentieth century, moreover, this religious work ethic of early modern Japan was picked up by the social teachings of the new religions. Davis observes that many new religions continue to preach "a feudalistic morality in the context of a capitalist economy" (p. 261). Mrs. God, for example, teaches her followers that "each person should remind himself of his responsibilities to God and his employer and make certain he renders his best efforts to both." Consequently, Davis remarks, Japan's folk religion may have more to do with the implementation of the popular work ethic than any other symbolic factor.

However, Davis also notes that Japanese industry takes pain to transmit this religious work ethic to workers (from the "top down") through various initiation rites, training sessions, and "spiritual education." In addition, the work ethic is propagated in the Japan theory of Morishima's work. Stressing the uniqueness of the Japanese national character, this Japan theory advocates that "to be Japanese, a person must work hard, be loyal and sincere." Through the sponsorship of the Japanese government and industry, work is made part of the values of harmony, unity, consensus, loyalty, sincerity, and altruistic service to the individual's family, company, and nation.

As there is a mixture of civil religion and work ethic, so there is a mixture of civil religion and business ideology. Davis (1987, p. 262) observes:

> During the Tokugawa period, Confucian schools aimed at producing men who would be useful to their fief. Later on, the same ambition was legitimated in the name of Japanese nationalism. The nouveaux riches in Japan justified its wealth in the name of family and nation, as much as early English entrepreneurs dedicated the fruits of their labor to the glory of God and the improvement of man's estate.

Nevertheless, Davis argues that the mixing of civil religion and business ideology was unsuccessful. In the 1920s, the traditional Confucian "barricades" held ground. The business elite failed to formulate a persuasive rationale for capitalism, and they were condemned for their selfishness and profit-mongering. This failure led to the rise of militarism and fascism, leaving little space for Western democracy to develop.

Japan as a Post-Confucian Industrial Society

Davis argues that by the 1980s, little remained of the barricades that defended traditionalism. Instead of being embedded in the

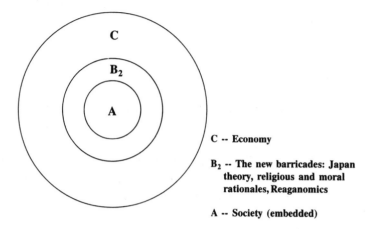

Figure 4.3. Davis's Model of Post-Confucian Industrial Society
SOURCE: Davis (1987). Reprinted by permission of the author.

society in the traditional phase, the economy now expanded and took charge of the modern society. Today, it is industry that asks to be made safe from society, and new barricades rise up to protect the economy from the intrusion of society. For Davis (1987, p. 264-265), the new barricades include the "secular preachers of the gospel of wealth, Reaganomics, administrative reform, Japan theory. Standing beside them, however, are the evangelists, shamans, magicians, and high priests of both traditional and New Religions who now bless the very institutions they once cursed" (see Figure 4.3).

In sum, Davis recapitulates that his three figures (reproduced here as Figures 4.1-4.3) are not intended to be interpreted as a unilinear model of development per se. Instead, they merely highlight the way in which religion sanctifies society, and the way the economy has become "secularized." Davis also wants to remind his readers of the functional or legitimating role of religion, and how religion itself has been transformed in order to accommodate its new role in development. Davis asserts that the decline of religion should no longer be taken for granted, and that folk

religion and magic can continue to exist and collaborate with the
institutions of modern society.

BANUAZIZI: ISLAMIC REVOLUTION IN IRAN

Like Davis, who examines the role of folk religion in development, Banuazizi argues for a greater appreciation of tradition in its
own right. Following the trend of the late 1960s, Banuazizi (1987)
criticizes the classical modernization theorists for (1) evoking an
ideal image of contemporary Western society, (2) defining tradition in residual and negative terms, and (3) arguing that the Third
World has to get rid of its traditional obstacles before modernization can occur. Banuazizi advocates bringing tradition back;
tradition can be as reflective, creative, and responsive to individual
and collective needs as its modern counterpart can, and tradition
has immense potential for social mobilization and change.

From this perspective, Banuazizi observes the revival of a traditionalist movement in the form of the "Islamic resurgence." In
the 1980s, there was hardly a Muslim country in which the Islamic
revival had not already had a noticeable impact—on the form and
content of politics, on the rejection of Western values and life-
styles, or on the strict observance of Islamic codes and enforcement
of sacred laws. In particular, Banuazizi examines one of the most
dramatic outbursts of the Islamic revival—the Iranian Revolution
of 1977-1979. The Iranian case is especially noteworthy because it
is the only revivalist movement that has actually brought a fun-
damentalist Islamic regime to power. What were the causes of the
Iranian Revolution? How can this interesting case enhance our
understanding of the new modernization studies?

In the Western media, Islamic resurgence movements have been
portrayed as extremist, anachronistic, and retrogressive. From the
point of view of classical modernization studies, these movements
have been indicative of a "breakdown" in institution building
under the strains of mass politics and rapid social mobilization. It
has been feared that these movements would bring about authoritarian regimes, escalation of ethnoreligious conflicts, and political

disintegration. With respect to the Iranian Revolution of 1977-1979, the Islamic resurgence is generally portrayed as a backlash of reactionary elements, such as the Islamic clerics, who adopted a defensive reaction against modernization in Iran.

Banuazizi argues that these interpretations are one-sided because they fail to examine factors such as the structural bases, the cultural division, and the nature of the Shi'ite religion, as well as the intricate coalitions of different social forces that explained the origins of the Iranian Revolution.

First, Banuazizi points to the structural roots of the Iranian Revolution. In the 1970s, Iran underwent extensive modernization, including heavy industrialization, urbanization, expansion of formal education, and growth of the mass media. However, this wave of modernization favored mainly the Westernized, predominantly urban, upper and middle strata, and "labor aristocracy" in the modern industrial sector. Side by side with modernization were growing structural inequalities, the subservience of the shah to the United States, the contempt of the shah for Islamic culture, and the repression and endemic corruption of the shah's regime. These conflicts led to resentment against the shah by virtually every segment of the population.

Second, the forces of modernization had produced a profound cultural division between a small modern segment of Western-educated elite and a large traditional segment of peasants, the urban poor, small merchants, and artisans. The modern segment favored such Western values as individualism, freedom, liberty, and democracy, while the traditional segment adhered to Islamic values, life-styles, and behavior.

Third, the unique nature of the Shi'ite religion acted to propel the revolution. On an ideological level, Shi'ism in Iran never lost its inherently oppositional potential. Banuazizi (1987, p. 304) explains:

Its powerful symbolism of steadfastness, suffering and self-sacrifice in pursuit of truth and justice displayed in its various dramatic rituals; its remarkable capacity for redefining political conflicts in religious terms; its populist logic and vocabulary of pitting the "disinherited" against the "oppres-

sors"; and its messianic promise of a just social order with the
return of the "Hidden Imam" make it an unusually powerful
religion of protest.

In addition, the Shi'ite *ulama* (Islamic clerics) acted ably as the
politicocultural elite to lead the revolution forward. They could
play such a role because they had long been active in every major
oppositional movement over the past century, had close economic
and personal ties with the traditional urban middle and lower
strata, possessed financial resources, and could use mosques,
shrines, and associations to voice public grievances and criticize
the regime with relative impunity. Finally, there was the factor of
religious charisma. Khomeini was enormously popular among the
various oppositional groups, and his militant followers launched
a well-coordinated revolutionary mobilization, using every traditional and modern form of communication and agitation to realize
their aims.

Fourth, the Iranian Revolution was a mass-based social revolution, involving a coalition of social forces and political ideologies.
At the ideological level, there was no single, monolithic "Islamic
ideology," but a number of Islamic and secular ideologies. Each of
these ideologies appealed to a particular social group that played
a role in the revolutionary struggle. On the Islamic side alone,
Banuazizi points out that there were four variants:

- *radical Islam:* the ideology of the young intellectuals who wanted to
  turn Iran into a classless Islamic society
- *militant Islam:* the ideology of the *ulama*, the petty bourgeoisie, and
  the dispossessed—groups that wanted to establish "God's" government on earth
- *liberal Islam:* the ideology of the bourgeoisie and the middle class—
  groups that wanted to share power with the state through non-
  violent means
- *traditional Islam:* the ideology of the old middle strata, a group that
  desired the return of the old order

Banuazizi argues that the ideals and values of Islam could be made
so elastic that they would fit the interests and proclivities of any
particular group. In addition, the clerics and the charismatic lead-

ers acted as coalition builders to bring all these groups together for revolutionary mobilization.

What have we learned from this analysis of the Iranian Revolution? First, like Davis, Banuazizi points out that modernization does not necessarily bring about secularization. Religious movements such as that of Islam can easily be revived when institutional and historical conditions are favorable. Thus the Islamic revolution in Iran has to be seen in relation to the historically specific processes that took place in that society, particularly the growing social inequalities, cultural divisions, unpopularity of the shah's regime, and inherent oppositional character of Shi'ite Islam.

Second, Banuazizi remarks that traditionalist actors do not seem to be hampered by their "traditionalist" traits. Consequently, traditional ideologies seem to be at least as efficacious in articulating the demands of a movement for social change as any of their modern secular counterparts. This applies to Shi'ite Islam as well as to ultra-Orthodox Judaism in Israel, "liberation theology" in Latin America, and the Catholic church in the Polish workers' movement.

Third, traditionalist religious movements can also appeal to those who have extensive exposure to modernizing institutions (such as the new middle class), as well as to marginal social elements (such as the poor and the dispossessed).

Finally, since 1979, Banuazizi has observed the triumph of a traditionalist element and the elimination of virtually all other groups that had participated in the revolutionary coalition in Iran. There is an Islamic campaign, extending its control into all spheres of public and private life. Given this observation, Banuazizi asserts that the dialogue concerning tradition and modernity should be reopened, this time with an emphasis on tradition.

HUNTINGTON: WILL MORE
COUNTRIES BECOME DEMOCRATIC?

As Banuazizi provides a sophisticated analysis of the Iranian Revolution, Huntington presents a comprehensive review of the crucial factors relating to the development of democracy in Third

World countries. In the 1960s, Lipset optimistically entertained the hypothesis that more economic development would lead to democracy. In the 1970s, with the breakdown of many democratic regimes, researchers in the modernization school became more pessimistic about the prospects for democracy in the Third World. In the 1980s, however, the prospects seem to have brightened once again, and there is a trend toward research on the possibilities of transitions to democracy.

It is within such a context that Huntington (1984) raises the question: Will more countries become democratic? In researching this question, Huntington distinguishes two sets of factors: (1) the preconditions that favor democratic development and (2) the political processes by which democratic development has occurred.

Preconditions of Democratization

After two decades of research, Huntington provides a more sophisticated analysis of the preconditions of democracy than Lipset's one-variable analysis. In addition to economic wealth and equality, Huntington has included social structure, external environment, and cultural context for consideration.

First is the factor of *economic wealth*. Lipset's (1963) pioneering research postulates that the more well-to-do a nation, the greater its chance of becoming democratic. The literature's explanation of this strong correlation between wealth and democracy is that a wealthy economy makes possible high levels of literacy, education, and mass media exposure, all of which are conducive to democracy. A wealthy economy also moderates political tensions through providing alternative opportunities for unsuccessful political leaders. In addition, an advanced, complex, industrialized economy cannot be governed efficiently by authoritarian means; decision making is necessarily dispersed, power is shared, and rules must be based on the consent of those affected by them. Furthermore, a country with a wealthy economy tends to have more equally distributed income than do poor countries, and thus a smaller impoverished mass.

However, Huntington raises the question as to what level of economic development is required to make possible the transition to democracy. Various countries have become democratic at widely varying levels of development. On the other hand, there are many countries, especially in East Asia and Latin America, that have gone through economic development and yet turned away from democracy. In opposition to Lipset's wealth-democracy theory, O'Donnell (1978) has developed a theory of bureaucratic authoritarianism that accounts for the emergence of a new and stronger form of authoritarian rule when a country is undergoing the strains of import substitution.

In trying to reconcile the contradictory evidence in the literature, Huntington proposes a new concept of the zone of transition (or choice). According to this concept, as countries develop economically, they move into a zone of transition in which traditional political institutions become increasingly difficult to maintain. Development alone does not determine what political system will replace those institutions. Instead of moving in a linear direction toward Western-style democracy, countries in the zone of transition may have choices among different alternatives, and their future evolution is dependent upon the historical choices made by their political elites. In short, although economic wealth is a necessary condition for democracy, it is not a sufficient one. A study of democratic transition, therefore, must consider other factors.

The second factor that Huntington discusses is *social structure*. If there is a widely differentiated and articulated social structure with relatively autonomous groups (such as business, occupational, religious, and ethnic groups), then these groups will provide the basis for the checking of state power and the groundwork for democratic political institutions. If there is no autonomous intermediate group, then the society will likely be dominated by a centralized power apparatus in the form of an absolute monarchy, an oriental despotism, or an authoritarian or totalitarian dictatorship.

Of all the intermediate groups, Huntington stresses the existence of an autonomous bourgeoisie as the most significant. Agreeing with Barrington Moore (1966), Huntington remarks, "No bourgeois, no democracy." The problem with Third World countries is that they lack a strong, autonomous bourgeois class. Although there is some economic growth in the Third World, it is mostly carried out by the state and by multinational enterprises. When economic development runs ahead of the development of a bourgeoisie in Third World countries, there tends to be a failure of democracy.

Another key element in the social structure that promotes democracy is the existence of market-oriented economies. All political democracies have market-oriented economies, although not all market-oriented economies are paired with democratic political systems. The reason, Huntington explains, is that a market economy requires a dispersion of economic power, thereby creating a check to state power. A market economy thus enables the bourgeoisie to limit state power and to exploit democratic means to serve its interests. In addition, a market economy is likely to give rise to economic wealth and to more equitable distribution of income, which provides the infrastructure of democracy.

The third factor that Huntington highlights is *external environment*. As Huntington succinctly states, democratization is the result of diffusion rather than of development, ascribed in large part to British and American influence, through settlement, colonial rule, defeat in war, or fairly direct imposition. Where American armies went in World War II, democracy followed. Where Soviet armies went, communism followed. In this respect, the rise and fall of democracy on a global scale is a function of the rise and decline of the most powerful democratic states. The spread of democracy in the nineteenth century went hand in hand with the Pax Britannica, and the extension of democracy after World War II reflected the global power of the United States. Conversely, the decline of democracy in East Asia and Latin America in the 1970s was a reflection of the waning of the American influence. This democratic influence, as Huntington (1984, p. 206) points out, "is felt both directly, as a result of the efforts of the American government to affect political processes in other societies, and also indirectly by providing a powerful and successful model to be followed."

Moreover, Huntington notices that in some regions, a regional trend may exist. By and large, Latin American governments moved in a democratic direction in the late 1950s and early 1960s, then in an authoritarian direction in the late 1960s and early 1970s, and then once again in a democratic direction in the late 1970s and early 1980s. These regional shifts might have been the result of economic development, the influence of neighboring countries, and the promotion of the U.S. government.

The fourth factor Huntington discusses is the *cultural context*. Examining the impact of religion on political culture, Huntington finds that Protestantism has a high correlation with democracy, that Catholicism has a moderate and delayed impact on the growth of democracy, that Hindu and Shinto cultures did not prevent democratization, and that Islam, Confucianism, and Buddhism have been conducive to authoritarian rule.

How can these differences be explained? Huntington distinguishes two types of religious culture. A *consummatory* religious culture—where intermediate and ultimate ends are closely related—is less favorable to democracy. In Islam, for example, there is no distinction between religion and politics (or between the spiritual and the secular), and political participation has historically been an alien concept. An *instrumental* religious culture is characterized by the separation of intermediate ends from ultimate ends. Hindu tradition, for instance, tolerates diversity and conflict among groups, recognizes the legitimacy of compromise, and thus should pose no barrier to democratization.

In sum, Huntington concludes that the preconditions of democratization are economic wealth, pluralistic social structure (an autonomous bourgeoisie and a market-oriented economy), greater influence vis-à-vis the society of existing democratic states, and a culture that is tolerant of diversity and compromise. He argues that with the exception of a market economy, no single precondition is necessary to produce such a development. Some combination of the above preconditions is required for a democratic regime to emerge, but the nature of the combination can vary greatly from one case to another.

Processes of Democratization

In addition to focusing on the preconditions of democracy, Huntington examines the political processes through which democratic development has occurred. He discusses three models of democratization. The first is a *linear* model that draws from both British and Swedish experience. In the British case, democratization progressed from civil rights to political rights, to gradual development of parliamentary supremacy and a cabinet government, and finally to an incremental expansion of suffrage over the course of a century. In the Swedish case, it took the following route: national unity, prolonged and inconclusive political struggle, a conscious decision to adopt democratic rules, and finally habituation to the working of those rules.

The second model of democratization is a *cyclical* one of alternating despotism and democracy. This model is most common in Latin American nations. In this model, key elites normally accept the legitimacy of democratic forms. Elections are held from time to time, but rarely is there any substantial succession of government coming to power through the electoral process. Governments are as often the product of military intervention as they are of elections. The military intervenes when a radical party wins election, when there is economic chaos (e.g., high inflation and unemployment), or when there is widespread political unrest. Once a military junta takes over, it usually promises to return power to civilian rule in the near future. It does so, however, only if it is forced to by mass protest or by its own inability to govern effectively. In a praetorian situation like this, Huntington points out that neither authoritarian nor democratic institutions are effectively institutionalized. Once a country enters into this cyclical pattern of alternating military authoritarian and civil democracy, it appears to be difficult for it to break the cycle.

The third model of democratization discussed by Huntington is *dialectical*. In this model, the development of an urban middle class leads to growing pressures on the authoritarian regime for political participation and contestation. At some point there is an "urban breakthrough," the replacement of the existing authoritarian regime with a democratic one. The new middle-class regime, however, finds it hard to govern effectively, and usually there is an overthrow of the democratic regime and a return to the authoritarian system. In due course, however, the authoritarian regime collapses and a transition is made to a long-lasting democratic system; this model characterizes the experience of Germany, Italy, Greece, and Spain.

In addition to his discussion of the linear, cyclical, and dialectical models, Huntington addresses the issue of the best sequence for democratic development. His preferred overall process is as follows:

(1) Define national identity.
(2) Develop effective political institutions.
(3) Expand political participation.

Huntington stresses that political participation must occur late in the sequence of change, after the installation of effective political institutions such as electoral and party systems. If participation expands too early in the sequence, it will lead to political instability and violence. To reinforce this point, Huntington asserts that democratic regimes that last have seldom been instituted by popular action. Instead, democracy has come as much from the top down as from the bottom up. It is only when political elites, after calculating their own interests, decide to negotiate and compromise with one another that democratic institutions come into existence.

Stressing the elitist origins of democracy, Huntington refutes Barrington Moore's (1966) argument that democracy can be inaugurated by bloody revolution. Although all guerrilla insurgences and revolutionary regimes claim to be democratic, they turn out to be authoritarian once they achieve power through violence, often imposing even more repressive regimes than those they overthrew. Huntington emphasizes that democracy tends to be the result of gradual evolutionary process with minimum violence, rather than the result of revolutionary outflow of existing hegemonies.

After surveying the preconditions and processes of democratization, Huntington applies these criteria to an examination of the prospects for democratization in the 1980s. He has high hopes for democratization in Latin America because of the current regimes' cultural traditions, levels of economic development, previous democratic experience, social pluralism, and the elites' desires to emulate European and North American models. However, he is not as optimistic about regimes in East Asia. Although the East Asian states have achieved some economic development and have experienced some influence from the United States, their cultural traditions, social structure, and weaknesses of democratic norms serve to impede democratic development. Huntington points out that the East Asian states present the issue of whether economics or culture has the greater influence on democratization. With respect to the Islamic countries in the Middle East and most African countries, prospects for democracy are slim, due to their religion, poverty, or the violent nature of their politics. The likelihood of democratic development in Eastern Europe is virtually nonexistent. The Soviet presence is a decisive overriding obstacle, and Huntington argues that no communist country has become democratic through internal causes.

In conclusion, Huntington suggests that the United States can contribute to the democratic development in Third World nations in the following ways: by assisting their economic development, by fostering their market economies and the growth of a vigorous bourgeoisie, by exercising greater influence than it has in world affairs, and by helping the elites of these countries enter the transition zone to democratization.

POWERS OF THE
NEW MODERNIZATION THEORIES

According to Almond (1987, p. 454), "the test of any research approach is its productivity. Does it generate novel ways of looking at the subject matter? Does it increase our knowledge and make it more reliable?" Using Almond's criteria, we can see that the new modernization studies have gone beyond the relatively crude analyses of the classical modernization studies. After dropping some of the shaky assumptions of the classical modernization studies—such as characterizing modernization as an irreversible, progressive, and lengthy Americanization progress, and treating tradition as an obstacle to modernization—the new modernization studies open up new research agendas and provide a more sophisticated analysis than the old modernization studies.

Bringing tradition back in. Guided by new concepts such as entrepreneurial familism, the theory of barricades, and Islamic resurgence, the new modernization studies have taken a much closer look at what tradition is, how it interacts with Western forces, and what role it has played in the process of modernization. Although the classical modernization studies focused on the negative role of tradition, the new modernization studies reveal the intricate relationship between tradition and modernity. Thus Wong shows that paternalistic management, nepotism, and a family mode of ownership have promoted the economic development of Hong Kong. Davis argues that Japanese industry takes pains to transmit a traditional religious work ethic to workers through spiritual education. Banuazizi points to the crucial role played by the Shi'ite religion and the Shi'ite ulama in propelling the Iranian Revolution forward. And Huntington takes note of the differential impacts of religion on democracy.

Bringing history back in. The new modernization studies have also adopted a different methodology. Instead of typological construction at a highly abstract level, the new modernization studies have brought history back into the picture, focusing on the unique development of each case study. Thus instead of adapting cases to illustrate theory, the new modernization studies use theory to explain individual case studies. For example, Wong concludes that his findings on Hong Kong familism may not be applicable to other places, such as mainland China, Korea, and Japan. Davis rewrites the religious history of Japan by emphasizing how folk religion and magic can continue to exist and collaborate with modern industrialism. Banuazizi focuses on how the historical combinations of social, political, and religious factors in 1979 gave rise to the unique Iranian Revolution. And Huntington stresses that it is important to examine the historical processes and sequences of democratic development.

Toward a more sophisticated analysis. The new modernization studies have avoided making simplistic statements or presenting single-variable analyses. Instead, they pay attention to multi-institutional (social, cultural, political, and economic) analysis, to multilineal paths of development, and to the interaction between external and internal factors. For instance, Wong brings in the factor of colonial government of Hong Kong and entertains the possible divergent pattern of modernization in East Asia. Davis's new barricades theory is more sophisticated than the old hurdles model because it takes into account the defending actors of traditional religion, charismatic leaders, exploitation, and militarism in Japanese history. Banuazizi examines the structural roots, cultural divisions, and religious elements of the Iranian Revolution. And Huntington provides a comprehensive analysis of a variety of factors—wealth, social structure, external environment, cultural context, political process, and sequence—in his exploration of whether more countries will become more democratic.

In light of the modifications demonstrated in this chapter, it seems that the modernization school has recovered from its crisis of the late 1960s and should be able to continue its fruitful line of research with vigor in the 1990s. Furthermore, it is possible that, as Portes (1980, p. 224) points out, modernization studies "may emerge in a new guise as correctives to the exclusive external focus of the new [dependency and world-system] perspectives."

Part II

THE DEPENDENCY SCHOOL

CHAPTER 5

The Dependency Perspective

THE HISTORICAL CONTEXT

Just as the modernization school can be said to examine development from the point of view of the United States and other Western countries, the dependency school can be said to view development from a Third World perspective. According to Blomstrom and Hettne (1984), the dependency school represents "the voices from the periphery" that challenge the intellectual hegemony of the American modernization school.

The dependency school first arose in Latin America as a response to the bankruptcy of the program of the U.N. Economic Commission for Latin America (ECLA) in the early 1960s (Bodenheimer 1970a; Dos Santos 1973). Many populist regimes in Latin America tried out the ECLA developmental strategy of protectionism and industrialization through import substitution in the 1950s, and many Latin American researchers had high hopes for a trend toward economic growth, welfare, and democracy. However, the brief economic expansion in the 1950s quickly turned into economic stagnation. In the early 1960s, Latin America was plagued by unemployment, inflation, currency devaluation, declining terms of trade, and other economic problems. Popular protests were followed by the collapse of popular regimes and the setting up of repressive military and authoritarian regimes. Needless to say, many Latin American researchers were disappointed. They became disillusioned with both the ECLA program and the American modernization school, which proved unable to explain economic stagnation, political repression, and the widening gap between rich and poor countries.

The dependency school was also a response to the crisis of orthodox Marxism in Latin America in the early 1960s. From an orthodox communist viewpoint, the Latin American countries had to go through the stage of "bourgeois" industrial revolution before they could wage a "proletarian" socialist revolution. However, the Chinese Revolution in 1949 and the Cuban Revolution in the late 1950s showed that Third World countries could skip the stage of bourgeois revolution. Attracted to the Chinese and Cuban models of development, many radical Latin American researchers wondered whether their own countries could also move into the stage of socialist revolution.

This indigenous Latin American dependency school then quickly spread from Latin America to North America. Andre Gunder Frank, who happened to be in Latin America in the early 1960s, was instrumental in disseminating the ideas of the dependency school to the English-speaking world. In fact, outside Latin America, the dependency school has generally been identified with Frank and the American journal *Monthly Review,* to which Frank is a frequent contributor.

The dependency school received a warm welcome in the United States in the late 1960s because it resonated with the sentiments of a new generation of young radical researchers who came of age during the campus revolts, antiwar protests, women's liberation activities, and ghetto rebellions of that time. In Chirot's (1981, p. 259-260) words:

> The American debacle in Vietnam and the eruption of major racial troubles in the mid-1960s, followed by chronic inflation, the devaluation of the American dollar, and the general loss of America's self-confidence in the early 1970s, ended the moral conviction on which modernization theory had come to base itself. A new type of theory became popular among younger sociologists, one that reversed all of the old axioms.

America became the very model of evil, and capitalism, which had been seen as the cause of social progress, became a sinister exploiter and the main agent of poverty in most of the world. Imperialism, not backwardness and lack of modernity, was the new enemy.

Emerging from the historical context of the 1960s, the dependency school was therefore a response to the failure of the ECLA program, the crisis of orthodox Marxism, and the decline of the modernization school in the United States. The following section provides a brief review of the ECLA program and the Marxist theories as background for discussion of the dependency perspective.

THE INTELLECTUAL HERITAGE

The ECLA

The formulation of a distinctly Latin American school of development is intimately related to the ECLA. In what is known as the "ECLA Manifesto," Prebisch (1950), who was the head of the ECLA, criticized the outdated schema of the international division of labor. Under this schema, Latin America was asked to produce food and raw materials for the great industrial centers, and, in return, Latin America would receive industrial goods from these centers. It was Prebisch's contention that this scheme was at the root of the developmental problems of Latin America. Reliance on exports of food and raw materials would inevitably lead to a deterioration of Latin America's terms of trade, which would further affect its domestic accumulation of capital.

Prebisch's strategy for Latin American development called for the one-sided international division of labor to be stopped, and for Latin America to undergo industrialization:

- The process of industrialization was to be speeded up by the substitution of a large part of current imports by domestic production.

Initially, domestic industries were to be protected from foreign competition by tariffs and other support measures, but once their competitive ability had improved, the local firms should be able to manage on their own.

- The production of raw materials would continue to play an important role in Latin American economies. The income earned from exporting raw materials should be used to pay for imported capital goods, and thus help increase the rate of economic growth.
- Governments should actively participate as coordinators of the industrialization program. Increased government involvement was necessary to break the chains of underdevelopment (Blomstrom and Hettne 1984, p. 41-42).

Initially, this ECLA strategy was rather coldly received by Latin American governments in the 1950s. This resistance explains why the ECLA could not push forward radical measures such as land reforms. In fact, structural changes have never been placed high on the priority list of necessary changes. To a certain extent, the ECLA strategy can be considered overly optimistic. It assumes that the various characteristics of an underdeveloped society would automatically disappear in the process of industrialization—that is, industrialization would put an end to all problems of development.

Unfortunately, the ECLA program did not succeed. Economic stagnation and political problems came to the fore in the 1960s. As Blomstrom and Hettne (1984, p. 45) explain, the shortcomings of the policy of import substitution were obvious:

The purchasing power was limited to certain social strata, and the domestic market showed no tendency to expand after its needs had been fulfilled. The import dependency had simply shifted from consumption goods to capital goods. The conventional export goods had been neglected in the general frenzy of industrialization, the result was acute balance-of-payment problems in one country after another. The optimism of growth changed into deep depression.

The failure of the moderate ECLA program prompted the dependency school to propose a more radical program, as will be seen in the next section.

Neo-Marxism

Another theoretical tradition upon which the dependency school draws is neo-Marxism. The success of the Chinese and Cuban revolutions helped to spread a new form of Marxism to Latin American universities, giving rise to a radical generation whose members described themselves as "neo-Marxists." According to Foster-Carter (1973), neo-Marxists are different from orthodox Marxists in the following respects:

(1) While orthodox Marxists see imperialism in a "center's" perspective as a stage of monopoly capitalism in Western Europe, neo-Marxists see imperialism from the "peripheral" point of view, focusing on the indictments of imperialism on Third World development.

(2) Orthodox Marxists tend to advocate a strategy of two-stage revolution. A bourgeois revolution has to take place before a socialist revolution occurs. Since most Third World countries are backward, orthodox Marxists have high hopes for the progressive bourgeoisie to carry out the present stage of bourgeois revolution. Neo-Marxists, on the other hand, believe that the present situation in the Third World is ripe for socialist revolution. They want revolution now. They perceive the bourgeoisie as the creation and tool of imperialism, incapable of fulfilling its role as the liberator of the forces of production.

(3) If socialist revolution occurs, orthodox Marxists would like it to be promoted by the industrial proletariat in the cities, while neo-Marxists are attracted to the path of socialist revolution taken by China and Cuba. Neo-Marxists have high hopes for the revolutionary potential of the peasantry in the countryside, and guerrilla warfare by the people's army is their favorite strategy of revolution.

As will be seen in the following discussion, this tradition of neo-Marxism has provided many key concepts for the dependency school's criticisms of both the ECLA program and the modernization school in the mid-1960s.

FRANK: THE DEVELOPMENT OF UNDERDEVELOPMENT

Before presenting the concept of underdevelopment and the model of metropolis-satellite exploitation, Frank (1967, 1969) starts with a critique of the modernization school. According to Frank, most of the theoretical categories and development policies in the modernization school have been distilled exclusively from the historical experience of European and North American advanced capitalist nations. To this extent, these Western theoretical categories are unable to guide our understanding of the problems facing Third World nations.

First, the modernization school is deficient because it offers an "internal" explanation of Third World development. The modernization school assumes that there is something wrong inside Third World countries—such as traditional culture, overpopulation, little investment, or lack of achievement motivation—and this is why Third World countries are backward and stagnant. In addition, by ignoring the history of Third World countries, the modernization school assumes that these countries are now at the early stage of development according to the experience of Western countries, and therefore they need to look to Western countries as mentors and follow the Western path of development in order to reach modernity.

According to Frank, Third World countries could never follow the Western path because they have experienced something that Western countries have not experienced. To put it plainly, Western countries have not experienced *colonialism,* while most Third World countries are former colonies of Western countries. It is strange that the modernization school seldom discusses the factor of colonialism in detail, given that many Third World countries were colonies for more than a century. The colonial experience has totally restructured Third World countries and has drastically altered their paths of development.

In reaction to the "internal" explanation of the modernization school, Frank offers an "external" explanation for Third World development. According to Frank, the backwardness of Third World countries cannot be explained by feudalism or traditionalism. In fact, it is wrong to characterize Third World countries as "primitive," "feudal," or "traditional," because many countries—such as China and India—were quite advanced before they encountered colonialism in the eighteenth century. Instead, the historical experience of colonialism and foreign domination have reversed the

development of many "advanced" Third World countries and forced them to move along the path of economic backwardness. In trying to capture this historical experience of the degeneration of Third World countries, Frank formulates the concept of "the development of underdevelopment" to denote that underdevelopment is not a natural condition but an artifact created by the long history of colonial domination in Third World countries.

In addition, Frank has formulated a "metropolis-satellite" model to explain how the mechanisms of underdevelopment work. This metropolis-satellite relationship has its origins in the colonial period, when the conqueror implanted new cities in the Third World with the aim of facilitating the transfer of economic surplus to Western countries. According to Frank, the national cities then became the satellites of the Western metropolis. This metropolis-satellite relation, however, is not limited to the international level—it penetrates to the regional and local levels of Third World countries as well. Therefore, just as the national cities have become the satellites of the Western metropolises, so these satellites immediately become the colonial metropolises with respect to the provincial cities, which in turn have local cities as satellites surrounding them. A whole chain of constellations of metropolises and satellites is established to extract economic surplus (in the forms of raw materials, minerals, commodities, profits) from Third World villages to local capitals, to regional capitals, to national capitals, and finally to the cities of Western countries.

Frank argues that this national transfer of economic surplus has produced underdevelopment in Third World countries and development in Western countries. In other words, the historical process that generates development in the Western metropolises also simultaneously generates underdevelopment in Third World satellites. Based on this metropolis-satellite model, Frank has proposed several interesting hypotheses concerning Third World development:

- *Hypothesis 1:* In contrast to the development of the world metropolis, which is no one's satellite, the development of national and other subordinate metropolises is limited by their satellite statuses. For instance, although São Paulo has begun to build up an industrial establishment, Frank does not believe that Brazil can break out of the cycle of satellite development, which is characterized by non-autonomous and unsatisfactory industrial development.

- *Hypothesis 2:* The satellites experience their greatest economic development when their ties to the metropolis are weakest. Frank observes that Latin America experienced marked autonomous industrialization during the temporary isolation caused by the crisis of World War I and by the depression in the world metropolis in the 1930s.

- *Hypothesis 3:* When the metropolis recovers from its crisis and reestablishes the trade and investment ties that then fully reincorporate the satellites into the system, the previous industrialization of these regions is choked off. Frank points out that Brazil's new industries suffered serious adverse consequences from American economic invasion right after World War I, leading to balance-of-payments problems, inflation, and political difficulties.

- *Hypothesis 4:* The regions that are the most underdeveloped and feudal today are those that had the closest ties to the metropolises in the past. For example, Frank points out that when the market for West Indies sugar and the wealth of Brazilian mines disappeared, the world metropolis simply abandoned these countries. Due to their satellite status, their already-existing structure was unable to generate autonomous economic growth, leaving them with no alternative but to degenerate into the extreme underdevelopment in which we find them today. Frank argues that the archaic institutions in the satellites are historical products of the penetration of metropolis capitalism.

More of Frank's hypotheses could be listed here, but the above are sufficient to show that they represent an approach to the examination of Third World development different from that offered by the modernization school.

DOS SANTOS: THE STRUCTURE OF DEPENDENCE

As the theory of imperialism focuses on the expansion and domination of the imperialist powers, the concept of dependence highlights the fundamental problems facing underdeveloped countries. In spelling out the classical definition of dependence, Dos Santos (1971, p. 226) states that the relationship between two or more countries "assumes the form of dependence when some countries (the dominant ones) can expand and can be self-starting, while other countries (the dependent ones) can do this only as a reflection of that expansion." He further argues that relations between dominant and dependent countries are unequal because development of the former takes place at the expense of the latter. For example, through monopolistic control of the market in trade relations, and through loans and the export of capital in financial relations, there is a transfer of surplus generated in dependent countries to dominant countries. For dependent countries, this transfer results in the limitation of the development of their internal markets and their technical and cultural capacities, as well as of the moral and physical health of their people.

In addition to formulating the commonly used definition of dependence, Dos Santos has distinguished three historical forms of dependence. The first two of these are *colonial* dependence and *financial-industrial* dependence. In colonial dependence, the commercial and financial capital of the dominant country, in alliance with the colonial state, monopolized the control of land, mines, and human resources (serf or slave) and the export of gold, silver, and tropical products from the colonized country. However, by the end of the nineteenth century, financial-industrial dependence emerged. Although still dominated by the big capital of the European centers, the economies of the dependent countries were then centered upon the export of raw materials and agricultural products for consumption in European countries. Unlike that in the previous epoch, the production structure in this stage was characterized by an export sector with rigid specialization and monocultivation in entire regions (e.g., the Caribbean and the Brazilian northeast). Alongside these export sectors, there were complementary economic activities (like cattle raising and some manufacturing) that were dependent on the export sector to which they sold their products. Then there was also a subsistence sector that both produced human resources for the export sector in boom periods and absorbed unemployment during periods of economic decline.

Dos Santos's greatest contribution, however, is his formulation of the third historical form of dependence: *technological-industrial* dependence. This form emerged in the post-World War II era, when industrial development began to take place in many under-

developed countries. According to Dos Santos, there are fundamental structural limitations placed on the industrial development
of underdeveloped economies. First, industrial development is
now dependent on the existence of an *export sector.* Only the export
sector can bring in the needed foreign currency for the purchase of
advanced machinery by the industrial sector. In order to preserve
its traditional export sector, an underdeveloped nation must maintain the preexisting relation between production and the maintenance of power by the traditional decadent oligarchy. In addition,
since the export sector (especially the marketing network) is usually controlled by foreign capital, it signifies political dependence on
foreign interests too.

Second, industrial development is strongly influenced by fluctuations of the *balance of payments,* leading to a deficit. The causes
of the deficit are three: (1) A highly monopolized international
market tends to lower the price of raw materials and to raise the
price of industrial products. There is also a tendency for primary
products to be replaced by synthetic raw materials. As such, dependent countries suffer a trade deficit because of their reliance on
the export of raw materials. (2) Since foreign capital retains control
of the economy of dependent countries, it carries off a high volume
of profit (from freight transport, royalty payments, technical aid,
and so on). Thus Dos Santos points out that the amount of capital
leaving dependent countries is actually much greater than the
amount entering. For example, for the period 1946-1967, for each
dollar that entered dependent countries, $2.73 left. This process
produces a deficit in capital accounts and limits the importation of
foreign inputs for industrialization. (3) The result is that "foreign
financing"—in the form of foreign capital and foreign aid—becomes necessary to cover the existing deficit and to finance further
development. Nevertheless, Dos Santos (1971, p. 231) argues that
the purpose of this foreign financing is "in large part to finance
North American investments, to subsidize foreign imports which
compete with national products, to introduce technology not
adapted to the needs of underdeveloped countries, and to invest
in sectors not necessarily of high priority."

Third, industrial development is strongly conditional on the
technological monopoly exercised by the imperial centers. On the one

hand, transnational corporations do not sell machinery and process raw materials as simple merchandise. Instead, they either demand payment of royalties for their utilization or convert these goods into capital and introduce them in the form of their own investments. On the other hand, dependent countries are short of foreign currency to pay for the utilization of machinery and raw materials that are patented. These factors oblige the governments of dependent countries to facilitate the entry of foreign capital into their domestic markets in order to obtain needed technology and patented raw materials. Under such conditions, Dos Santos (1971, p. 232) states that "foreign capital enters with all the advantages: in many cases, it is given exemption from exchange controls for the importation of machinery; financing of sites for installation of industries is provided; government financing agencies are available to facilitate industrialization; loans from foreign and domestic banks, which prefer such clients, are available; in many cases, foreign aid for the strengthening of industrialization is available."

What are the effects of this latest form of technological-industrial dependence on the productive structure of underdeveloped countries? First, the unequal capitalist development at the international level is reproduced internally in an acute form, with the productive structure of underdeveloped countries torn between a "traditional" agrarian export sector and a "modern" sector of technological and economic-financial concentration.

Second, the context of a local cheap labor market combined with the utilization of a capital-intensive technology has led to profound differences among various domestic wage levels. From a Marxist perspective, Dos Santos labels this high concentration of income a "high rate of exploitation" (or superexploitation) of labor power.

Third, this unequal production structure has imposed limits on the growth of internal markets in underdeveloped countries. The growth of consumer-goods markets is limited by the low purchasing power of the labor force and by the small number of jobs created by the capital-intensive sector. In addition, the growth of capital-goods markets is limited by the remittance abroad of profits, which carries away part of the economic surplus generated in the domestic economy.

Dos Santos concludes that the economic backwardness of underdeveloped countries is not due to a lack of integration with capitalism. Those studies that say so are "nothing more than ideology disguised as science." Instead, it is the monopolistic control of foreign capital, foreign finance, and foreign technology at national and international levels that prevents underdeveloped countries from reaching an advantageous position, resulting in the reproduction of backwardness, misery, and social marginalization within their borders.

AMIN: TRANSITION TO PERIPHERAL CAPITALISM

Amin's (1976) theory of the transition to peripheral capitalism has the following key assertions. First, transition to peripheral capitalism is fundamentally different from transition to central capitalism. The onslaught from without carried out by central capitalism upon the precapitalist formations caused certain crucial retrogression to take place. For example, local crafts were destroyed without being replaced by domestic industrial production. Amin notes that the agrarian crisis of the contemporary Third World is largely a result of these setbacks.

Second, peripheral capitalism is characterized by *extraversion*— the distortion toward export activities. Amin (1976, p. 200) points out that "extraversion does not result from inadequacy of the home market but from the superior productivity of the center in all fields, which compels the periphery to confine itself to the role of complementary supplier of products for the production of which it possesses a natural advantage: exotic agricultural produce and minerals." With such extraversion distortion, the level of wages in the periphery becomes lower than that at the center.

Third, another form of distortion is the *hypertrophy* of the tertiary sector at the periphery. At the center, hypertrophy of the tertiary sector reflects the difficulties in realizing surplus value in monopoly capitalism, so more resources have to be spent in the marketing and the accounting of commodities. However, at the periphery, hypertrophy of the tertiary sector is mainly a result of the contradictions inherent in peripheral capitalism, namely, sluggish industrialization, increasing unemployment, desperate migration from rural to urban areas, and so on. According to Amin, this hypertrophy of unproductive activities hampers capital accumulation in peripheral countries.

Fourth, the theory of the multiplier effects of investment cannot be extended in a mechanical way to the periphery. At the center, the Keynesian multiplier does work in monopoly capitalism, but at the periphery, the export of the profit of foreign capital has nullified this multiplier effect. Instead of benefiting the periphery, the export of foreign profit transfers the multiplier effect from the periphery to the center, serving to accelerate the latter's development.

Fifth, Amin warns that researchers should not confuse underdeveloped countries with the now-advanced countries as they were at earlier stages of their development. This is because underdeveloped countries possess the following distinctive structural features: (1) the extreme unevenness that is typical of the distribution of productivity at the periphery, (2) disarticulation due to the adjustment of the orientation of production at the periphery to the needs of the center, and (3) economic domination by the center, which is expressed in the forms of trade and financial dependence.

Sixth, as a result of the above structural features of underdevelopment, it necessarily leads to the blocking of the growth of the peripheral countries. In other words, peripheral capitalism is unable to attain autocentric and autodynamic economic growth without challenging the domination of foreign monopolies and central capitalism.

Finally, the specific form of underdevelopment assumed by these peripheral formations depends upon (1) the nature of the precapitalist formation that was there previously, and (2) the forms and the periods in which the peripheries were integrated into the capitalist world-system. However, while not neglecting the differences among peripheral countries, Amin asserts that they all tend to converge toward a typical model, characterized by the dominance of agrarian capital, comprador or commercial capital, and central capital. And with the domination of central capital over the system as a whole, this model severely limits the development of peripheral national capitalism.

BASIC ASSUMPTIONS OF THE DEPENDENCY SCHOOL

Like the modernization school, the dependency school is highly heterogeneous. Its members come from many social science disciplines, focus on different countries in Latin America as well as on other regions, and have different ideological orientations and political commitments. Nevertheless, members of the dependency school tend to share the following basic assumptions (see Blomstrom and Hettne 1984, p. 71-76).

First, dependency is seen as a very *general* process, applicable to all Third World countries. The aim of the dependency school is to outline the general pattern of dependency in the Third World throughout the history of capitalism from the sixteenth century to the present. Thus national variations and historical complexity are downplayed in order to present the "ideal type" construct of dependency.

Second, dependency is understood to be an *external* condition, that is, imposed from the outside. The most important obstacle to national development, therefore, is not lack of capital, entrepreneurial skills, or democratic institutions; rather, it is to be found outside the domain of the national economy. The historical heritage of colonialism and the perpetuation of the unequal international division of labor are the greatest obstructions to the national development of Third World countries.

Third, dependency is analyzed mostly as an *economic* condition. It is seen as a result of the flow of economic surplus from Third World countries to Western capitalist countries. Thus Third World countries generally suffer from declining terms of trade with Western countries.

Fourth, dependency is treated as a component of *regional polarization* of the global economy. On the one hand, the flow of surplus from Third World countries leads to their underdevelopment; on the other, the development of Western countries is benefited by this influx of economic surplus. Thus underdevelopment in the periphery and development in the core are two aspects of a single process of capital accumulation, leading to regional polarization in the global economy.

Conclusion overall opinion

Finally, dependency is seen as *incompatible* with development. Is development possible in the periphery? For the dependency school, the answer is generally no. Although minor development can occur during periods of isolation, such as during a world depression or a world war, genuine development in the periphery is highly unlikely with the continual flow of surplus to the core.

POLICY IMPLICATIONS OF THE DEPENDENCY SCHOOL

Definition of dependency.

Proponents of the dependency school feel that there is a need to redefine the term *development*. It should mean more than just more industry, more output, and rising productivity. Instead, it should be defined in terms of improving the living standard for all the people in the periphery. Thus developmental programs should not cater to elites and urban dwellers, but should attempt to satisfy the human needs of rural peasants, the unemployed, and the needy. Any developmental program that benefits only a small sector at the expense of the suffering majority is no good at all.

What are the political implications of the dependency perspective? It appears that the dependency school's views are exactly opposite to those of the modernization school. As the modernization school proposes that the periphery should receive more contacts (more aid, more technology, more modern values) from Western countries, the dependency school argues that it is harmful for peripheral countries to have more contact with core countries. In fact, the dependency school asserts that the periphery has too much harmful core contact already. Since the era of colonialism, the political economy of the periphery has been totally restructured to suit the needs of the core, thereby leading to the development of underdevelopment.

Consequently, the dependency school suggests that peripheral countries should sever their ties with core countries. Instead of relying upon foreign aid and foreign technology, peripheral countries should adopt a self-reliance model—relying upon their own resources and planning their own paths of development so as to achieve independence and autonomous national development.

Self-reliance, of course, does not mean complete isolation from other nation-states. It means only that peripheral countries should not be dominated by core countries. They should trade with other peripheral countries on equal and mutually beneficial terms.

From the dependency school perspective, the old elites in peripheral countries most likely would not accept such a complete break from core countries and their multinationals. The interests of the old elites are too closely tied to foreigners for them to accept such an option. As a result, many dependency researchers propose that a socialist revolution may be necessary for a country to get rid of the old ruling elites. In the words of Chilcote and Edelstein (1974, p. 21), "Development requires the profound alteration of economic, social, and political relationships in the overthrow of the market and the mobilization of domestic populations in a nationally oriented effort. Thus, development requires the elimination of foreign penetration, which supports the status quo, and the creation of a socialist context for development." Only when there is a new power group whose mission is to satisfy the human needs of the peasantry and the workers would the radical policies of total restructuring be carried out, as is revealed by the experience of the Chinese and Cuban revolutions.

COMPARISON OF THE DEPENDENCY
AND MODERNIZATION SCHOOLS

In conclusion, it may be useful to review the extent to which the classical dependency perspective is similar to and different from the classical modernization perspective (see Table 5.1 for a summary).

Similarities

First, the two classical perspectives share the same research focus: They are concerned with Third World development, and they want to find out what factors promote Third World develop-

Table 5.1 Comparison of Classical Modernization Perspective
and Classical Dependency Perspective

	Classical Modernization Perspective	*Classical Dependency Perspective*
Similarities		
research focus	Third World development	same
methodology	high-level abstraction, focus on the general process of development	same
polar theoretical structure	tradition versus modernity	core versus periphery
Differences		
theoretical heritage	evolutionary and functionalist theories	ECLA program and radical neo-Marxist theories
causes of Third World problems	mostly internal	mostly external
nature of national linkages	generally beneficial	generally harmful
prediction for direction of development	optimistic	pessimistic
solutions for development	more Western linkages	fewer core linkages, socialist revolution

ment. Second, the two perspectives adopt similar methodologies.
They anchor their discussions at a highly abstract level, with an
eye toward explaining the very general process of development
applicable to all of the nations. Third, the two perspectives have
developed a polar theoretical framework, although the classical
modernization perspective tends to call it "tradition versus modernity" while the classical dependency perspective calls it "core
(metropolis) versus periphery (satellite)."

Differences

Despite the above similarities, these two classical perspectives in fact differ from each other in basic ways. First, they come from different theoretical backgrounds. The classical modernization perspective is strongly influenced by European evolutionary theories and American functionalist theories, while the classical dependency perspective is strongly influenced by the liberal ECLA program and radical neo-Marxist theories.

Second, with respect to the causes of Third World problems, the classical modernization perspective offers an internal explanation, pointing to such traits as traditional culture, lack of productive investment, and absence of achievement motivation in Third World countries. The classical dependency perspective, in contrast, offers an external explanation, stressing the roles played by colonialism and neocolonialism in shaping the underdevelopment of Third World countries.

Third, the classical modernization perspective characterizes the linkages between Third World countries and Western countries as beneficial. From this perspective, Western countries are assisting Third World countries to develop. The classical dependency perspective, on the other hand, sees the linkages as harmful—Western countries are exploiting Third World countries for their own benefits.

Fourth, in predicting the future direction of development, the classical modernization perspective is generally optimistic. With patience, Third World countries will eventually catch up with Western countries and modernize themselves. The view of the classical dependency perspective concerning the future of Third World countries is pessimistic. If the present exploitative linkages remain unchallenged, Third World countries will become more and more dependent on Western countries, leading to further underdevelopment and bankruptcy.

Finally, regarding solutions to the backwardness of Third World countries, the classical modernization perspective has advocated more linkages with Western countries, such as more foreign aid, more cultural exchanges, and more technological transfers. Classical dependency researchers offer a totally different approach. They advocate reduction of core linkages so that Third World countries may attain autonomous, independent development, and they realize that radical socialist revolution may be required to achieve this goal. Examples of classical dependency studies incorporating the orientations discussed above are presented in the next chapter.

CHAPTER 6

The Classical Dependency Studies

In this chapter, three classical dependency studies are examined: Baran on colonialism in India, contributors to the *Monthly Review* on the debt trap in Latin America, and Landsberg on manufacturing imperialism in East Asia. These are "classical" studies because they set the direction that dependency research has taken. They have led to a chain of empirical studies on the harmful impact of colonialism and the debt crisis. They have also steered researchers away from studying the developmental potential of the East Asian industrialization process by labeling it merely a variant of manufacturing imperialism. Further, these studies represent the dependency approach to development because they are informed by the basic assumptions of the dependency perspective.

BARAN: COLONIALISM IN INDIA

Baran's (1957, p. 144-150) study of India has become one of the classical statements on what can happen to a Third World country after it goes through the historical experience of colonialism.

Economic Impact

According to Baran (1957, p. 144), India was one of the most developed countries in the world in the eighteenth century: "The economic condition of India was relatively advanced, and Indian methods of production and of industrial and commercial organization could stand comparison with those in vogue in any other part of the world. . . a country which has manufactured and exported the finest muslins and other luxurious fabrics and articles." The products of the Indian loom, in fact, supplied the markets of Asia and Europe in the eighteenth century. In the same period, Britain had yet to undergo the Industrial Revolution, and the British textile industry was still in its infancy. "Prior to 1760, . . . the machinery used for spinning cotton in Lancashire was almost as simple as in India; while about 1750 the English iron industry was in full decline."

However, Britain possessed military superiority. It had a strong navy, and its warships assisted its colonization of Third World countries. Consequently, after defeating India's armed forces, Britain turned India into its colony. According to Baran (1957, p. 145), the present backwardness of India was caused by "the elaborate, ruthless, systematic despoliation of India by British capital from the very onset of British rule." This process of underdevelopment began with the plunder of the wealth of India. It has been estimated that the volume of wealth that Britain derived from India during the early decades of colonization was between $500 million and $1 billion. In the early twentieth century, Britain appropriated annually, under one title or another, over 10% of India's gross national income. Even this figure is an understatement of the draining of Indian wealth, because it refers only to direct transfers and does not include India's losses due to unfavorable terms of trade imposed by the British.

In addition to plundering, Britain also used other means to extract resources from India. By the mid-eighteenth century, rural industries began to appear in the British countryside on a massive scale. In order to expand its rural industrialization and capture the world textile market, Britain believed that it was necessary to eliminate the strong competition of the Indian textile industry, find a stable supply of cotton for its manufacturers, and expand its overseas markets. Britain naturally turned to its colonies for help in the pursuit of these goals.

Consequently, after Britain had conquered India, the East Indian Company and the British Parliament began a policy of *deindustrialization*. Quoting Romesh Dutt (1901), Baran (1957, p. 147) notes that the British

> discouraged Indian manufacturers in the early years of British rule in order to encourage the rising manufacturers of England. Their fixed policy, pursued during the last decades of the eighteenth century and the first decades of the nineteenth, was to make India subservient to the industries of Great Britain, and to make the Indian people grow raw produce only, in order to supply the material for the looms and manufacturies of Great Britain. This policy was pursued with unwavering resolution and with fatal success; orders were sent out, to force Indian artisans to work in the Company's factories; commercial residents were legally vested with extensive powers over villages and communities of Indian weavers; prohibitive tariffs excluded Indian silk and cotton goods from England; English goods were admitted into India free of duty or on payment of a nominal duty.... The invention of the power-loom in Europe completed the decline of the Indian industries; and when in recent years the power-loom was set up in India, England once more acted towards India with unfair jealousy. An excise duty has been imposed on the production of cotton fabrics in India which ... stifles the new steam-mills of India.

In addition to the deindustrialization process, Britain also wanted to turn India into a cotton-growing nation that could provide an adequate supply of materials to British textile manufacturers. As a result, India moved backward, from a relatively advanced industrial nation to a backward agricultural nation. As Baran asserts, agriculture was virtually the only remaining source of national wealth for India in the nineteenth century. However, the shift to export agriculture failed to enrich the Indian peasants. Quoting Dutt again, Baran (1957, p. 147) notes:

> What the British Government ... take as Land Tax at the present day sometimes approximates to the whole of the economic rent.... This ... paralyses agriculture, prevents

saving, and keeps the tiller of the soil in a state of poverty and indebtedness. . . . In India the State virtually interferes with the accumulation of wealth from the soil, intercepts the incomes and gains of the tillers . . . leaving the cultivators permanently poor. . . . In one shape or another all that could be raised in India by an excessive taxation flowed to Europe, after paying for a starved administration. . . . Verily the moisture of India blesses and fertilizes other lands.

In sum, Baran argues that the transfer of economic surplus from India to Britain, the deindustrialization of Indian industries, the flooding of Indian society with British manufactured goods, and the pauperization of the Indian countryside led to the underdevelopment of India on the one hand and capital accumulation for Britain on the other. British colonialism, however, had more than economic impact on India; it had profound impacts on the country's political and cultural spheres as well.

Political and Cultural Impacts

From a dependency perspective, the goals of establishing a colonial government were to maintain peace and order, to ensure the smooth extraction of raw materials and minerals from the colony for the mother nation, and to facilitate foreign imports into the periphery. The colonial government was never meant to be an institution for promoting the economic development of the periphery.

In turning a Third World nation into a peripheral nation, a colonial government generally does not hesitate to use coercion to secure the compliance of the native population. In fact, peace and order in colonial countries have often been the historical product of violent repression of the natives. If necessary, colonial governments might exterminate entire native populations, as the Spanish wiped out the Aztec population in Latin America.

Only after the natives have been turned into a docile population do colonial administrators begin to shape the local society to fit their own interests. Thus Baran (1957, p. 149) reports that the British administration of India systematically destroyed all the fibres and foundations of Indian society. Its land and taxation policy ruined India's village economy and substituted for it the parasitic landowner and moneylender. Its commercial policy destroyed the Indian artisan and created the infamous slums of the Indian cities filled with millions of starving and diseased paupers. Its economic policy broke down whatever beginnings there were of an indigenous industrial development and promoted the proliferations of speculators, petty businessmen, agents, and sharks of all descriptions eking out a sterile and precarious livelihood in the meshes of a decaying society.

After a colonial government is firmly in control, it begins to rely on the natives to rule the colony. Of course, not every native is eligible—usually only those native elites are chosen who have sworn loyalty to the colonial administration and whose interests are closely tied to those of the foreigners. The dependency school calls these native elites the "clientele social class" and identifies native landlords as the most likely candidates to be recruited into colonial administration, because they are afraid of peasant protests and need the colonial government to back them up with power. In return, the colonial government wants the landlords to keep peace in the countryside and to promote export agriculture.

Thus Baran (1957, p. 149) asserts that in India, Britain

consolidated itself by creating new classes and vested interests who were tied up with that rule and whose privileges depended on its continuance. There were the landowners and the princes, and there were a large number of subordinate members of the services in various departments of the government, from the patwari, the village headman, upward. . . . To all these methods must be added the deliberate policy, pursued throughout the period of British rule, of creating divisions among Indians, of encouraging one group at the cost of the other.

In order to facilitate political domination, the British adopted an educational policy that aimed "to keep the natives of India in the profoundest state of barbarism and darkness." According to Baran (1957, p. 145):

> The British-organized-and-supervised educational system did all it could not to promote but to repress the growth of scientific and industrial aptitude among the Indians. . . . Do we not find that, instead of teaching the people to understand the world about them and how natural forces can best be utilized and controlled, they have been taught to write notes on archaic phrases in the works of sixteenth- and seventeenth-century Englishmen and to learn by rote the personal history of obscure rulers of a foreign land?

Since the Indian political economy had been so thoroughly restructured by the British colonial government for more than a century, Baran asserts, the formal removal of the colonial government from India could not have possibly eradicated her colonial heritage. Even after political independence, the structure of dependence was still very much alive in India and would continue to haunt Indian development. Quoting Nehru, Baran (1957, p. 149) agrees that "nearly all our major problems today have grown up during British rule and as a direct result of British policy: the princes; the minority problem; various vested interests, foreign and Indian; the lack of industry and the neglect of agriculture; the extreme backwardness in the social services; and, above all, the tragic poverty of the people."

THE *MONTHLY REVIEW* AUTHORS:
THE DEBT TRAP IN LATIN AMERICA

If colonialism is the crucial factor that explains the historical backwardness of India, then the debt trap is the key factor that explains the present crisis facing Latin American countries. Chinweizu (1985), MacEwan (1986), Magdoff (1986), Pool and Stamos (1985), and Sweezy and Magdoff (1984), all contributors to the *Monthly Review,* have presented a dependency perspective on the debt trap facing Latin American countries in the 1980s. This debt trap can be observed in Brazil, one of the most advanced countries in Latin America. Brazil's foreign debt was just about $4 billion in the early 1970s. It quickly increased to around $50 billion in the late 1970s, and then suddenly jumped to $121 billion in 1989. But Brazil was not alone—other Latin American countries such as Mexico, Argentina, Venezuela, Chile, and Colombia also sank deeply in foreign debt. Mexico's foreign debt, for example, also jumped from around $7 billion in the early 1970s to around $38 billion in the late 1970s, and then further to $106 billion in 1989. The extent of this debt problem can be demonstrated by the fact that the foreign debt in Mexico in the mid-1980s amounted to about 76% of its GNP (*Time*, January 8, 1989, p. 33). About 80% of Mexico's export earnings were used to keep up with the interest payment on its foreign debt alone.

From the dependency perspective, the foreign debt problem represents an intensification of *financial dependency*, a process that has played a crucial role in the shaping of the development of Latin American countries in the 1980s. Consequently, it is important to ask: What are the causes of the debt problem? How has the debt problem affected Latin American countries? What are the solutions to the debt problem?

Origins of the Debt Problem

First of all, to illustrate how Latin American countries developed a debt problem, we can focus on the development of Mexico over the past two decades. In the mid-1970s, the progressive Luis Echeveria government in Mexico instituted a number of social spending programs, such as provision of education, health care, and welfare services to the poor and the unemployed. The Echeveria government also promoted heavy industry and infrastructure construction, such as building freeways and airports. However, financing all these large-scale projects resulted in an increase in government deficit, since the government had spent more money than it could collect.

Another issue facing the Echeveria government was the growing problem of imbalance of payments. In order to develop domestic industries, the government needed to import many foreign products, such as machinery, trucks, computers, and steel. This resulted in more goods being imported than exported. The government therefore needed more foreign currency to pay for the expanding imports.

Fortunately, Mexico discovered that it possessed one of the richest oil fields in the world, comparable to that in the Middle East. Moreover, there was an oil boom in the 1970s. Oil prices were rising, and so was the demand for oil. Consequently, the Echeveria government was very hopeful. It borrowed money from the World Bank, the International Monetary Fund (IMF), and the giant American banks in order to finance oil exploration projects. After the oil industry and domestic industries got started, the Echeveria government estimated that its exports should enable Mexico to earn enough foreign currency to reduce the government deficits and solve the balance-of-payments problem. Filled with optimism based on the rich oil reserve, the Mexican government started to borrow money—from $4 billion to $6 billion a year from foreigners in the mid-1970s.

However, the Mexican oil export plan did not materialize because of poor timing. In the early 1980s, there was a sharp drop in oil prices and demand. Due to the world oil glut, the price of oil dropped from a high of $30 a barrel to a low of about $20 a barrel. The OPEC nations were forced to cut back production so as to prevent oil prices from falling further. Consequently, Mexico earned much less from its oil exports than it had expected.

This miscalculation of foreign earnings led Mexico to fall into a *debt trap*. In the mid-1970s, borrowing $4-6 billion a year seemed to be a matter of minor importance, since the projected annual earnings from oil exports would easily cover the loan payments. But when the new source of export earnings failed to materialize, the debt burden suddenly became intolerable. Due to a compound interest rate, the foreign debt grew at a fairly fast rate once it reached a certain size.

Consider the following hypothetical example given in Sweezy and Magdoff (1984): Suppose a Latin American nation has been borrowing $1,000 every year for seven consecutive years at an interest rate of 10%, and the loan is to be repaid in 20 years. In the eighth year, when the nation borrows again, the $1,000 it borrows is just enough to cover the interest and principal amortization payments on the loans it has taken out over the past seven years. In other words, after the eighth year, the nation in our example has to keep on borrowing just to meet the deadline for interest and amortization payments.

This example illustrates how a foreign debt creates its own momentum for rapid expansion. Thus Mexico, after borrowing for a few consecutive years, found that it already had a debt of $55 billion in 1982. On this debt Mexico needed to pay $9 billion every year, just for interest and principal amortization. Consequently, it did not take long for the debt to reach another peak—$106 billion in 1989.

Because of the rapid accumulation of foreign debt, dependency researchers have compared the debt burden to drug addiction. Like drug addicts, who need to take more and more drugs in order to satisfy their appetites, debtor nations need to borrow more and more money in order to meet interest and amortization payments. The debtors, like addicts, soon find that it very difficult to "kick the habit."

Impact of the Debt Problem

How did the debt problem affect Third World political economy? Falling oil prices, the world economic recession, and the piling up of foreign debts finally forced Mexico and Brazil to declare in 1982 that they could not keep up with the interest payments anymore. This news of debt default sent shock waves through the financial world and created a near crisis, as the default involved more than $300 billion. A rescue mission from the World Bank, the IMF, and the U.S. banks quickly adopted the following policies to settle this default of interest and amortization payments. First, the Latin American nations were allowed to reschedule their loan payments for a later date. This rescheduling helped to avert a financial crisis that could have sparked another world depression. However, dependency researchers argue that it was the foreign banks that were rescued, not the Latin American nations. Second, in order to help the Latin American nations to meet the payments, the banks decided to lend them more money. However, there were new conditions attached to the new loans. These new loans were short-term, emergency loans, and they carried a higher interest rate than the market rate.

According to the dependency school, these rescue policies actually provided more profit for the banks and enabled them to extend their control over the Latin American nations. Since the rescue mission, the Western banks have exercised a closer supervision of the financial statements of the debtor nations than before. The IMF can visit the Latin American debtor nations and inspect their accounts and books. The debtor nations' budgets and economic programs must be approved by the IMF before they can be carried out. Furthermore, the IMF demanded that the Latin American nations adopt an austerity policy before they could obtain new loans. The austerity policy called for the following actions:

(1) massive reduction in government spending, such as the cancellation or reduction of social spending on welfare, education, health care, and the like

(2) increase in government revenue through raised taxes

(3) reduction of foreign imports in order to reduce the balance-of-payments problem

(4) increase in exports so as to earn more foreign currency

In addition, dependency researchers point out that the debt trap exerted a profound impact on the domestic societies of the debtor nations. First, there was the problem of currency devaluation. The Mexican peso, for example, plunged from 25 pesos to $1 U.S. in 1982 to 200 pesos to $1 U.S. in 1984. Many Mexicans, worried that the Mexican economy was going to collapse at any moment, created a financial panic by rushing to convert their pesos to American dollars.

Second, since the domestic currency was worth less than before, there was a trend toward rising inflation. In the early 1980s, Mexico's annual inflation rate was approximately 80%. Brazil was even worse, with an inflation rate of over 200% in 1985 and around 500%

in 1986. But it seemed that Peru experienced the worst inflation rate—around 1,700% in 1989.

Third, due to cutbacks in state investment in the industrial sector and restrictions on foreign imports such as machinery, the optimistic economic growth of Latin American nations in the 1970s vanished. Instead, the debtor nations experienced a drastic economic decline in the 1980s. Mexico's GNP, for instance, dropped from +8% in 1978 to –5% in 1983. Economic decline resulted in massive unemployment, with many debtor nations having an unemployment rate of over 50%.

Fourth, currency devaluation, rising inflation, and economic decline inevitably led to the intensification of political conflict in the societies of the debtor nations. The people were highly dissatisfied with the high rates of unemployment and inflation (which, of course, cut into their buying power). Strikes and demonstrations became quite common in Latin American nations in the 1980s. In 1983 there was a hunger riot in Brazil, with city dwellers looting supermarkets for food. *Time* magazine reported in March 1986 that there was a "life and death struggle" taking place in Latin America that stirred social unrest, pushed the Latin American people toward leftist political parties, and destabilized their governments.

Fifth, there was an increase in anti-Americanism in Latin American nations. The Latin American people began to blame the lowering of their living standards and their suffering on American banks and the American government. Every year, billions of dollars were taken out of Latin American nations just to meet the payment of their foreign debts. From the dependency perspective, the people in Latin America would have been much better off if these billions of dollars had been spent on domestic welfare and employment programs instead of given to foreign banks.

Future of the Debt Problem

How can this debt problem be solved? What are the options available to the debtor nations and to the creditors? If the Latin American nations really cannot meet their loan payments, is there a possibility that they will not honor their debts? Can they just declare their debts null and void?

Debt default may be an option, but it is unlikely that it would be adopted by the debtor nations. From the dependency perspective, the debtor-creditor relationship is a political one. If the creditors are powerful and the debtors are powerless, then it is very difficult for the debtors to run away from the debt. Historical experience tells us that the default of a national debt has frequently led to the colonization of that nation—as happened in Egypt with the British and in the Dominican Republic with the Americans at the turn of the twentieth century. The creditors could send armies to overthrow the government that defaulted on the loans, install a new government, levy taxes, and collect customs in order to make sure that the debts would be repaid.

However, unlike in the old colonial days, creditors may not be able to send armies to debtor nations in the 1980s. Nonetheless, the Latin American nations are borrowing money from some of the most powerful organizations in the world—the multinational financial institutions. The foreign banks could easily wage an economic war to overthrow the debtor governments. The creditors could ask for a freeze of the assets of the debtor nations in the United States, set up an economic blockade to cut off all trade with and loans to the debtor nations, and request that foreign companies pull their business out of the debtor nations. Since the debtor nations are already in deep economic trouble, any of the above offensive policies used against them would send them into economic chaos and political turmoil.

Consequently, the domestic economic elites and the ruling class in the debtor nations would most likely not favor the strategy of defaulting on their debt payments. The domestic elites in the Latin American nations have formed a partnership with foreign corporations, and they would be hurt most by the economic reprisals of the multinational corporations. Instead of defaulting, therefore, the dominant economic elites have chosen to transfer some of their economic assets secretly from Latin America to the United States, or to the Swiss banks. Magdoff estimates that about $180 billion of Latin America capital—about half of the debts owed to the foreign banks—is now outside of the debtor nations. Dependency researchers point out the interesting fact that the larger the foreign debt, the greater the outflow of domestic capital to the core nations.

Therefore, instead of defaulting, the domestic elites have asked for concessions from the foreign banks. In March 1986, the debtor nations in Latin America held a meeting to deal with the debt trap. The meeting reached the following conclusions:

(1) There should be a reduction of the interest rate on past and future loans. The Latin American nations borrowed at a peak of 14-16% interest rate in the late 1970s. Since the interest rate was much lower in the mid-1980s, the Latin American nations hoped that the foreign banks could cut 2-4% from the interest rate on their loans.

(2) There should be a longer extension of the loan repayment period. The longer period could ease the burden of interest payment considerably.

(3) There should also be a limit on how much export earnings could be used to pay interests on the debt. The debtor nations could not afford to pay 80% or more of their export earnings on debt, because then they would not have enough money to import the needed foreign technology for domestic industrialization.

In sum, the debtor nations asked the foreign banks to make concessions.

The foreign banks were also concerned about the prospect of default of over $300 billion in Third World debt. Many U.S. banks had lent too much to Latin American nations. For example, the Bank of America, Citibank, and the Chase Manhattan Bank had about 30-40% of their capital tied up in Third World debt. If Third World nations defaulted on their loans and declared bankruptcy, the U.S. banks and other multinational corporations would have to do so also, because they were inextricably connected with the debtor nations. Facing this impending world economic crisis, the foreign banks were willing to take a "soft" stand and to negotiate with the debtor nations on how to reduce the interest rate and to extend the loan term. In effect, the foreign banks did not want to kill the goose that laid the golden eggs.

In 1989, Nicholas F. Brady, the U.S. secretary of the treasury, put forward a plan that sought to reduce Latin American debt burdens by asking the banks to forgive portions of the loans and to swap other parts of the debt for new securities—an exchange that would be underwritten by guarantees from the IMF and the World Bank. However, the banks were unwilling to forfeit their profits from Third World debts. Due to resistance from the banking community, the latest proposal by Brady, as of July 1989, placed far more emphasis on new lending than on debt reduction for the debtor nations. Also, the role of the IMF and the World Bank in underwriting debt reduction has proved far smaller than what Brady had initially envisioned.

In sum, the dependency perspective has contributed by pointing out the origins of the debt trap, the impact of the debt problem on the debtor nations, and the complicated issues that are involved in solving the debt problem. From the study on Latin America, the dependency perspective quickly spread to the study of other parts of the world, including a study on the prospects for East Asian industrialization.

LANDSBERG:
MANUFACTURING IMPERIALISM IN EAST ASIA

In observing export-led industrialization (ELI) in South Korea, Taiwan, Singapore, and Hong Kong, Landsberg (1979) entertained the research question of whether these nations should be looked upon as models for Third World development. However, after examining the historical context and the nature, origins, and impact of this new wave of industrialization in East Asia, Landsberg concludes that ELI is just part of a new form of imperialist domination, and that it will lead the Third World only to dependent industrialization instead of to self-expanding development.

The Historical Context

Landsberg argues that foreign domination of Third World countries did not break up at the end of World War II. Domestic development of Third World countries suffered for the following reasons. First, with little industrial base, Third World countries were forced to spend large sums of foreign currency to import almost all manufactured goods. Second, in order to earn the needed foreign currency, Third World countries had to rely upon primary commodity exports (e.g., sugar, rubber, tea) that were subject to fluctuations in the international market. Third, the lack of foreign currency led to the incurrence of a substantial foreign debt, with continued foreign domination as the end result.

Consequently, the strategy of import-substituted industrialization (ISI) was proposed to help Third World countries break out of this dependence on primary commodity exports. In addition, instead of importing all manufactured goods, through ISI these countries would pursue the replacement of these imports by boosting domestic industrial production.

However, according to Landsberg, the logic of imperialism prevented the strategy of ISI from succeeding. First, since the majority of the population in Third World countries remained poor, there was a lack of a consumer-goods market. Thus domestic production was geared toward a tiny urban market of luxurious and consumer durables. Second, the domestic bourgeoisie did not have the capital or technology to start domestic industrialization. The result was the incurrence of foreign debts and dependent industrialization under the dominance of foreign capital. Third, instead of resulting in the import of foreign manufactured goods, ISI speeded up the import of foreign capital and technology. This was followed by a massive outflow of profits back to the home countries of the transnational corporations (TNCs). As a result, the deficit from imbalance of payments in Third World countries continued to grow under the ISI program. In sum, Landsberg argues that the results of the ISI were anything but positive: growing income inequalities, limited industrialization, foreign domination, and large deficits and debts.

By the early 1960s, most Third World countries realized that the strategy of ISI was a failure, and a new strategy called export-led industrialization (ELI) was proposed. Unlike ISI, the goal of which was to capture the domestic market, the goal of ELI was to increase the export of manufactured goods to the world market. Through this strategy, Third World capitalists hoped to promote industrialization and employment, earn foreign currency, and stimulate domestic capital accumulation.

Using figures from the United Nations, Landsberg shows that manufactured exports as a percentage of total Third World exports increased from 9.2% in 1960 to almost 17% in 1969. He also points out that the manufactured exports of Third World countries increased at an annual rate of 14% between 1970 and 1976, a rate that was four times as high as the rate of growth of manufacture output in the developed capitalist countries. In observing these impressive figures, a researcher would ask the following questions: What is the nature of this new wave of ELI? How can we explain its emergence? What is its impact on Third World development?

The Nature of the ELI: Who Is Exporting to Whom?

Landsberg found that a few Third World countries produced the great majority of manufactured exports to the developed capitalist countries. Within this small number of Third World exporters, Landsberg distinguished two groups. The countries in Group A—including Mexico, Brazil, Argentina, and India—had significant natural resources, relatively large domestic industrial bases and domestic markets, and established infrastructures. Yet their exports to the developed capitalist countries were concentrated on traditional manufactured goods such as textiles, leather, footwear, wood, and food products. The countries in Group B—including Hong Kong, Singapore, South Korea, and Taiwan—had small domestic markets, few natural resources, and relatively undeveloped industrial infrastructures in the early 1960s. Yet these small countries specialized in the production of nontraditional manufactured goods such as light manufactures, clothing, and engineering, metal, and electronic products. Furthermore, these small countries had become very successful exporters, outcompeting the more developed Third World countries in the world market.

What then was behind the growth of exports in the Group B countries? What explains their sudden impetus toward ELI in the 1960s?

Origins of ELI

For Landsberg, the explanation lies in the policy of "international subcontracting" designed by the transnational corporations. In order to capture the markets in the advanced capitalist countries, the TNCs made use of Third World firms to produce entire products or components of products. A variety of legal relationships were formed between the TNCs and the subcontractors, ranging from wholly owned subsidiaries to joint ventures and independent producers. From the viewpoint of international subcontracting, ELI signaled a new stage in the international division of labor in which manufacturing activities were transferred from the advanced capitalist countries to Third World countries.

Landsberg mentions several reasons for the growth of international subcontracting. First, there was an expansion of the consumer market in the advanced capitalist countries. The transnational corporations therefore competed with one another to capture the expanding consumer markets in the core countries.

Second, the cost of production was on the rise in the advanced capitalist countries. For instance, by the mid-1960s, American capitalists were forced to yield to the working class's demands for material and political gains. In fact, labor costs in the United States had risen so high that American TNCs found it difficult to compete with Japanese and German firms for the U.S. market. Market rivalry, therefore, compelled U.S. firms to engage in international subcontracting in order to enhance their competitiveness.

Third, new technological innovations in transportation and communication greatly facilitated the growth of international subcontracting. Landsberg (1979, p. 57) points out that "with improved air freight, containerization, and telecommunication, transnational corporations could dispatch products and components quicker, cheaper, and safer."

Fourth, international subcontracting was highly profitable. Productivity tended to be high under subcontracting because labor problems—such as union demands, strikes, and absenteeism—were kept to a minimum by the fear of starvation and repressive labor legislation. In addition, the wage level in Third World countries was much lower than that of the United States. In 1967, the basic wage per hour in South Korea was only $0.10, compared to the American basic wage of $2.01 per hour.

Finally, the Group B countries were ideal candidates for subcontracting. Landsberg (1979, p. 58) explains:

> Since labor is the key variable, the poorer countries—those with less industry to compete for workers—appear most desirable. Since the final market to be served is the developed capitalist market, the internal market size of the Third-World country is not a key factor. Economies of scale, and modern capital-intensive technology are all possible, even in a small, underdeveloped Third-World country, because production is geared for export.

Since manufacturing industries now exist in several Third World countries, does this mean that these exporting countries have an opportunity to attain a self-expanding economy?

Impact of ELI

From a dependency perspective, ELI represented a false promise for establishing a self-expanding capitalist economy. In other words, Landsberg argues that ELI is merely a new form of international capitalist domination and cannot serve as a model for indigenous Third World development.

First, for those Third World countries that had carried out ELI, their industrial production was largely for export. Since their investment, technology, and resource use were largely shaped by the consumer demands of the advanced capitalist countries, their industrial production was mostly unrelated to the needs of their workers and peasants.

Second, subcontracting operations normally specialized in the use of low-skilled labor for elementary production processes (such as assembly work in the semiconductor industry). Consequently, the nature of subcontracting made it unlikely that advanced technology would be transferred to Third World countries, that there would be an upgrading of the skill level of its work force, or that the technological know-how pertaining to the entire production process would be revealed to the subcontractor nations.

Third, irrespective of whether a Third World firm was a joint venture with a transnational corporation or independent, it generally failed to gain the upper hand in the subcontracting process. Landsberg (1979, p. 59) states that the transnational corporations always "retain complete control over the entire process (research, design, transport, processing, storage, and marketing)." The Third World firms thus were dependent upon the TNCs for raw material input, modern technology, service and technical assistance, access to markets, and direct exporting. It was impossible for Third World firms to achieve a self-generating capitalist industrialization under such dependent conditions of subcontracting.

Fourth, although he notes that the Group B countries are trying to upgrade and diversify their exports in order to build a more dynamic base of industrialization, Landsberg is pessimistic about their ability to succeed, because the transnational corporations possess the power to relocate their subcontracting from the Group B countries in East Asia to other countries in Southeast Asia, Africa, and Central America. In order to compete for the subcontracting, many Third World countries offered generous tax holidays, subsidized credit, bonus exchange rates, and duty-free importation of supplies and equipment. Some countries were even willing to turn over the governance of their free-trade zones to foreign capitalists. Landsberg predicts that after losing some of the subcontracts to the newly established export centers, the efforts of the Group B countries toward export diversification and industrial upgrading will be retarded. Accordingly, Landsberg asserts that ELI can lead only to the dependence and the underdevelopment of Third World countries.

Finally, Landsberg argues that the instability of the global economy has also hindered the industrial growth of the Group B countries. For example, the cyclical downturn of 1974-1975 cut down the output and export of Third World countries, and the economic stagnation of the advanced capitalist countries in 1979 led to growing pressure for protectionism. With more and more import quotas, special levies, and unofficial cartels, protectionism could set a limit on how far Third World countries can proceed along the path of ELI.

In sum, Landsberg (1979, p. 61-62) concludes that although ELI "leads to growth in industrial production and the industrial work force, it will not lead to the creation of an indigenous, self-expanding capitalist economy. Moreover, in the context of deepening economic stagnation in the core capitalist economies, such an externally based development strategy is likely to produce increased poverty and suffering for workers and peasants in the Third World."

POWERS OF THE DEPENDENCY PERSPECTIVE

To what extent do the three empirical studies discussed above represent the typical dependency approach to the study of Third World development? They all share these assumptions: The imposition of external conditions on Third World countries results in dependency, and dependency in turn steers Third World countries in the direction of underdevelopment.

Dependency as an externally imposed condition. The powerful insight of the classical dependency theories has directed researchers to examine the process by which foreign domination had shaped the development of Third World countries. For example, Baran traced how British colonialism contributed to the underdevelopment of India through plundering, deindustrialization, and the uprooting of the local society. On the issue of the debt trap, dependency researchers point out that after the Latin American countries had borrowed money from the World Bank, the IMF, and the Western banks, they came under the tight control of these financial institutions. And Landsberg argues that the TNCs, through the policy of subcontracting, retained complete control over the research, design, transportation, and marketing of the new wave of industrialization in East Asia.

Dependency as an economic condition. By conceptualizing that dependency is produced through unequal economic exchanges, the classical dependency theories have directed researchers to examine the economic dimension of dependency. Thus political and cultural dimensions of dependency are often taken to be the natural consequences of the economic dimension of dependency. For instance, the economic dimensions of colonialism (such as deindustrialization, export agriculture, and the transfer of economic surplus) laid the foundation for the institutionalization of the clientele social classes in India. In contemporary Latin America, the debt crisis has led to a devaluation of domestic currency, rising inflation, declining GNP, and unemployment, which have further instigated political unrest and anti-Americanism. Landsberg describes the economic origins of recent East Asian industrialization by highlighting such factors as high labor costs in advanced capitalist countries, new technological innovations in transportation and communication, and high productivity and low wages in the East Asian states.

Dependency as incompatible with development. The classical dependency theories are at their best in delineating the harmful effect of dependency on Third World countries. In doing so, they often lead researchers to argue that substantial, autonomous development in Third World countries is impossible without a reversal of the dependency situation. Thus Baran argues that the historical heritage of colonialism still haunts the present development of India. Borrowing money from Western banks has only aggravated the problem of financial dependency for Latin American countries, pushing them further toward economic chaos and political turmoil. And while export-led industrialization may lead to an increase in industrial production and the size of the work force, it is unable to promote indigenous, self-sustaining economic growth in East Asia. The low-skilled production process, the stringent controls exerted by transnational corporations, and the instability of the world economy would nullify any attempt by East Asian countries toward diversification and industrial upgrading.

CRITIQUE OF THE CLASSICAL DEPENDENCY STUDIES

The dependency perspective has been the subject of a great deal of criticism since the 1970s (Almond 1987; Brenner 1977; Chilcote 1982; Chirot 1981; Fagen 1983; Fitzgerald 1981; Hermassi 1978; Howe and Sica 1980; Koo 1984; Laclau 1977; O'Brien 1975; Petras 1978; Portes 1976; Seers 1981; Smith 1982; Trimberger 1979; Weaver and Berger 1984; Worsley 1982). The critics are not satisfied with the methodology and the concept of dependency, or with the policy implications of the dependency studies.

On Methodology

The dependency school arose as a critique of the mainstream modernization school, denouncing the latter's studies as providing ideological justification for Western countries to exploit Third World countries. In response to this criticism, modernization theorists fought back, characterizing the dependency perspective as a propaganda fragment of Marxist revolutionary ideology. Dependency studies are seen by them as more like exercises in pamphleteering than as products of scholarly work. It has been argued that the dependency school gave up the battle for science after it lapsed into rhetoric. Consequently, instead of providing a scientific analysis of what has actually happened in Third World countries, the concept of dependency has become an all-purpose explanation for everything that is wrong with Third World countries.

In addition, the dependency perspective is accused of being highly abstract. Aiming to outline the general pattern of dependency in Third World countries, the dependency perspective is said to have committed the major error of treating all peripheral areas as if they were the same. As a result, dependency researchers tend to take a deductive approach to national studies, making them conform to what is logically expected on the basis of the dependency model. Dependency studies seldom make a serious attempt to bring out the historically specific development of each particular Third World country. In fact, by treating the concept of dependency as a global phenomenon, dependency studies have little room left for analysis of national variants.

On the Concept of Dependency

From the viewpoint of the dependency school, dependency is the result of the imposition of a set of external conditions on Third World development. Thus Marxist critics of the school charge that the dependency perspective has overemphasized the factor of external conditions, and has neglected the role of internal dynamics such as class conflict and the state. Where exactly do class analysis and the state fit in the dependency theory? Fagen (1983, p. 16), for instance, is highly dissatisfied because "the clarity with which classical Marxism located the question of class struggle at the center of development and decay of capitalism has been lost." Similarly, Petras (1982, p. 149) indicates that "to conceptualize the issues of the Third World in terms of dependency ... is to lose sight of the most decisive processes of class formation and social relations which beget change." Although the Marxist critics agree that it is important to examine the transfer of surplus from the periphery, they suggest that dependency researchers need to bring social classes, the state, and political struggles back into their analyses in order to answer the crucial questions of how and why this transfer of surplus takes place.

Political struggles have been neglected because dependency studies generally assume that Third World industrialists are a "lumpen bourgeoisie" class dependent on foreign capital, that Third World governments are "administrative committees" of foreign capital and the imperial state, and that Third World workers are merely a class of "labor aristocracy" whose interests are tied to foreign capital. Consequently, the dependency school does not believe that these domestic classes and institutions could resist foreign domination and promote independent development for Third World countries.

Due to this negligence of internal dynamics and domestic political struggles, the dependency school is accused of presenting an inaccurate picture of passive peripheries with a very small "degree of freedom." The critics charge that the dependency school has exaggerated the power of the external forces to such an extent that they believe that the phenomenon of dependency can completely determine the fate of Third World countries irrespective of local resistance. As Trimberger (1979, p. 128) points out, "Such a model sees the dynamic of the system as flowing completely from the center. The periphery, whether originally in Europe or today in the Third World countries, becomes a passive victim of capitalism from without."

The dependency school's critics argue that no matter how strong the dominating effects of the core countries, they also represent opportunities for ideas, institutions, and technologies that can be used by peripheral countries for change. Portes (1976, p. 79) remarks that "all historical evidence points to the existence of certain 'degrees of freedom' for national government and their ability to carry out, under certain circumstances, fairly drastic policies of internal and external transformation."

On Policy Implications

The dependency perspective emphasizes the harmful effects of colonialism and international division of labor. It argues that as long as the present unequal exchange relationship remains intact, there will be extraversion, hypertrophy, technical dependency, the development of underdevelopment, and so on in Third World countries. Consequently, many dependency researchers have proposed a radical strategy of socialist revolution in order to eradicate this externally imposed dependency situation.

The critics, however, are of the opinion that dependency and development may coexist, and that dependency may not necessarily lead to underdevelopment (Warren 1973). For example, South Korea and Taiwan were once colonies of Japan, yet these two countries have attained rapid economic development since World

War II. Countries such as Canada are "dependent" in the sense that their economies have been penetrated by foreign-owned subsidiaries, yet Canada exhibits a standard of living higher than that of most Third World countries.

Furthermore, the critics contend that the dependency perspective is vague on policy conclusions and that it has failed to spell out in concrete details how the newly independent states should proceed in order to achieve their national goals. The critics argue that the elimination of imperialist influence may not automatically bring about national development, that a socialist revolution may not necessarily produce positive results for development.

How does the dependency school answer the above criticisms? The next chapter presents a discussion of the rise of the "new" dependency studies, which utilize a "historical-structural" methodology to analyze and explain how the internal dynamics of political struggles can promote a certain degree of development in Third World countries.

CHAPTER 7

The New Dependency Studies

RESPONSES TO THE CRITICS

Cardoso is usually singled out as the key figure of the new dependency studies. His works have set the research agenda for a new generation of radical scholars (see, e.g., Cardoso 1973, 1977; Cardoso and Faletto 1979). This section examines what is so attractive about Cardoso's new dependency studies.

First, unlike the general analysis of the classical dependency school, Cardoso's methodology is "historical-structural." Since Cardoso wants to bring history back in, he employs the term *dependency* not as a theory to generalize the universal pattern of underdevelopment, but as a methodology for the analysis of concrete situations in Third World development (Palma 1978). Cardoso's goal is to delineate historically specific new situations of dependency in the search for differences and diversities. Consequently, his key research questions are as follows: How can the researcher bring out the historical uniqueness of a given dependency situation? How is a particular dependency situation different from previous ones? What is the historical origin of a particular dependency situation, and when and how will the situation change? How do the existing dependency structures themselves generate possibilities for transformation? What impact will a change in dependency have on the historical development of a Third World country?

Second, unlike classical dependency researchers, who focus on the external conditions of dependency, Cardoso is more inclined to emphasize internal structures of dependency. And instead of stressing the economic foundation of dependency, Cardoso is more interested in analyzing the sociopolitical aspect of dependency, especially class struggles, group conflict, and political movements. To Cardoso, "the problem of development in our days cannot remain restricted to a discussion about import substitution, not even to a debate on different strategies for growth, in terms of export or non-export policies, internal or external markets, orientation of the economy, etc. The main issue is people's movements and consciousness of their own interests" (quoted in Hettne and Wallensteen 1978, p. 32). Consequently, according to Cardoso (1977, p. 14), "what was significant was the 'movement,' the class struggles, the redefinitions of interest, the political alliances that maintained the structures while at the same time opening the possibility of their transformation."

However, while Cardoso contributes by reexamining the role of internal political struggles in dependency situations, he also makes it clear that he conceives "the relationship between external and internal forces as forming a complex whole whose structural links are . . . rooted in coincidences of interests between local dominant classes and international ones, and, on the other side, are challenged by local dominated groups and classes" (Cardoso and Faletto 1979, p. xvi). For example, external domination appears as an "internal" force, through the social practices of local groups and classes that try to enforce foreign interests because they may coincide with values and interests that these groups pretend are their own. Thus Cardoso calls for an analysis of the "internalization of external interests."

Third, unlike researchers of the classical dependency school, who emphasize the structural determination of dependency, Cardoso views dependency as an open-ended process. Given similar structures of dependency, there is a range of possible responses depending on the internal political alliances and movements. Thus if dependency structures delimit the range of oscillation, then political struggles of classes, groups, and the state can revive and transfigure these structures and may even replace them with others that are not predetermined.

Thus unlike the classical dependency school, which predicts a unidirectional trend of underdevelopment in Third World countries, Cardoso (1977, p. 20) argues that it is possible to have dependent-associated development—"that there can be development and dependency and that there exist more dynamic forms of dependence than those characterizing enclave or quasi-colonial situations."

In sum, many basic assumptions of the classical dependency studies—such as external, economic dependency and structural underdevelopment—have been modified in Cardoso's works (see Table 7.1). This change of orientation has opened up new areas of research in dependency studies. In this chapter, we will examine how dependent development took place, how internal factors (such as the bureaucratic-authoritarian state and its political alliance with local and foreign capital) have shaped the path of development in Latin America, and how the economic miracle in East Asia can be interpreted in the light of Cardoso's historical-structural methodology.

CARDOSO: ASSOCIATED-DEPENDENT DEVELOPMENT IN BRAZIL

In 1964, the Brazilian populist regime was overthrown and replaced by a military regime. In the impassioned aftermath of 1964, much of the discussion in the literature of development revolved around the nature of the new military regime. How should this turning point in Latin American history be interpreted? Was it just another reactionary military coup or did it represent a new political-economic order for Third World development?

From a classical dependency perspective, Furtado (1968) characterizes the new Brazilian regime as a military state, arguing that, like any other military state, this Brazilian regime had social stability as its major goal and would use every means to preserve the

Table 7.1 Comparison of Old Dependency Studies and
New Dependency Studies

	Old Dependency Studies	New Dependency Studies
Similarities		
focus of research	Third World development	same
level of analysis	national level	same
key concepts	core-periphery, dependency	same
policy implications	dependency harmful to development	same
Differences		
methodology	high-level abstraction, focus on general pattern of dependency	historical-structural, focus on concrete situation of dependency
key factors	emphasis on external: unequal exchange, colonialism	emphasis on internal: class conflict, the state
nature of dependency	mostly an economic phenomenon	mostly a sociopolitical phenomenon
dependency and development	mutually exclusive: lead only to underdevelopment	can coexist: associated-dependent development

status quo and its perpetuation of power. The economic model
corresponding to this political environment was the reduction of
urban-industrial investment in favor of agricultural production—
that is, promoting pastoralization at the expense of industrialization. The new regime pursued such stagnant economic policy
because of its social basis—the agrarian oligarchy. From this classical dependency perspective, the new military state was therefore
nothing but the instrument of the agrarian oligarchy, regardless of
the military's own corporate interest.

Cardoso (1973), however, is highly dissatisfied with Furtado's
interpretation of the new Brazilian regime. He asks: "How much

of this is an objective attempt to analyze real, existing tendencies, and how much is simply the preferred, normative model?" (p. 156). To Cardoso, the classical dependency analysts have failed to take note of many new activities that occurred in the military regime, thus they were unable to recognize this regime as pursuing a new model of "associated-dependent development" in Brazil.

New Activities in the Military Regime

Cardoso has pointed to the following new activities in the military regime in Brazil. First, international capitalism became more interested in direct investment in the manufacturing sector, such as establishing factories and plants in Latin American countries. In Brazil, for example, the level of foreign private investment grew so much and became so sustained that the state sector and national entrepreneurs no longer played a dominant role in the dynamic industrial sectors. Cardoso reports that foreign capital occupied 72.6% of the capital-goods sector, 78.3% of the durable consumer-goods sector, and 53.4% of the nondurable consumer-goods sector for the ten largest firms in each sector in Brazil in 1968. This growing industrial power of foreign-owned manufacturing firms that sold their products to the Brazilian market was also reflected in the advertising business. In 1967, the twelve major advertisers in Brazil included Volkswagen, Gillette, Ford, Nestle, Coca-Cola, and Shell. And by being the largest advertising sponsors, foreign firms exercised influence on the mass media—newspapers, magazines, and television.

Second, the antipopulist sector of the military and the technocracy, which had been relatively uninfluential in the populist era, suddenly gained considerable influence as the new economic trend emerged. Not only did the military-technocratic sector carry out the repressive function in the political arena, it also took on the task of modernizing the economy and the state administration.

Third, as a result, the populist sector lost its power. Cardoso observes that the union leaders, who mediated between the workers and the state in the previous era, had completely disappeared from the political scene due to political repression in the new military regime. Cardoso (1973, p. 147) further argues that capital accumulation would require, among other things, "keeping down the wage level and therefore dismantling an array of union and political organizations through which, in the populist period, the wage earners were able to resist part of the pressure for accumulation."

Finally, the old ruling sectors had lost their relative power position also. Not only the traditional agrarian sector (*latifundiarios*), but even industrial and merchant interests that had not adapted to the new economic trend found themselves at a political disadvantage under the new regime. By accepting military intervention to destroy the influence of the workers, the Brazilian bourgeoisie unintentionally supported measures that destroyed its own direct political expression (such as elections, political parties, and free speech).

To summarize, the new activities since 1964 were the increasing foreign direct investment in manufacturing, the economic and repressive functions of the military sector, the dismantling of working-class power, and the erosion of bourgeois political expression. However, in interpreting these new activities, Cardoso cautions against falling back on the classical dependency school's assertion that foreign domination allows no room for national development. Instead, researchers should focus on the particularity of these activities and formulate a new model to capture their dynamics. Thus Cardoso presents his model of "associated-dependent development."

The Model of Associated-Dependent Development

Cardoso deliberately uses the phrase *associated-dependent development* because it combines two notions that generally have appeared as separate and contradictory—dependency and development. Classical modernization theories focus only on modernization and development, while classical dependency theories and imperialism view the basic relationship between a dependent capitalist country and an underdeveloped country as one of extractive exploitation that perpetuates stagnation. But Cardoso asserts that a new phase has emerged as a result of the rise of multinational corporations, the immersion of industrial capital into peripheral economies, and a new international division of labor. Cardoso (1973, p. 149) argues that "*to some extent,* the interests of the foreign corporations become compatible with the internal prosperity of the dependent countries. In this sense, they help to promote development." Since foreign corporations aim to manufacture and sell consumer goods to the domestic market, their interests coincide with economic growth in at least some crucial sectors of the dependent country. From this angle, development implies a definite articulation with technological, financial, organizational, and market connections that only multinational corporations can assure.

Thus, unlike the classical dependency model, associated-dependent development is not without dynamism in the industrial sector. It is not based on ruralization at the expense of industrialization, and it will not lead Third World countries to export only raw materials. However, Cardoso is not willing to go all the way to join the modernization school, for he immediately stresses the costs of associated-dependent development. For example, he points out that the Brazilian economic boom was based on a regressive profile of income distribution, emphasizing luxurious consumer durables as opposed to basic necessities, generating increasing foreign indebtedness, contributing to social marginality and the underutilization and exploitation of manpower resources, and thereby leading to an increase in relative misery.

In addition, Cardoso points to the objective limitations of this type of dependent development. Dependent development is crippled because it lacks "autonomous technology"; it is compelled to utilize imported technology and must bear all the consequences of absorbing capital-intensive, labor-saving technology. It is also crippled because it lacks a fully developed capital-goods sector. The accumulation, expansion, and self-realization of local capital require and depend on a dynamic complement outside the dependent country—it must insert itself into the circuit of international capitalism.

In underscoring the costs and structural limitations of dependent development, Cardoso therefore stays within the confines of the dependency school. In fact, what Cardoso tries to accomplish is to examine both dependency and development, to study both foreign domination and domestic political forces, in order to show how the historically specific interaction between these actors has managed to produce some dynamic development within the structural confines of dependency. Thus it is interesting to examine what the various political forces in Cardoso's model are.

The Political Dynamics

There are three types of political actors in Cardoso's model—the military (bureaucratic-technocratic) state, the multinational corporation, and the local bourgeoisie. Cardoso argues that these three groups have formed a political alliance to promote associated-dependent development in Brazil since 1964.

First, there was the emergence of the *military state*. The military established tight control of the executive by redefining the role of the presidency, broadening the scope of the National Security Council, creating a national intelligence service, and setting up security departments in all ministries and state enterprises. After accomplishing the centralization of administration, the military state began to repress all forms of social protest. Using the doctrine of national security, the military state dismantled workers' organizations and achieved a high degree of "political tranquillity." Then the military state tried to accelerate economic growth through a combination of public and private enterprises, such as the promotion of the petrochemical industry by means of establishing PETROBRAS (the state oil monopoly). It also promoted the ideology of social mobility, with the aim to "keep socially open a politically closed society."

Second, the local bourgeoisie's nationalist developmentalist fraction was deposed by the military state and replaced by the *bourgeoisie's internationalized sectors*. Later, after the bourgeoisie had relinquished its political control instruments (parties, elections, freedom of the press, and so on), an agreement was reached between the military state and the bourgeoisie. The military implicitly assumed an identity between the economic interests of the entrepreneurs and the general interests of the nation. They defined some areas in which Brazilian capital would be preferentially encouraged to act. With the support of the state, very promising opportunities were opened up for the Brazilian bourgeoisie to make a profit, and the productive forces of modern capitalism were unleashed.

Third, according to Cardoso, the Brazilian economy was increasingly restructured in accordance with the new patterns of international economic organization. The Brazilian bourgeoisie frequently associated with *multinational corporations* as a dependent and junior partner, so new forms of production involving international monopolies and local enterprises appeared. Cardoso argues that multinational corporations had the upper hand over the Brazilian bourgeoisie because the former controlled finances and advanced technology.

Based on the above analysis, Cardoso (1973, p. 163) concludes that it is reasonable to perceive of the 1964 political event in Brazil as a revolution:

> A bourgeois economic revolution did take place, brought into being by a reactionary political movement. It was economically revolutionary to the extent that it pushed the local bourgeoisie to adapt to the beat of international capitalist development, thereby establishing an effective subordination of the national economy to modern forms of economic domination.

Cardoso's research has shaped the direction of empirical studies in the dependency school and has started a whole new series of investigation on the bureaucratic-authoritarian state; on the triple alliance among the state, the multinational corporations, and the local bourgeoisie; and on dependent development in the Third World. The influence of Cardoso's research can be seen in the following discussion of the new dependency studies.

O'DONNELL: THE BUREAUCRATIC-AUTHORITARIAN
STATE IN LATIN AMERICA

O'Donnell (1978, p. 4) notes that the concept of "dependence explains so much so fully that it becomes senseless to question how it is linked with factors whose dynamism is far from being the mere reflection of dependency itself." Not satisfied with the classical dependency theory, O'Donnell argues that researchers should adopt Cardoso's "historical-structural" approach to investigate the interrelationships through time between capitalism and its pattern of political domination. O'Donnell has contributed by delineating the defining characteristics, the emergence, the development, and the collapse of a specific type of political domination that he calls the "bureaucratic-authoritarian" (BA) state.

Defining Characteristics

In Latin America, the BA state emerged in the 1960s, first in Brazil and Argentina, and then in Uruguay and Chile. O'Donnell points out that, unlike other forms of political domination such as traditional authoritarianism and Fascism, the BA state possesses the following defining characteristics:

(1) *Dominance of bureaucrats:* High government positions usually are occupied by persons who come to them after successful careers in bureaucratic organizations such as the armed forces, the public bureaucracy, and large private firms.

(2) *Political exclusion:* The BA state closes channels of political access to the popular sector either through repression or through the imposition of vertical (corporatist) controls by the state on such organizations as labor unions.

(3) *Economic exclusion:* The BA state reduces or postpones indefinitely aspirations to economic participation by the popular sector.

(4) *Depoliticization:* Social issues are reduced to "technical" ones that can be solved by the rational planning of state bureaucrats.

(5) *Deepening of dependent capitalism:* The emergence of the BA state corresponds to a stage of the deepening of peripheral and dependent capitalism in the Third World.

The following sections offer discussion of how the BA state emerges and explanations for the rise of the BA states in Latin America.

Emergence of the BA State

Why did the BA state emerge only in the 1960s but not earlier? According to O'Donnell, the BA state was a response to the economic and political crises of dependent capitalism in Latin America in the post-World War II era. In the 1950s, many Latin American states adopted the policy of import substitution. Instead of importing foreign consumer goods, the Latin American states decided that they would manufacture consumer goods themselves for their domestic markets. To the extent that domestic demands had already been created by imports and the production of simple industrial consumer goods entailed small requirements of capital, technology, and organization, the policy of import substitution initially led to an expansion of local capital and thus a horizontal expansion of industrial activities. However, this horizontal expansion lasted only briefly and soon led to the appearance of many symptoms of economic crisis—balance-of-payments pressures, inflation, negative redistribution of income, declining GNP and investment rates, flight of capital, and so on.

These economic problems led to the political activation of the popular sector. The working masses asked for higher wages, lower inflation, more government services, tighter control of foreign corporation, and higher taxes on the rich. According to O'Donnell, this political activation was perceived by the dominant classes and sectors as a threat to their interests and to their international affiliations. O'Donnell argues that the greater the level of threat, the greater the polarization and visibility of the class context of the conflicts. This, in turn, tended to produce stronger cohesion among the dominant classes, to lend more weight to the "hardline" groups in the military and in the bureaucracy, to promote a more complete subordination of the middle sectors, and to provoke a more drastic defeat of the popular sector.

The BA state is a historical product of these economic and political crises. Realizing that the horizontal expansion of industrial consumer goods had reached its limit, the military-bureaucratic elites tried a new economic strategy that O'Donnell labels the "deepening of industrialization." The aim of the deepening strategy was to produce intermediate and capital goods—such as petrochemical products, automobiles, industrial inputs, equipment, machinery, and technology—that were more complex and more removed from final consumption. This movement toward basic industrial production, if successful, would generate significantly more vertically integrated industry in Latin America, open the door to future exports, and reduce the balance-of-payments problem by cutting back on technology imports.

In order to carry out this deepening policy, the military-bureaucratic elites realized that they must institute a BA state to generate the social peace for large-scale capital investment. Compared to investment in consumer goods, investment in capital goods requires a longer maturation period, greater technological content, more organizational management, and much more capital input. No corporation is willing to undertake such large-scale, lengthy, and risky investment unless there is a high degree of future certainty of profitable environment.

Consequently, in order to solve the economic crisis, the military-bureaucratic elites first had to solve the political crisis by instituting a BA state. The military-bureaucratic elites had to eliminate the threat entailed politically by the activation of the popular sector. Thus came into being the authoritarian nature of the state—eliminating the leaders of the popular sector, turning the workers' organizations at the factory level into an arm of the state, banning strikes, discontinuing periodic elections, and so on. According to O'Donnell, political exclusion of the popular sector led to "order," created the necessary conditions to stabilize the domination relationship, guaranteed the predictability of profitable investment, and provided a new impulse toward the deepening of production structure. Conversely, if the state had not increased its capacity for control over the civil society enormously through political repression, the deepening process would not have been possible.

Dynamics of the BA State

If the BA state corresponds to a stage of the deepening of industrialization in Latin America, what then are its dynamics? From O'Donnell's perspective, international capital is a necessary condition for the deepening process, because only the transnational corporations have sufficient capital, advanced technology, and modern equipment to take part in such a process. In addition, the foreign currency that the TNCs bring in serves to relieve immediate balance-of-payments problems and to show internal allies the external support that the BA state enjoys.

Thus during the *initial stage* of the BA state, its inaugural problem is to eliminate the threat from the activation of the popular sector, to provide an attractive investment environment so as to lure the entry of international capital. However, O'Donnell contends that this task takes time and is intrinsically precarious. It takes time to curtail popular protests and to demonstrate to the international capitalists the seriousness and ability of the BA state to carry out the deepening process. In addition, the BA state has to fight against not only the allies of the popular sector, but also its old allies who became disillusioned with the BA state. The national bourgeoisie, for instance, is not pleased with the BA state's policy of eliminating its subsidies and lowering import tariffs. Only when the BA state receives the support of the World Bank and the International Monetary Fund can international capital start to enter and invest in capital-goods industries.

The distinguishing elements of the initial phase of the BA state, then, are political isolation from the popular sector, the disillusionment of its original allies (especially the national bourgeoisie), and dependence on international capital. O'Donnell argues that the initial stage of the BA state is the time at which it is most open to deep penetration by international capital.

Only when international capital begins to enter in sustained fashion has the BA state consolidated its power and moved beyond the initial stage. At this *consolidation stage* there is a significant recovery of the GNP's growth rate, and there are external economies resulting from the previous entry of the TNCs. The BA state therefore has more bargaining power and more room for action than before. O'Donnell argues that the successful BA state may adopt a policy of selective reopening to the national bourgeoisie, thus forming a triad consisting of the BA state, international capital, and local capital.

With the inclusion of national and private components, the BA state can now claim representation of the incarnation of the general interests of the nation. In pretending to express the general interest, the BA state represents itself as working for everyone's long-term benefit, although some of the beneficiaries may not as yet be able to recognize it. O'Donnell (1978, p. 20) further points out that at this stage, "the new role of international capital and the state expansion are presented as instruments for the attainment of the true goal: the grandeur of a nation in which even those excluded and repressed are invited to participate vicariously."

Obviously, the formation of a triad generates a much more complex situation than existed before. On the one hand, the BA state actively orchestrates the reentry of the national bourgeoisie—the BA state becomes more nationalist and more protectionist, it again subsidizes the bourgeoisie, it reserves for the national bourgeoisie hunting grounds forbidden to the direct access of international capital. Thus the BA state must come to restrict international capital to a degree almost unthinkable during the initial stage. On the other hand, the BA state still requires a high and sustained flow of international capital, due to the difficulties of generating internal technology, mounting foreign indebtedness, large investments for the capital-goods industry, and so on.

From the viewpoint of international capital, despite its nationalistic whims, the BA state continues to be the political guarantee of the order and stability necessary for profitable investment in capital-goods industries. International capital, of course, wants to "restrict the pruning of its domestic expansion attempted by the state and the national bourgeoisie. But to the extent that the pruning does not seem to entail greater costs than the surrender of the market, international capital continues to need the guarantee of stability and predictability extended by the BA" state (O'Donnell 1978, p. 23). O'Donnell uses the term "mutual indispensability" to characterize the relationship between the BA state and international capital during this consolidation phase, and remarks that the above conception of the BA state and the national bourgeoisie takes "it well beyond the nullity or marginality postulated by simplistic versions of imperialism and dependence" (p. 23).

In the end, O'Donnell entertains two different paths for the *collapse or transformation of the BA state*. On the first path, many BA states may not even have a chance to go beyond the initial stage. Take the Argentina BA state, for example. In 1968, two years after a coup, international capital began to enter Argentina. At the same time, Argentina's national bourgeoisie and middle sectors had begun to turn back toward the popular sector and its nationalist popular expression of *Peronismo*. By mid-1969, with rising popular unrest, it was clear that Argentina's BA state had failed to fulfill its role as the guarantor of social peace and economic stability. Consequently, the flow of foreign investment halted, hot money left the country, international reserves fell, private investments in equipment and machinery declined, and so on—leading to the failure of the deepening project and the end of the short-lived partnership of the BA state and international capital. In this light, Argentina provides a classic case in which the civil society invaded and demolished a state that, under these attacks, began to water down its bureaucratic-authoritarian characteristics in terms of having more sensibility toward social problems and curtailing international capital. O'Donnell (1978, p. 24) points out that although defeated politically, the dominant classes were still powerful and backed by the armed forces. As a result, the dominant classes "inaugurated a defensive strategy in which what remained of the BA was used as a bargaining card against the guarantee that its successors would not transgress the limits of those institutional and class interests."

On the second path, after a successful BA state has consolidated its power, it renationalizes itself, orchestrating the reentry of the national bourgeoisie, distancing itself somewhat from international capital, and thus opening up again toward civil society. On this point, O'Donnell observes a paradox between the BA state and democracy. A successful BA state that has established a triad has more bargaining power with the popular sector. It can demand full protection from dominant class interests as compensation for democratic development. Having promoted rapid economic growth, the BA state may even have a chance to win democratic elections over its opponents. Thus a successful BA state has also the capacity to transform itself into a democratic state. However, since there is no urgency (in the form of popular protests) to compel the BA state to develop democratic institutions, those within the BA state and the dominant classes who favor democratic transition exert less leverage. It is hard for this tiny democratic faction to convince other members that the BA state needs to democratize itself before it is too late. Why bother to change if the status quo is accepted by the majority of the population?

Writing as he did during the height of the success of the BA state in the 1970s, O'Donnell only briefly discusses the downfall of successful BA states. Peter Evans, however, writing during the ebb of the BA state about a decade later, gives a fascinating analysis of the prospect of the successful BA state in Brazil in the 1980s. His work is discussed in the next section.

EVANS: THE TRIPLE ALLIANCE
IN BRAZIL IN THE 1980s

In the late 1960s and early 1970s, Brazil experienced an economic miracle. Its gross domestic product grew at about 10% per year during this period, production of capital goods and consumer durables grew at rates of over 20% per annum, manufactured exports increased by about 30% per annum, and, as industrialization deepened, the value added in manufacturing in Brazil in 1970 exceeded that of all other developing countries.

However, by 1981 Brazil had entered a period of economic uncertainty. For example, Volkswagen do Brasil, perennially profitable for a quarter of a century, recorded its first annual loss in 1980 and dismissed over 3,000 workers. Economic problems then were quickly translated into political unrest. Enraged by a 60% increase in bus fares, the people of Salvador exploded and destroyed 750 buses. In response to the layoff of over 5,000 workers, 500 workers invaded the factory yard of Mercedes-Benz, manufacturer of the bulk of Brazil's buses and trucks.

What is the explanation for this transition from economic miracle to economic uncertainty in just two decades? According to Evans (1983), it was the result of the changing nature of the external environment and the internal contradictions in the late 1970s. Specifically, Evans presents a model of "triple alliance" of state, multinational, and local capital, and shows how the interaction of external and internal contradictions have worsened Brazilian dependent development, making the leadership of the triple alliance increasingly problematic.

Dependent Development and the Triple Alliance

For Evans (1983, p. 141), dependent development is a contradictory concept:

> Development implies the accumulation of capital in the context of an increasingly differential internal division of labour, an expansion of the variety of goods that may be produced locally, more flexibility as to the goods that can be offered on international markets and therefore less vulnerability to the international system.

Defined in this way, development is the opposite of dependence. Yet Evans points out that in Brazil, development has been linked to continued dependence on international capital. What makes Brazilian dependent development possible, according to Evans, is the formation of a triple alliance among transnational capital, local capital, and the entrepreneurial fraction of state capitalism.

To a certain extent, the three partners in the alliance have found it mutually beneficial to participate in the pact. The transnational corporations were attracted to the large Brazilian market and the favorable investment climate set up by the state, such as strict controls on labor, generous subsidies to investors, and protection of those willing to produce locally from competitors producing elsewhere. In return for enjoying the fruits of operating in such a profitable market, Evans (1983, p. 141) points out, the "TNCs had to moderate the degree to which they gave global accumulation

priority over local accumulation," and they had to share ownership and managerial controls with local partners.

Local private capital, of course, benefited from the same investment climate that made Brazil profitable for the TNCs. In addition,
local capital enjoyed extra privileges such as having access to
low-interest loans and monopolization of certain niches (such as
insurance and commercial banking). However, the degree to
which local capital could be protected from TNC competition was
limited. Evans (1983, p. 142) remarks that "the denationalization of
certain industries and the destruction of certain local capital
groups was the price that local capital as a whole paid for what
was otherwise a very profitable arrangement."

For the "state bourgeoisie" (the entrepreneurially oriented segment of the state apparatus) the triple alliance was an ideal means
of capital accumulation. The partnership with local capital enhanced the legitimacy of the state bourgeoisie in the eyes of the
local population. Collaboration with the TNCs brought in technology, foreign currency, and marketing expertise. Although the state
then took an active role in promoting capital accumulation, state-
owned enterprises had to take care not to encroach upon the space
that could be filled by private capital.

However, despite the mutual benefits, the triple alliance was
not without internal conflict. Although the partners shared an
interest in a "profitable business climate," they were also keen
competitors in the pursuit of profit. First, the state bourgeoisie and
local capitalists understood very well that the "TNCs continued to
look for ways to use their operations in Brazil as a means of
increasing the return on assets held elsewhere." If the investment
climate in Brazil had worsened, the TNCs would not have hesi-
tated to abandon their commitment to local capital accumulation.
Thus neither the state nor local capital wanted the TNCs to gain
too much leverage over the Brazilian economy. Second, local capitalists were afraid that state enterprises would use their legal and
financial leverage to encroach upon the industrial territory of
private capital. Third, the TNCs knew that they were at risk. They
were the ones that invested huge amounts of capital and technology, and they would suffer tremendous losses if there were any
changes in the rules of the triple alliance. So the TNCs had to be

cautious and wary of any nationalistic outburst in Brazil. Thus Evans labels the triple alliance an "uneasy partnership," full of tensions.

According to Evans, in addition to the formation of the triple alliance, there were two more factors that facilitated the miracle of economic growth in Brazil between the late 1960s and early 1970s. First, the interests of a large portion of the Brazilian population were sacrificed in order to promote economic growth. While the Brazilian GNP rose at record rates, the real income of Brazil's workers fell. At the same time color television sets were first produced, infant mortality rates remained at levels double those of countries with comparable per capita income. In addition, Brazil's economic growth was aided by a favorable international climate. During this period there was unusual growth in international liquidity, making it easy for Brazil to borrow funds externally to finance its state enterprises. Also there was a buoyant market for exports, thereby attracting the TNCs to commit long-term capital investment that made dependent development possible.

If the triple alliance, the sacrifices of the Brazilian population, and the favorable international climate explain the Brazilian economic miracle, what then explains the later transition to economic and political uncertainty? On this point, Evans mentions two factors—the changing external environment and internal contradictions in Brazil in the late 1970s.

The External Environment

Evans observes that the worldwide recession of 1974-1975 changed the buoyant nature of the credit and capital markets. As the external environment changed, so did the long-term optimism of investors and the flow of capital to Brazil.

In 1973 the influx of direct investment was 2.5 times larger than the outflow of capital. However, in the late 1970s, profit outflow climbed to double or triple its earlier levels, and the amount of this profit outflow came to represent an increasing proportion of capital inflow. Evans reports that the role of loan capital followed a similar shift. With rising interest rates in the late 1970s, an increasing proportion of new loans went directly to making debt service payments. By 1979, debt service payments amounted to 95.5% of the new finances obtained.

Capital outflow and debt service payments naturally aggravated the balance-of-payments problem. According to Evans, this hostile external environment had (1) reduced the Brazilian state's flexibility in dealing with conflicts among the other two partners in the triple alliance, (2) limited its ability to respond to an increasing internal pressure for redistribution, and (3) limited its ability to use economic growth as a solvent for internal tensions. Thus the shift in the external environment set new internal economic and political dynamics into motion.

Growing Internal Contradictions

Facing this hostile external environment, the state needed more cooperation from international capital, in the form of both increased exports by TNC subsidiaries and external financing. In order to gain cooperation on the export front, the state was tempted to grant concessions to the TNCs. For example, in 1980, the state planners gave Dow Chemical the tentative go-ahead to produce ethylene and granted Dow a subsidy worth about $173 million U.S., on the grounds that such chemical products would generate a total of around $800 million in export sales over a ten-year period. This concession would give Dow Chemical a vertically integrated empire in ethylene-based products.

In addition to its desire to increase exports, the state also struggled to increase the supply of foreign loans. There was a case in the aluminum industry in which, in order to secure a loan of $2 billion U.S. from Japan, the state granted concessions to the Japanese companies. Japanese firms in Brazil were allowed to buy electricity from the Brazilian state at a subsidized rate, and the aluminum exported to Japan sold below the Brazilian market price.

However, to the extent that the state granted special favors to international capital, it antagonized local capital. In the early

1970s, the state promised low-interest financing, and its ambitious program of capital expenditure made it a major source of the increased demand in the industry. Local capital was to be given first priority on government bids. But during the late 1970s, the state withdrew its promises. With rising inflation rates and a deteriorating balance of payments, the state cut back its ambitious program and the state's demand for capital goods fell accordingly. Consequently, local capital-goods producers, who had heeded the state's invitation to expand, found themselves in trouble. The purchase orders that they had counted on were simply not there, and the loans they took out were a burden. Local capitalists were frustrated because the state failed to support them in hard times. They protested that the state favored the TNCs at the expense of the local capitalists. This gave rise to the "entrepreneurial rebellion," with the local bourgeoisie becoming prominent in the democratic struggle to make its influence felt in the decision-making process of the state.

On the one hand, the state could not ignore the entrepreneurial rebellion. Gaining the support of local capitalists was important for the state to maintain its legitimacy, otherwise it would face problems in presenting itself as the incarnation of the general interests of the nation. Furthermore, if accused of selling the nation to foreign interests, the state would have difficulty in getting the support of the military. Thus the state simply could not allow its nationalistic credentials to deteriorate beyond a certain point.

On the other hand, if the state moved in a more nationalistic direction, it might jeopardize relations with the TNCs. The TNCs might doubt the future investment climate in Brazil, suspend their plans for future investments, and reduce their attempts to expand exports. If this happened, the entire economy would be at stake. Without billions of dollars in new loans, and without strong linkages to the international market, the profitable growth that had held the triple alliance together would be a thing of the past.

In Evans's (1983, p. 158) words, the dilemma facing the Brazilian state was this: It could not "embark on nationalist policies that appear to prejudice the profits of TNCs. Yet the regime badly needs to impress its nationalist credentials by improving its relations with local capital." In such a dilemma, what were the options available to the Brazilian state?

First, the state could have tried to subsidize the profits of both local and TNC capital, and, to a certain extent, this has been the state's strategy all along. But Evans remarks that this is a very expensive and demanding proposition. Support for local capital may backfire, and local capital may use state subsidies as a means of extracting personal gains rather than as a means of reviving their firms. In addition, subsidies make rational economic planning difficult and have been known to be a mechanism that propagates inflation.

Second, the state may turn to state capital itself and sell its enterprises to the private sector. Not only should privatization be attractive to both local and international capital, but it also requires no expenditure of resources on the part of the state. But Evans notes that privatization is not a good solution to the dilemma. Weakening the state enterprise sector will weaken the state's ability to support the local bourgeoisie, undermine the state's role in the local adoption of advanced technology, and decrease the state's capacity to attract international investment—thereby further undermining the entrepreneurial dynamism of capital accumulation in Brazil.

Third, the state may impose further sacrifices on the excluded majority of the population, thus providing a more favorable labor condition for capital accumulation. Again, Evans does not think this solution is workable. Since the late 1970s, there has been active opposition from the working class against the regime, with over half a million workers joining in an unprecedented wave of strikes. In fact, the current political environment in the 1980s has pointed to a direction of progressive redistribution of income for the Brazilian population.

In the end, Evans argues that the state has far fewer options for solving the dilemma in this period of uncertainty than it would have had in the previous decade of miracle growth. Thus Evans entertains several scenarios with respect to the future of the triple alliance. These are discussed in the following section.

Prospects for the Future

A pessimistic scenario is that with faltering inflow of foreign direct investments, with local capitalists becoming unwilling to risk investments in production, with state enterprises crippled by inflation and privatization programs, and with protectionism in the world-economy, the Brazilian economy will eventually collapse. Civilian politicians will come to power just in time to be forced to take on the responsibility of imposing the IMF's policy of regressive austerity.

An optimistic scenario is that current difficulties will push Brazil toward the model of "redistribution with growth." The state will invest in basic public services and in basic wage goods in the private sector. This scenario is attractive from an equity viewpoint, but Evans argues that it will be resisted by both international capital and local capital.

An apocalyptic scenario is that the hard-line faction of the military will bear with the political activation of the popular sector no more. It will shut down the electoral process, impose its own candidate for the presidency, and assume power. Its goal will be to preserve the existing structure of power and privilege by whatever means necessary, and it will not have the same commitment to economic growth as the post-1964 regime. Evans believes this scenario is also highly unlikely, given the pragmatic and partial solutions that have characterized past Brazilian regimes.

So, finally, the most probable scenario, as Evans sees it, is that of Brazil's "muddling through" the current difficulties, since there will always be ingenious and unexpected ways of coping with the unfriendly international environment and internal contradictions.

GOLD: DYNAMIC DEPENDENCY IN TAIWAN

Although claiming to follow the path of Cardoso's study of associated-dependent development, O'Donnell's study of the BA state, and Evans's study of the triple alliance, and although still using the term *dependency*, Gold's (1986) study is actually a testing of how far a dependency researcher can go in the direction of stressing dynamic development without abandoning the basic assumptions of the dependency theory. This new emphasis on dynamic development may in fact be due to the research problem that Gold imposed upon himself. Instead of studying economic uncertainty and political chaos, Gold has tackled the research problem of explaining the miracle of Taiwan's development. In other words, Gold employs the concept of dependency to explain the economic growth and political stability of Taiwan.

From Gold's perspective, although the concept of dependency is originally derived from studies of the underdevelopment of Latin America countries, it can be disengaged from that region and used as an approach (or a methodology) to examine development. Gold argues that Taiwan's starting point of development was in most ways very similar to that of Latin American countries.

The Phase of Classical Dependence

On the eve of transfer to Japanese colonial rule in 1895, Taiwan's socioeconomic situation was characterized by an agricultural economy premised on small peasant owners and tenant cultivators. There was a landlord-gentry class that provided political leadership for local regions. With the expansion of external commodity trade with mainland China, Taiwan's agricultural economy became increasingly commercialized. The export sector, however, was dominated by mainland Chinese and foreign merchants rather than by local Taiwanese merchants.

Then Japan defeated China and turned Taiwan into her first colony. Like other colonial governments, the Japanese implanted a structure of dependent capitalism in Taiwan: (1) The economy was skewed to the production of two primary goods (rice and sugar), the bulk of which was exported to Japan by Japanese trading houses; (2) Taiwan imported manufactured consumer and producer goods from one source—Japan; (3) the Japanese monopolized capitalist production and the financial sector, and they used legal statutes to obstruct Taiwanese participation in any but a subordinate way; and (4) the population as a whole was excluded from political participation.

Nevertheless, Gold (1986, p. 44-45) points out that the Japanese legacy in Taiwan was different from the typical dependent structure in other countries. The Japanese colonial state created a good investment climate in Taiwan, "enforcing law and order; unifying weights, measures, and currency; guaranteeing private property rights; building a modern infrastructure; mobilizing natural resources; increasing agricultural productivity; making investment capital available; and developing human capital, including the provision of public education and employment for women." Thus Gold remarks that "Taiwan was undeniably restructured by its dependent relation with Japan; it was not underdeveloped."

After Japan was defeated in World War II, Taiwan was suddenly yanked out of the Japanese orbit and appended to China in another colonial relationship. In the late 1940s, the nationalist government of mainland China (the Kuomintang, or KMT) needed every resource it could get in its struggle against its communist rival. Thus Gold (1986, p. 50) remarks that "before long, Taiwan's resources were siphoned off to the mainland by private carpetbaggers and government agencies charged with confiscating enemy assets. Factories were dismantled and shipped to China along with raw materials, thus devastating the part of Taiwan's economic base that had escaped American bombs."

Economic plundering was followed by political repression. With the Taiwanese relegated to the lowest position of the provincial government, the KMT brought "lawlessness, corruption, plunder, inflation, disease, and an environment of general disorder." In response, the Taiwanese elite voiced their protest on February 28, 1947. This alarmed the KMT, and led it to dispatch quickly more than 10,000 troops to Taiwan. In what is now known as the "2-28 incident," the KMT declared war on the Taiwanese elites and masses, unleashing a fortnight of terror and looting, and killing over 10,000 of them. Since this incident, Gold observes that "the reconquered Taiwanese again became leaderless, atomized, quiescent, and apolitical."

The Phase of Dependent Development

The year 1950 proved to be the turning point in Taiwan's history. After the KMT was defeated by the Chinese Communist Party (CCP) in mainland China, it took refuge in Taiwan. Within a short time, 1-2 million civilian and military refugees from the mainland descended on Taiwan, which in 1945 had a population of only about 6 million.

Then the Korean War started. President Truman reversed the American hands-off policy toward the KMT and dispatched the Seventh Fleet into the Taiwan Straits to protect the KMT from imminent communist invasion. This was the beginning of the Cold War. After Taiwan became "Free China" and an ally of the United States, American military and economic aid was sent in massive scale to help the KMT achieve political and economic stability. With the military backing and financial assistance of the United States, the KMT was afforded security and breathing space, and thus was able to adopt a fresh strategy toward political and economic reform.

The KMT quickly transformed itself into what O'Donnell calls a bureaucratic-authoritarian state in the 1960s. The KMT proclaimed a general state of siege on Taiwan and declared martial law. It extended party cells into civil organizations such as schools, enterprises, clubs, and overseas Chinese communities. Among other things, it set up overt and covert quasi-military security agencies to suppress dissent, imposed universal conscription of males, and exercised strict control over the mass media. All these policies were easily accomplished because those who opposed the KMT had already been liquidated during the 2-28 incident in 1947. Thus the KMT basically had a free hand to impose its policies on the general population.

Learning from their own mistake of neglecting the peasant problem on the mainland, the KMT quickly instituted land reform. Land was given to the small cultivators, and the landlords were compensated 70% with land bonds in kind and 30% with shares of stock in four government enterprises. Since then, small landholding families have become the dominant force in Taiwan's countryside.

The KMT's next reform program was to promote industrialization. Since American aid was tied to economic reforms, the KMT was encouraged to adopt a developmentalist attitude. Although the KMT dominated most industries, it devised measures such as the Small Industry Loan Fund and Model Factory Program to promote investment by the private sector in key industries. The KMT also turned Taiwan's economy toward *import substitution* in light consumer industry to conserve funds, absorb labor, supply the domestic market, and accumulate capital rapidly.

However, by the early 1960s, Taiwan's economy came to another turning point. Import-substitution industrialization had reached its limit due to the fairly small size of the domestic market. In addition, the United States made clear its intention of phasing its aid program to Taiwan out of existence by 1968, since the Taiwanese economy had recovered. At this stage, the Taiwanese economy was still pretty fragile. Unlike the big Latin American states, Taiwan lacked capital, foreign exchange, global credit, technology, internal markets, and labor shortages to justify the prestigious but costly deepening of capital-goods production.

Upon analyzing the available options, the KMT chose to liberalize and internationalize the economy. It loosened controls on trade and industry, promoted exports, reduced tariffs on imported products, unified multiple exchange rates, and created a business climate designed to stimulate private local and foreign investment. In short, the state adopted a strategy of *export-led industrialization*.

Gold (1986, p. 95) argues that "the source of dynamism moved to external markets. The leading industry, textiles, turned outward, producing goods under contract for foreign buyers. The most dynamic sector, electronics, originated as a TNC enclave but rapidly established ties with local industry, spawning domestic suppliers and imitators." Especially in the export processing zones, the triple alliance among the state, local capital, and TNCs took shape and stimulated economic growth in Taiwan. This ever-increasing opportunity for investment and employment, together with fluid mobility, contributed to the maintenance of stability and the spread of wealth in Taiwan.

The Phase of Dynamic Dependency

However, by the early 1970s, political and economic problems arose again. In 1971, there was a nationalist movement in Taiwan to protest against Japan's takeover of the Taio-yu-t'ai (Senkaku) island, leading to an uncharacteristic outburst of political activity on college campuses. Then mainland China was invited to join the United Nations, while Taiwan (the Republic of China) was asked to withdraw. All of Taiwan was further shocked by President Nixon's visit to mainland China and the signing of the Shanghai Communique in 1972. A new generation of intellectuals in Taiwan began to be highly critical of the authoritarian rule of the KMT, pressing for reforms to end martial law and advocating the protection of human rights, democratic elections, and so on.

The economic front was in trouble too. Gold (1986, p. 94) argues that Taiwan's economy fell victim to its own success:

> The vulnerabilities inherent in the export-oriented strategy all seemed to appear simultaneously: Taiwan's trading partners raised protectionist quotas against its exports; with full employment and a rising standard of living, wages and other costs rose; other less developed countries with even lower labor costs and more abundant resources began to hone in on Taiwan's markets; and the infrastructure, most of which dated from the Japanese era, was stretched beyond capacity.

Needless to say, the oil crisis of 1975 further exacerbated these vulnerabilities.

The KMT state, again, was the only actor capable of responding to these political and economic problems. Gold (1986, p. 133) labels the state managers as having an attitude of "dynamic dependency: assessing the economy and society's capabilities and needs and then linking to the world system in such a way as to utilize these and improve one's situation."

The strategy that the KMT state adopted was the *deepening of industrialization*—upgrading of industries and vertically integrating them. From 1978 to 1981, the state issued a Six-Year Plan, emphasizing the buildup of heavy and capital-intensive industries (such as steel and petrochemical) and modernization of the infrastructure (the Ten Major Development Projects). Later, in the early 1980s, the state began to stress strategic technology-intensive industries, such as computers, telecommunications, and robotics. The state also nurtured within Taiwan its own research and development program to develop new products, raise value added, and vertically integrate the electronic industry. In 1980, the state established a new type of industrial zone, the Science-Based Industrial Park in Hsin-chu, to cultivate these technology-intensive and information industries.

Gold argues that this deepening strategy is promising because a new generation of capitalists—better educated, more cosmopolitan, and more independent-minded than their predecessors—has sprung up. There is also a new generation of foreign-educated and liberal technocrats and politicians. This new generation should help Taiwan's industry to get a better deal in the triple alliance, and should set in motion the transition from an authoritarian to a democratic regime in the near future.

In fact, Gold (1986, p. 16-17) seems to argue that by the mid-1980s, Taiwan had escaped the problems of underdevelopment:

> Capital for investment was primarily from domestic savings, and the state's coffers were flush with foreign reserves. . . . Taiwan was exporting its own capital goods, technology, and whole plants to less developed countries. Taiwan-based transnational corporations were making direct foreign investments in the United States, Europe, and the Third World. . . . the domestic production structure, including foreign-owned enterprises, had become increasingly integrated vertically and horizontally. The social dislocations commonly associated with dependency, such as impoverished rural sector and glaring inequality, had been largely eliminated.

Unlike classical dependency theorists (e.g., Landsberg), who portray the miracle of East Asian development as "manufacturing imperialism," Gold (1986, p. 133) approaches the study of development using the concept of "dynamic dependency," which enables him to conclude his study on a hopeful note, saying that "in-

formed, selective, and managed linkages" to the capitalist world
market "need not be tantamount to turning one's nation over to
foreign masters."

POWERS OF THE NEW DEPENDENCY THEORIES

The new dependency perspective has modified some of the
basic assumptions of the classical dependency perspective. Instead
of treating dependency as a general, external, economic process
that leads to regional polarization and underdevelopment, new
dependency theorists now conceptualize it as a historically specific, internal, sociopolitical process that can lead to dynamic development. Thus the new dependency perspective has put forward
many original concepts, such as those discussed in this chapter:
associated-dependent development; the bureaucratic-authoritarian state; the triple alliance among the state, local capital, and
international capital; and dynamic dependency. These new concepts have opened up new research frontiers and have promoted
a new wave of empirical studies on the changing situations of
dependency in Third World countries.

Bringing history back in. The new dependency studies have paid
more attention to historically specific situations of dependency
than did classical dependency studies. For example, Cardoso highlights the new activities of the military regime in Brazil after the
1964 coup. O'Donnell shows that the emergence of the bureaucratic-authoritarian state is historically contingent upon the success of the responses of military-bureaucratic elites to the political
and economic crises in the early 1960s. Evans's analysis of the
triple alliance reveals how the changing external environment and
the growing internal contradictions have both affected the path of
Brazilian development in the 1980s. And Gold traces the historical
process of the transformation of Taiwan from classical dependency
to dependent development, and then further into the latest phase
of dynamic dependency.

Stressing internal and sociopolitical activities. From the viewpoint
of the new dependency studies, the state in the Third World is no
longer perceived as a dependent state for foreigners, but as an

active agency that tacitly works together with local capital and international capital. In addition, it is the political struggle among the state, local capital, and international capital that shapes the ever-changing situations of dependency. Thus Cardoso and O'-Donnell point to the success of the military elites in Brazil in the late 1960s in setting up the triple alliance at the expense of the popular sector, while Evans writes about the same state having much less maneuvering room in holding the alliance together during the period of economic uncertainty and popular protests in the 1980s. Compared to the Brazilian state, Gold observes that Taiwan has done very well in responding to political crises (expulsion from the United Nations and student protests) and economic crises (the oil crisis and the vulnerabilities in the world market) in the 1970s. Taiwan has not only carried out the deepening of industrialization but tolerated a high degree of political liberalization in the 1980s.

Dependency and development. The final characteristic of the new dependency studies is their willingness to acknowledge the co-existence of two contradictory processes—dependency and development. Thus not only are Cardoso, O'Donnell, and Evans able to explain the economic success of Brazil in carrying out the deepening process in the late 1960s, but Gold is also able to interpret the miracle of Taiwan economic development in reference to the concept of dynamic dependence.

All in all, it seems that the new dependency studies are more sophisticated than the classical dependency studies. Therefore, the new dependency perspective should be able to continue as a living tradition in Third World research in the 1990s.

Part III

THE WORLD-SYSTEM SCHOOL

CHAPTER 8

The World-System Perspective

THE HISTORICAL CONTEXT

When the United States became a superpower after World War II, American social scientists were called upon to study the problems of Third World development. This started the modernization school, which dominated the field of development in the 1950s. However, the failure of modernization programs in Latin America in the 1960s led to the emergence of a neo-Marxist dependency school. This dependency school was highly critical of the modernization school, frequently attacking it as a rationalization of imperialism. From Latin America this dependency school quickly spread to the United States, since it fit nicely with the antiwar sentiments of many American students.

Although the dependency school was unable to "destroy" the modernization school, the modernization school was unable to exclude competing views as illegitimate. The coexistence of contrasting perspectives in the field of development made the 1970s a time of intellectual fertility. By the mid-1970s, the ideological battle between the modernization school and the dependency school began to subside. The debate on Third World development became less ideological and emotional. A group of radical researchers led by Immanuel Wallerstein found that there were many new activities in the capitalist world-economy that could not be explained within the confines of the dependency perspective.

First, East Asia (Japan, Taiwan, South Korea, Hong Kong, and Singapore) continued to experience a remarkable rate of economic growth. It became harder and harder to portray this East Asian economic miracle as "manufacturing imperialism," "dependent development," or "dynamic dependence" because the these East Asian industrial states had begun to challenge the economic superiority of the United States.

Second, there was a crisis among the socialist states. The Sino-Soviet split, the failure of the Cultural Revolution, the economic stagnation in the socialist states, and the gradual opening of the socialist states to capitalist investment have signaled the bankruptcy of revolutionary Marxism. Many radical researchers began to rethink whether delinking from the capitalist world-economy is an appropriate model for Third World countries to apply.

Third, there was a crisis in U.S. capitalism. The Vietnam War, the Watergate crisis, the oil embargo in 1975, and the combination of stagnation and inflation in the late 1970s, as well as the rising sentiment of protectionism, the unprecedented government deficit, and the widening of the trade gap in the 1980s—all signal the demise of American hegemony in the capitalist world-economy. In addition, there has been a steady movement toward a structuring of the alliances in the interstate system. The latest alliance among Washington, D.C., Beijing, and Tokyo makes no ideological sense at all, certainly not in terms of the ideological lines of the Cold War in the 1950s.

In order to rethink the critical issues that emerged out of the changing world-economy over the last two decades, Wallerstein and his followers have developed a new world-system perspective. This school had its genesis at the Fernand Braudel Center for the Study of Economies, Historical Systems, and Civilization at the State University of New York at Binghamton. The Fernand Braudel Center publishes *Review*, a journal that calls for "the primacy of analysis of economies over long historical time and large space, the holism of the socio-historical process, and the transitory (heuristic) nature of theories." The center also publishes a working paper series as well as an annual newsletter on its research activities. In addition, the world-system school holds a professional meeting every year and publishes its conference papers.

According to Chirot and Hall (1982, p. 93), this new world-system perspective has "seized the imagination of a new generation of sociologists" and exerted a profound impact on the discipline of sociology. A new section titled "The Political Economy of the World-System" was established in the American Sociological Association in the 1970s. Having originated in sociology, the world-system school has now extended its impact to anthropology, history, political science, and urban planning (Bergesen 1983; Bergquist 1984; Chase-Dunn 1982b; Chirot 1976; Evans et al. 1985; Friedman 1982; Goldfrank 1979; Hechter 1975; Henderson and Castells 1987; Hopkins and Wallerstein 1980, 1982; Kaplan 1978; Moulder 1977; Nash 1981; Rubinson 1981; Thompson 1983).

THE THEORETICAL HERITAGE

Before presenting an examination of the key concepts and theories of the world-system school, this section retraces its intellectual heritage. According to Kaye (1979), Wallerstein's world-system perspective has drawn on two major intellectual sources—the neo-Marxist literature of development and the French Annales school.

Wallerstein started out as a specialist on Africa. His earlier works present studies of the developmental problems facing Africa after independence (Wallerstein 1964, 1967; see also Ragin and Chirot 1984). Consequently, during his initial stage of formulating the world-system perspective, Wallerstein was strongly influenced by the neo-Marxist literature of development. For example, he has incorporated many concepts from the dependency school—such as unequal exchange, core-periphery exploitation, and the world-market—into his world-system perspective. Wallerstein has also adopted many basic tenets of the dependency school, such as the argument that "the 'feudal' forms of production characteristic of much of American history are not 'persistent from the past' but rather products of Latin America's historical relations with the core" (Kaye 1979, p. 409). In fact, Wallerstein (1979a, p. 53) has included the concepts of Frank, Dos Santos, and Amin as part of his world-system perspective, on the grounds that these concepts have in common a critique of both the modernization school and the Marxist developmentalist perspective.

However, at a later stage, when Wallerstein had fully developed his world-system perspective, it seemed that he moved beyond the domain of the neo-Marxist dependency school. This shift in Wallerstein's orientation may be explained by the strong influence of Fernand Braudel and the French Annales school on Wallerstein's conception of the world-system (see Wallerstein 1978, 1979c, 1982, 1986, 1988a).

The Annales school arose as a protest against the overspecialization of social science disciplines within conventional academic boundaries. Through the works of its long-time leader, Fernand Braudel, the Annales school advanced the following arguments.

First, Braudel sought to develop "total" history or "global" history. Instead of subordinating history to other disciplines, from Braudel's viewpoint history is an all-embracing and catholic discipline. Braudel argues that historians must direct each observation to the totality of the field of social force. As Wallerstein (1988a, p. 5) remarks: "It is indeed this vision of history that emerges in his [Braudel's] *Mediterranean* when, not content to stop at the shores of the 'inland sea' . . . , the book starts in the mountains and extends not only to the hot deserts of Africa but to the cold deserts of China, half a world away; and westwards, it extends to Mexico and Lima, to Acapulco and Manila, and back to China."

Second, Braudel argues "for the synthesis of history and social sciences through an emphasis on *la longue duree* (the long-term). In that way, history would move away from the 'uniqueness of events' (eventism), and the social sciences would gain a historical perspective lacking in much of its attempts to formulate trans-historical theory" (Kaye 1979, p. 409). The *longue duree* is a historical process in which all change is slow, a history of constant repetition, even recurring cycles. It is only through the study of the long term that the totality, the deepest layers of social life, the "subterranean history," and the continuing structures of historical reality are revealed.

Third, Braudel was instrumental in shifting the center of concern in historical discourse from the histories of periods to problem-oriented history. As Wallerstein (1988a, p. 7) points out,

Braudel's work is characterized by "his willingness to ask 'big' questions: What is capitalism? What accounts for France's failure ever to have dominated the European world? How did 'Europe' grow to global dominance? Why did the center of economic gravity shift from the Mediterranean to the North Atlantic? . . . 'It is the fear of history, of history on the grand scale, which has killed History.' "

In the following sections, we will see how the quest for total history, the *longue duree*, and the "big" questions have provided the foundation on which Wallerstein has formulated his world-system perspective.

METHODOLOGY

For Wallerstein (1987, p. 309), world-system perspective is not a theory but a protest—"a protest against the ways in which social scientific inquiry was structured for all of us at its inception in the middle of the nineteenth century." Wallerstein criticizes the prevailing mode of scientific inquiry both for its "closing off rather than opening up" many important research questions and for its inability "to present rationally the real historical alternatives that lie before us." In particular, Wallerstein feels uncomfortable about the following five assumptions of traditional social scientific inquiry that have informed our research process over the past 150 years.

On Social Science Disciplines

In traditional scientific inquiry, "the social sciences are constituted of a number of 'disciplines', which are intellectually-coherent groupings of subject-matter distinct from each other" (Wallerstein 1987, p. 310). The disciplines include anthropology, economics, political science, sociology, and possibly geography, psychology, and history. The disciplines have organizations with boundaries, structures, and personnel to defend their collective interests in the universities as well as in the research world. Based upon this premise, proponents of interdisciplinary research and/or teaching argue that some problem areas can benefit from an approach that combines the perspectives of many disciplines.

But Wallerstein questions whether the disciplines can be separated from one another in the first place. Are the various social scientific disciplines really disciplines? And what exactly constitutes a discipline? Examining the historical origins of social sciences, Wallerstein (1987, p. 311) observes that "there emerged over the course of the nineteenth century a set of names, and then of departments, degrees and associations, that by 1945 (although sometimes earlier) had crystallized into the categories we use today." All these social science divisions are actually derived intellectually from the dominant liberal ideology of the nineteenth century, which argued that state (politics) and market (economics) were analytically separate domains, that sociology was thought to explain the irrational phenomena that economics and political science were unable to account for, and that anthropology specialized in the study of the primitive people beyond the realm of the civilized world. However, according to Wallerstein (1987, p. 312), "as the real world evolved, the contact line between 'primitive' and 'civilized', 'political' and 'economic', blurred. Scholarly poaching became commonplace. The poachers kept moving the fences, without however breaking them down."

From a world-system perspective, Wallerstein (1987, p. 313) rejects this artificial disciplinary boundary because it is a barrier to further knowledge rather than a stimulus to its creation:

The three presumed arenas of collective human action—the economic, the political and the social or sociocultural—are not autonomous arenas of social action. They do not have separate "logics". More importantly, the intermeshing of constraints, options, decisions, norms, and "rationalities" is such that no useful research model can isolate "factors" according to the categories of economic, political and social, and treat only one kind of variable, implicitly holding the others constant. We are arguing that there is a single "set of rules" or a single "set of constraints" within which these various structures operate.

In short, the various disciplines of social science are actually but a single one.

On History and Social Science

In traditional scientific inquiry, "history is the study of, the explanation of, the particular as it really happened in the past. Social science is the statement of the universal set of rules by which human/social behavior is explained" (Wallerstein 1987, p. 313). This is the famous distinction between idiographic and nomothetic modes of analysis, and there is a call to combine the two modes of analysis in the world of scholarship. The historian is said to serve the social scientist by providing the latter with wider, deeper sets of data from which to deduce lawlike generalizations. On the other hand, the social scientist is said to serve the historian by offering reasonably demonstrated generalizations that offer insight into the explication of a particular sequence of events.

Again, Wallerstein questions this "neat division" of intellectual labor—with historical analysis focusing on particular sequences while social scientific analysis examines universal generalizations. Is there a meaningful difference between sequence and universe, between history and social science? Are they two separate activities or one? Wallerstein (1987, p. 314) explains that "all description has time, and . . . unique sequence is only describable in non-unique categories. All conceptual language presumes comparisons among universes. Just as we cannot literally 'draw' a point, so we cannot literally 'describe' a unique 'event'. The drawing, the description, has thickness or complex generalization."

In response to the arbitrary separation between history and social science analysis, "world-system analysis offers the heuristic value of the *via media* between trans-historical generalizations and particularistic narrations." For Wallerstein (1987, p. 315), the method of world-system perspective

is to pursue analysis within systemic frameworks, long enough in time and large enough in space to contain governing "logics" and "determine" the largest part of sequential reality, while simultaneously recognizing and taking into account that these systemic frameworks have beginnings and ends and are therefore not to be conceived of as "eternal" phenomena. This implies, then, that at every instant we look both for the framework (the "cyclical rhythms" of the system), which we describe conceptually, and for the patterns of internal transformation (the "secular trends" of the system) that will eventually bring about the demise of the system, which we describe sequentially. This implies that the task is singular. There is neither historian nor social scientist, but only a historical social scientist who analyses the general laws of particular systems and the particular sequences through which these systems have gone.

On the Unit of Analysis:
Society Versus Historical System

In traditional social scientific inquiry, "human beings are organized in entities we may call societies, which constitute the fundamental social frameworks within which human life is lived" (Wallerstein 1987, p. 315).

In the nineteenth century, the concept of "society" was opposite to that of "state." The key intellectual issue was then the question of how to reconcile society and state. Unlike this formulation, although the state could be observed and analyzed directly through formal institutions, the society was referred to as the manners and customs that represent something more enduring and deeper than the state. Wallerstein states that as time has passed, we have become accustomed to thinking that the boundaries of a society and a state are synonymous, and that sovereign states are the basic entities within which social life is conducted. In traditional social science inquiry, therefore, it has often been assumed that "we live in states. There is a society underlying each state. States have histories and therefore traditions. Above all, since change is normal, it is states that normally change or develop. . . . They have the boundaries, inside of which factors are 'internal' and outside of which they are 'external'. They are 'logically' independent entities such that, for statistical purposes, they can be 'compared' " (Wallerstein 1987, p. 316).

However, Wallerstein questions this treatment of society/state as the unit of analysis. Where and when do the entities within which social life occurs exist? His world-system perspective argues that the basic unit of analysis should be the historical system rather than the state/society. For Wallerstein, this is more than a mere semantic substitution because the term *historical system* rids us of the central connotation that "society" has acquired its link to "state," and therefore of the presupposition about the where and when. Furthermore, *historical system* as a term underlies the unity of historical social science. The entity is systemic and historical simultaneously.

Wallerstein has put forward a set of hypotheses concerning the nature of this historical system. The defining boundaries of a historical system are "those within which the system and the people within it are regularly reproduced by means of some kind of ongoing division of labour." In human history, Wallerstein argues that there have been three known forms of historical systems: *mini-systems*, *world-empires*, and *world-economies*.

In the preagricultural era, there were a multiplicity of mini-systems that were small in space and brief in time (a life span of about six generations). The mini-systems were highly homogeneous in terms of cultural and governing structures, and they split up when they became too large. The basic logic was one of reciprocity in exchange.

In the period between 8000 B.C. and 1500 A.D., the world-empires were the dominant form of historical system. The world-empires were vast political structures, encompassing a wide range of cultural patterns. The basic logic was the extraction of tribute from otherwise locally self-administered direct producers that was passed upward to the center and redistributed to a network of officials.

Around 1500, the capitalist world-economies were born. These world-economies were vast, uneven chains of integrated production structures dissected by multiple political structures. The basic logic was that the accumulated surplus was distributed unequally in favor of those able to achieve monopolies in the market networks. By their inner logic, the capitalist world-economies then expanded to cover the entire globe, absorbing in the process all existing mini-systems and world-empires. Hence by the late nineteenth century, for the first time ever, there existed only one historical system on the globe.

On the Definition of Capitalism

In traditional social science inquiry, "capitalism is a system based on competition between free producers using free labour with free commodities, 'free' meaning its availability for sale and purchase on a market" (Wallerstein 1987, p. 318). This definition is adopted because most liberals and Marxists have taken England after the Industrial Revolution as an accurate description of the capitalist norm. In the English model of competitive capitalism, proletarian workers (essentially landless, toolless urban workers) labored in factories owned by bourgeois entrepreneurs (essentially private owners of the capital stocks of these factories). The owners purchased the labor power of (and paid wages to) the workers, who had no real alternative, in terms of survival, but to seek wage work. Wallerstein notes that out of this English model, a degree-of-capitalism scale is constructed in traditional social science inquiry. A state, as the locus of work situation, is classified as more or less capitalist depending on whether it is congruent with the presumed capitalist norm of free wage laborers.

However, Wallerstein (1987, p. 319-320) argues that "the situation of free labourers working for wages in the enterprises of free producers is a minority situation in the modern world. This is certainly true if our unit of analysis is the world economy." If this is true, if a deduced capitalist norm turns out not to be congruent with the reality of the capitalist world-economy, then researchers should wonder whether the prevailing definition of the capitalist norm serves any useful function at all. In other words:

> If we find . . . that the system seems to contain wide areas of
> wage and non-wage labour, wide areas of commodified and

non-commodified goods and wide areas of alienable and non-alienable forms of property and capital, then we should at the very least wonder whether this 'combination' or mixture of the so-called free and the non-free is not itself the defining feature of capitalism as a historical system. (Wallerstein 1987, p. 320)

Wallerstein further argues that if researchers have adopted this new definition of capitalism, it should have opened up new research questions, such as the search for structures that maintain the stability of a particular combination as well as the examination of the underlying pressures that may transform the combination over time. Thus "the anomalies now become not exceptions to be explained away but pattern to be analyzed, so inverting the psychology of the [traditional social] scientific effort."

On Progress

In traditional social science inquiry, "human history is progressive, and inevitably so" (Wallerstein 1987, p. 322). It seems that both liberal evolutionary theorists and Marxist developmentalists have shared this basic assumption of progress. For Wallerstein (1987, p. 322-323), however,

world-system analysis wants to remove the idea of progress from the status of a trajectory and open it up as an analytical variable. There may be better and there may be worse historical systems (and we can debate the criteria by which to judge). It is not at all certain that there has been a linear trend—upward, downward or straightforward. Perhaps the trend line is uneven, or perhaps indeterminate. Were this conceded to be possible, a whole new arena of intellectual analysis is immediately opened up. If the world has had multiple instances of, and types of, historical systems, and if all historical systems have beginnings and ends, then we will want to know something about the process by which there occurs a succession (in time-space) of historical system.

Finally, Wallerstein concludes that we are now living in the long moment of transition wherein the contradictions of the capitalist world-economy have made it impossible to continue to adjust its machinery. Thus we are living in a period of real historical choice, and "world-systems analysis is a call for the construction of a historical social science that feels comfortable with the uncertainties of transition, that contributes to the transformation of the world by illuminating the choices without appealing to the crutch of a belief in the inevitable triumph of good."

Equipped with a new methodology, the world-system school has developed a new perspective from which to reexamine the critical issues in the field of development. The following sections address the innovative concept of the semiperiphery as well as how the world-system perspective has provided a new interpretation of the history of the capitalist world-economy during the past four centuries.

THE SEMIPERIPHERY COUNTRIES

Wallerstein (1979b) has criticized the conception of a bimodal system. He argues that the world is too complicated to be classified as a bimodal system, with cores and peripheries only. There are many in-between nations that do not fit into either the core or the periphery category. Consequently, Wallerstein proposes a trimodal system consisting of *core, semiperiphery,* and *periphery.*

Wallerstein (1979b, p. 69-70) argues that the present capitalist world-system needs a semiperipheral sector for two reasons. First, a polarized world-system with a small, distinct, high-status sector facing a large low-status sector can lead rapidly to acute disintegration. "The major political means by which such crises are averted is the creation of 'middle' sectors, which tend to think of themselves primarily as better off than the lower sector rather than as worse off than the upper sector." Second, in response to the decline in comparative costs of production in the core countries, individual capitalists must be able to transfer capital from a declining leading sector to a rising sector in order to survive the effects of cyclical shifts in the loci of the leading sectors. As Wallerstein (1979b, p. 70) explains: "There must be sectors able to profit from the wage-productivity squeeze of the leading sector. Such sectors are what we are calling semiperipheral countries. If they weren't there, the capitalist system would as rapidly face an *economic* crisis as it would a *political* crisis."

In Wallerstein's formulation, semiperipheral states have two distinctive features. First, if the exchange between the core and the periphery of a capitalist world-economy is that between high-wage products and low-wage products, it would then result in an "unequal exchange," in which a peripheral worker would have to work many hours to obtain a product produced by a core worker in one hour. In reference to this system of unequal exchange, Wallerstein (1979b, p. 71-72) notes:

> The semiperipheral country stands in between in terms of the kinds of products it exports and in terms of the wage levels and profit margins it knows. Furthermore, it trades or seeks to trade in both directions, in one mode with the periphery and in the opposite with the core. . . . it is often in the interests of a semiperipheral country to *reduce* external trade, even if balanced, since one of the major ways in which the aggregate profit margin can be increased is to capture an increasingly large percentage of its *home* market for its *home* products.

This leads to a second distinctive feature of semiperipheral countries; that is, the state has a direct and immediate interest in controlling the domestic market. This politicization of economic decisions can be seen to be most operative for semiperipheral states at the following two moments of active change of status in the capitalist world-economy: (1) the actual breakthrough from peripheral to semiperipheral status, and (2) the strengthening of an already semiperipheral state to the point that it can lay claim to membership in the core.

From Peripheral to Semiperipheral Status

The process of a country's moving from peripheral to semi-peripheral status attracts the most attention in the development literature, although it is often treated as though it were a question of shifting from the periphery to the core. Why are some peripheral countries able to achieve semiperipheral status while others are unable to do so? According to Wallerstein, success in moving from periphery to semiperiphery depends on whether the country can adopt one of the following strategies of development: seizing the chance, promotion by invitation, or self-reliance.

First, by *seizing the chance,* Wallerstein (1979b, p. 76) refers to the activity that

> at moments of world-market contraction, where typically the price level of primary export from peripheral countries goes down more rapidly than the price level of technologically advanced industrial exports from core countries, the governments of peripheral states are faced with balance-of-payments problems, a rise in unemployment, and a reduction of state income. One solution is *"import-substitution"*, which tends to palliate these difficulties. It is a matter of "seizing the chance" because it involves aggressive state action that takes advantage of the weakened political position of core countries and the weakened economic position of domestic opponents of such policies.

However, only relatively strong peripheral countries (such as the Latin American states) with some small industrial bases already established would be able to expand such bases at a favorable moment; other relatively weaker peripheral countries would not be able to do so. In addition, the strategy of seizing the chance has certain built-in problems. Instead of importing foreign manufactured goods, prospective semiperipheral countries are now importing foreign machinery and technologies, thus essentially substituting "technological dependence" for "manufacturing dependence." Furthermore, the internal market cannot grow fast enough to absorb domestic industrial products due to the fact that the large landowners are opposed to the process of full prole-tarianization of the agricultural sector. Wallerstein notes that a way out of these developmental problems is to expand outward, to substitute an external market for an internal market, with the semiperipheral countries serving as purveyors of products that the core countries no longer bother to manufacture.

The second strategy is *semiperipheral development by invitation.* Wallerstein (1979b, p. 80) observes:

> Direct investment across frontiers grew up in part because of the flowering of infant industry protectionism and in part because of some political limitations to growth of enterprises in core countries (such as anti-trust legislation). The multina-tional corporations quickly realized that operating in col-laboration with state bureaucracies posed no real problems. For these national governments are for the most part weak both in terms of what they have to offer and in their ability to affect the overall financial position of the outside investor.

The prospective semiperipheral countries have competed with one another for multinational investment because there are dis-tinct advantages in getting it. With the presence of foreign invest-ment in the Ivory Coast, for instance, "in the countryside, the traditional chiefs, transformed into planters, have become richer, as have the immigrant workers from [upper Volta] who come out of a traditional, stagnant, very poor milieu; in the town, unemploy-ment remains limited in comparison with what it is already in the large urban centres of older African countries" (translation of Amin, 1971, quoted in Wallerstein 1979b, p. 80).

Wallerstein notes that the strategy of promotion by invitation is different from the strategy of seizing the chance in two ways. Done in more intimate collaboration with external capitalists, promotion by invitation is more a phenomenon of moments of expansion than of moments of contraction in the capitalist world-economy. Thus Wallerstein (1979b, p. 81) argues that "indeed, such collabo-rative 'development' is readily sacrificed by core countries when they experience any economic difficulties themselves. Second, it is available to countries with less prior industrial development than the first path but then it peaks at a far lower level of import-substitution light industries rather than the intermediate level of heavier industries known in Brazil or South Africa."

The third strategy is *semiperipheral development through self-reliance.* Wallerstein (1979b, p. 81) cites the Tanzania experience as an example showing that "a clearly enunciated and carefully pursued strategy of development including economic independence as a goal can be consistent with an accelerating rate of economic as well as social and political development." However, Wallerstein also cautions that this strategy can be pursued by only a few peripheral countries. In the case of Tanzania, its poverty and "rarity among Africa's regimes stand her in good stead of thus far minimizing the external pressure brought to bear against her economic policies."

From Semiperipheral to Core Status

How have once-semiperipheral countries, such as England, the United States, and Germany, been able to raise their status to that of core countries? According to Wallerstein, the key to a semiperipheral breakthrough is that a country must have a market available that is large enough to justify an advanced technology, and for which it must produce at a lower cost than the existing producers. A semiperipheral country can enlarge a market for its national products in one of the following ways:

(1) It can expand its political boundaries by unification with its neighbors or by conquest, thus enlarging the size of its domestic market.

(2) It can increase the costs of imported goods through tariffs, prohibitions, and quotas, thus capturing a larger share of its domestic market.

(3) It can lower the costs of production by providing subsidies for national products, thus indirectly raising the price of imported goods relative to the subsidized items. The cost of production can also be lowered by reducing wage levels, but this policy would increase external sales at the risk of lowering internal sales.

(4) It can increase the internal level of purchasing power by raising wage levels, but this policy may increase internal sales at the risk of lowering external sales.

(5) It can, through the state or other social institutions, manipulate the tastes of internal consumers through ideology or propaganda.

Obviously, there are many ways to achieve a perfect combination of the above policies. For example, the strategy that England adopted in the sixteenth century was a medium-wage route, involving

> a combination of a rural textile industry (thus free from the high guild-protection wage costs of traditional centres of textile production such as Flanders, Southern Germany, and Northern Italy), with a process of agricultural improvement of arable land in medium-sized units (thus simultaneously providing a yeoman class of purchasers and an evicted class of vagrants and migrants who provided much of the labor for the textile industry), plus a deliberate decision to push for the new market of low-cost textiles (the "new draperies") to be sold to the new middle stratum of artisans, less wealthy burghers, and richer peasants who had flourished in the expanding cycle of the European world-economy. (Wallerstein 1979b, p. 85-86)

Another perfect combination is the high-wage route undertaken by the white settlers in the United States, Canada, Australia, and New Zealand. In this pattern, high wage levels preceded industrialization, and physical distance from the world centers of production provided the natural protection of high transportation costs for imports.

The Soviet Union provides an example of yet another route to core status. At the turn of the twentieth century, Russia was the fifth industrial producer in the world. The Soviet state kept the industrial wage at a medium level and rural wage at such a low level that there was an extensive urban labor reserve. Last but not least, the Soviet Union is a very large country, which made possible the relatively long period of autarchy that it practiced. However, if the Soviet Union—with its strong prerevolutionary industrial

base, its firm control over external trade and internal wages, and
its enormous size—barely made it to the core of the world-economy, Wallerstein ponders what hope there is for semiperipheral
countries such as Brazil and Chile to transform their roles in the
world-economy.

A Note on the Socialist Semiperipheral Countries

In examining the case of the Soviet Union, it is interesting to
note that Wallerstein (1979b, p. 90), as early as 1974, had already
proposed a provocative thesis that "establishing a system of state
ownership within a capitalist world-economy does not mean establishing a socialist economy." Since the capitalist system is composed of owners who sell for profit, the fact that an owner is a
group of individuals (such as a joint-stock company) or a sovereign state (such as a so-called socialist state) rather than a single
person makes no essential difference. A state that collectively owns
all of the means of production is merely a collective capitalist firm
as long as it remains a participant in the market of the capitalist
world-economy. In short, Wallerstein argues that "state ownership
is not socialism," it is merely a variant of "classical mercantilism"
by which the semiperipheral countries are trying to achieve upward mobility in the capitalist world-economy.

Wallerstein (1979b, p. 91) argues that by identifying state ownership with socialism, researchers have contributed to an ideological screen that obscures the reality: "State ownership countries
have, in fact, lower standards of living than those countries that
have predominantly private enterprises; and, in addition, social
inequality in these so-called socialist countries is still manifestly
enormous."

What then is socialism? According to Wallerstein (1979b, p. 91):

> A socialist government when it comes will not look anything
> like the USSR, or China, or Chile, or Tanzania of today.
> Production for use and not for profit, and rational decision
> on the cost benefits (in the widest sense of the term) of
> alternative uses is a different mode of production, one that

can only be established within the single division of labor that is the world-economy and one that will require a single government.

From a world-system perspective, Wallerstein therefore contributes by formulating a new concept of semiperipheral states and by identifying the present socialist states as mere semiperipheral countries (or state-owned capitalist enterprises) trying to make it to the core in the capitalist world-economy. Obviously, this new perspective calls for a reinterpretation of the history of the capitalist world-economy over the past four centuries.

HISTORY OF THE CAPITALIST WORLD-ECONOMY

Wallerstein has discussed the history of the capitalist world-economy in several of his works, but his latest treatment on this subject is quite different from his earlier views. In "Development: Lodestar or Illusion," Wallerstein (1988b) divides the history of the world-economy into two periods: from the sixteenth century to 1945, and from 1945 to the present. In the same study, he also discusses the crisis of the antisystemic movements as well as what should be done in the present era of the transformation of the capitalist world-economy.

Prior to 1945

According to Wallerstein, a capitalist world-economy began to form centered in the European continent in the sixteenth century. This world-economy possessed a set of integrated production processes that Wallerstein calls "commodity chains." The total surplus extracted from these commodity chains was always concentrated to a disproportionate degree in some zones rather than in others. Peripheries are those zones that lost out in the distribution of surplus to the core zones.

What then explains the differentiation of capitalist world-economy into different zones? As Wallerstein (1988b, p. 2018) explains:

"Whereas, at the beginning of the historical process, there seemed little difference in the economic wealth of the different geographical areas, a mere one century's flow of surplus was enough to create a visible distinction between core and periphery." The core zones were able to extract surplus from the peripheral zones because the cores had monopolized some segment of the commodity chains to their advantages. "The monopolization could occur because of some technological or organizational advantage which some segment of the producers had or because of some politically-enforced restriction of the market."

Thus, by 1600, the emergent peripheral zones in east-central Europe already exhibited the following traits compared to the emergent core zones in north-west Europe: (1) Per capita consumption was lower, (2) the local production process relied heavily upon coerced labor, and (3) the state structures were less centralized internally and weaker externally. Wallerstein argues that although all of these three comparisons were true by 1600, none was true as of 1450. These comparative differences were the consequence of the operation of the capitalist world-economy.

However, Wallerstein (1988b, p. 2018) further contends, "that a given geographical zone occupies a given role in the world-economy is far from immutable." Whatever the source of the monopolistic advantage of the core zone, it is inherently vulnerable. The advantage can come under attack both within and between the states. For example, mercantilism was a means for the semi-peripheral zones to protect their domestic markets in order to overcome the cores zones' monopolistic advantages. Also, some nations could over a period of time copy in one way or another the technological or organizational advantage, or could undermine the politically enforced restrictions of the market. In this respect, Wallerstein (1988b, p. 2018) observes that "every time a major monopoly has been undermined, the pattern of geographical locations of advantage has been subject to reorganization," leading to the so-called interstate mobility in the world-economy. For instance, the undermining of the American monopoly in high-tech industries signals the emergence of Japan as another superpower in the world-economy.

In addition to the accentuation of the polarization of zones, another trait of the capitalist world-economy in the pre-1945 period was *incorporation*, which refers to the constant expansion of the outer boundaries of the world-economy from Europe to the other parts of the world. What explains this expansion of the frontiers of the world-economy? According to Wallerstein, incorporation was a result of the exhaustion of leading monopolies, which led to periodic stagnations in the world-economy (so-called Kondratieff B-phases). In order to restore the overall rate of profit in the world-economy and to ensure its continual uneven distribution, it is necessary to (1) reduce the cost of production by reduction of wage cost (both by further mechanization of production and by site relocation), (2) create new monopolized leading products via innovation, and (3) expand effective demand through further proletarianization of segments of the work force. The expansion of the boundaries of the world-economy, therefore, can be seen as a mode of incorporating new low-cost labor, which in effect compensated for the increase in real wages in the core (in order to promote effective demand) and thereby kept the global average wage down.

Nevertheless, the process of incorporation was not unproblematic. As Wallerstein points out, people everywhere offered resistance, of varying efficacy, to the process of incorporation because it "was so unattractive a proposition in terms both of immediate material interests and the cultural values of those being incorporated." Consequently, only when the core states were technologically advanced in armaments would they be able to conquer the states in the external arena during the long waves of colonialism.

Specifically, incorporation has involved the following major transformations in the external arena. First, there was the transformation of production processes in these areas such that they became integrated into the commodity chains of the world-economy through production of cash crops, mineral products, or food crops. In addition, there was the reconstruction of the existing political structures into states operating within the interstate system of the capitalist world-economy. Wallerstein (1988b, p. 2019) observes that this reconstruction "involved sometimes the remoulding of existing political structures, sometimes their dismemberment, sometimes the fusion of several, and sometimes the creation of entirely new and quite arbitrarily delimited structures." Whatever was the case, the resulting states (sometimes called colonies) had to operate within the rules of the interstate system. These states had to be strong enough to conduct the operation of the commodity chains, but they could not be so strong vis-à-vis the states in the core zone as to threaten the interests of the major existing monopolizers.

The process of incorporation started in the seventeenth century. By the late nineteenth century there was no area on the globe that remained outside the operations of the interstate system. The history of the capitalist world-economy from 1600 to 1945, therefore, was characterized by the polarization of zones and incorporation. As a whole, there was overall growth in the forces of production and levels of wealth in the world-economy during this period. However, Wallerstein argues that although the absolute wealth of 10-20% of the world's population (mostly in the core zones) has risen considerably over the past 400 years, the large majority of the world's population (mostly in the peripheral zones) are probably worse off than their ancestors were. Thus the gap between the rich and the poor has widened enormously over the past four centuries.

Since 1945

Wallerstein notes that the transformation of the capitalist world-economy since 1945 has been remarkable in two respects. First, the absolute expansion of the world-economy since 1945—in terms of population, value produced, forces of production, and accumulated wealth—has probably been as great as that for the entire period of 1500-1945. This remarkable development of the forces of production has meant a massive reduction of the percentage of the world population engaged in producing primary goods, including food products. In the process, nations have come close to exhausting the pool of low-cost labor that has hitherto existed. Virtually all households are now at least semiproletarianized (part peasant and part wageworker), and economic stagnations continue to produce the consequence of transforming segments of these semiproletarianized households into fully proletarianized ones. As such, this proletarianization of households translates into higher-cost wage labor and the decline of profit margins in the capitalist world-economy.

Second, the political strength of the antisystemic forces has increased by an incredible amount. Since 1945 there have been triumphs from all branches of the antisystemic movements, including the creation of socialist countries (due to the military prowess of the Soviet Union or to internal revolutionary forces), the triumph of national liberation movements, and the coming to power of social-democratic/labor parties in the Western world. Despite their differences, these variants of the antisystemic forces all share three elements: Each was the result of the upsurge of popular forces in its own country, each involved parties or movements that aimed at assuming government office, and each set for itself the double policy objective of economic growth and greater internal equality.

However, Wallerstein observes that recently all the above types of antisystemic forces have come under criticism from within their own countries, and often even from within the movements in power, for their failures to achieve the twin goals of economic growth and internal equality. Indeed, the prevailing mood in the 1980s was the disillusionment of the antisystemic movements.

The Crisis of the Antisystemic Movements

According to Wallerstein, the growing disillusionment of the antisystemic movements can be explained by the contradiction embedded in the movements' twin goals. On the one hand, the movements seek greater *internal equality* (which involves fundamental social transformations), and on the other they desire rapid *economic growth* (which involves catching up with the core states).

The movements bring together under one organizational roof those who wish to catch up economically and those who search for social change.

Prior to 1945, this contradiction was scarcely a problem. As long as the capitalist world-economy was still in secular expansion, as long as there was a growing pie to ensure that everyone could hope for more, the antisystemic movements remained politically weak. The prospects for upward mobility lured members away from the movements and unwound their sense of collective solidarity in the struggle. Because the antisystemic movements never rose to power, they did not have to confront the contradictions of their ideology.

Since 1945, however, there has been a "weakening of the political carapace of capitalism which, by allowing the anti-systemic movements to arrive at state power in large numbers, exposed the deep internal cleavage of these movements, the rift between those who sought upward mobility and those who sought equality" (Wallerstein 1988b, p. 2021). Since the 1970s, this contradiction in the movements' goals has become a glaring one, and the members of the movements have been asked to make different political choices.

Policy Implications: What Shall Be Done?

What political implications has Wallerstein drawn from his analysis? Given his assumption that the objective is "truly an egalitarian democratic world," Wallerstein argues that we should substitute a new world-level class movement for the prevailing national-level popular movements. First of all, Wallerstein (1988b, p. 2022) asserts that

national development may well be a pernicious policy objective. This is for two reasons. For most states, it is unrealizable whatever the method adopted. And for those few states which may still realize it, that is transmute radically the location of world-scale production and thereby their location on the interstate ordinal scale, their benefits will perforce be at the expense of some other zone.

This has been especially true since 1945, when the geography of the whole world-economy could no longer expand. As such, development in the world-economy was like a zero-sum game—when a new nation-state comes in, an old nation-state must go out. Wallerstein (1988b, p. 2022) gives an example:

> If in the next 30 years China or India or Brazil were in a true sense to "catch up", a significant segment of the world's population elsewhere in this world-system would have to decline as a locus of capital accumulation. This will be true whether China or India or Brazil "catches up" via delinking or via export-orientation or by any other method.

From this angle, Wallerstein (1988b, p. 2022) thinks that "popularly-organized national movements have found themselves in a dilemma for which there is no easy solution, and which has contributed strongly to the sense of impasse and frustration that has been growing of late." This is because the goal of the national movements was to capture the state power. It was hoped that the nation-state could go against the strong current of unequal exchange flow to the core zones. Nevertheless, Wallerstein argues that the economic self-interest of the state bureaucrats pushed them toward the economic growth and "catching-up" goals. As a result, the goal of internal equality and the interest of the popular strata were sacrificed. Very often, states governed by erstwhile antisystemic movements (such as Poland) may even adopt repressive policies toward their own popular strata (like Solidarity).

Instead of endorsing the national movements that have prevailed in the movement literature since the nineteenth century, Wallerstein advocates a new world-level strategy that requires implementation by a world-level movement. In particular, Wallerstein (1988b, p. 2022) calls for a worldwide attack on the flow of surplus at the point of production: "Suppose that anti-systemic movements concentrated their energies everywhere—in the

OECD countries, in the Third World countries, and yes, in the socialist countries as well, on efforts defined as retaining most of the surplus created. One obvious way would be to seek to increase the price of labor or the price of sale by the direct producers." Wallerstein (1988b, p. 2023) further explains that the concern of this world-level movement

> must be how at each point on very long commodity chains a greater percentage of the surplus can be retained. Such a strategy would tend over time to "overload" the system, reducing global rates of profit significantly and evening out distribution. Such a strategy might also be able to mobilize the efforts of all the many varieties of new social movements, all of which are oriented in one way or another more to equality than to growth. . . . [The premise of this strategy is that] global rates of profit are quite open to political attack at a local level. And, as the local victories cumulate, a significant cave-in of political support for the system will occur.

According to Wallerstein, this strategy of surplus retention by the producers could be more effective in the late twentieth century than before, because the world-economy has reached its geographic limit and is in the process of exhausting its reserve labor force. Thus this exhaustion will undermine the capitalist world-economy's ability to maldistribute surplus and to continue its accumulation process.

Finally, Wallerstein stresses that his world-level strategy of promoting surplus retention by the producers is different from the former strategy of national class struggle. In the nineteenth century, the fight against inequality through class struggle took place in the workplace (via trade unions) and in the political arena of the nation-state (via socialist parties). But the capitalists could easily fight back in several ways. They could recruit new workers from the worldwide pool of reserve households, they could use the state to repress such movements, and, if they failed to control the nation-state, they could relocate the locus of their capital to other zones without necessarily losing long-term control over it. In this respect, Wallerstein (1988b, p. 2023) argues that class struggle movements "cannot afford their close links to the state, even to the

Table 8.1 Comparison of Dependency Perspective and
World-System Perspective.

	Dependency Perspective	*World-System Perspective*
Unit of analysis	the nation-state	the world-system
Methodology	structural-historical: boom and bust of nation-states	historical dynamics of the world-system: cyclical rhythms and secular trends
Theoretical structure	bimodal: core-periphery	trimodal: core-semiperiphery-periphery
Direction of development	deterministic: dependency is generally harmful	possible upward and downward mobility in the world-economy
Research focus	on the periphery	on the periphery as well as on the core, the semiperiphery, and the world-economy

regimes they have struggled to bring to power." Instead, class struggle movements must be waged at the world level in order to be effective in forcing the pace of the transformation of the capitalist world-economy.

COMPARISON OF THE DEPENDENCY
AND WORLD-SYSTEM PERSPECTIVES

In its earlier formulation, the world-system perspective bore traces of the dependency perspective and therefore was frequently cited together with the dependency school (Barrett and Whyte 1982; Chirot and Hall 1982; Koo 1984; Moulder 1977; Petras 1982). However, as the world-system school became more advanced, students of development began to point out differences between the dependency perspective and the world-system perspective (Bach 1982; Chase-Dunn 1982a; So 1981). These differences are discussed in turn in this section (see Table 8.1 for a summary).

First, the *unit of analysis* for the world-system perspective is, of course, the world-system. Unlike the dependency perspective, which focuses on the national level, the world-system perspective insists that the whole world should be taken as a unit of social science analysis. Wallerstein argues that historical explanation should proceed from the viewpoint of the world-system, and all phenomena are to be explained in terms of their consequences for both the totality of the world-system and its subparts. Thus Wallerstein (1977b, p. 7) calls for the analysis of the holism of the sociohistorical process over a long historical time and large space.

This world-system perspective may shed new light on many familiar sociological concepts, as Wallerstein (1976, p. xi) explains:

> Once we assume that the unit of analysis is such a world-system and not the state or the nation or the people, then much changes in the outcome of the analysis. Most specifically we shift from a concern with the attributive characteristics of states to concern with the relational characteristics of states. We shift from seeing classes (and status groups) as groups within a state to seeing them as groups within a world-economy.

From the world-system perspective, there is only one world-system in the twentieth century. Even though world-system researchers recognize the profound impact of the socialist revolutions, they argue that the socialist states are still operating within the confines of the capitalist world-economy. Thus the socialist states' policies on economy, politics, and culture are, to a certain extent, constrained by the dynamics of the capitalist world-economy. Unlike classical dependency theorists, who formulate the strategy of socialist delinking as a solution to Third World development, world-system analysts doubt the viability of this delinking strategy.

Second, influenced by French *historical methodology*, Wallerstein (1984, p. 27) perceives social reality as in a state of flux. He points out that "we seek to capture a moving reality in our terminology. We thereby tend to forget that the reality changes as we encapsulate it, and by virtue of that fact." In order to capture this ever-changing reality, Wallerstein (1984, p. 27) suggests a study of

> provisional long-term, large-scale wholes within which concepts have meanings. These wholes must have some claim to relative space-time autonomy and integrity. . . . I would call such wholes "historical systems." . . . It is a system which has a history, that is, it has a genesis, an historical development, a close (a destruction, a disintegration, a transformation, an *Aufhebung*).

Unlike the dependency school, which focuses upon the boom and bust of nation-states, the world-system school studies the historical dynamics of the world-economy. Wallerstein (1984, p. 13-26) points out that the capitalist world-economy develops itself through the secular trends of incorporation, commercialization of agriculture, industrialization, and proletarianization. Along with these secular trends, the capitalist world-economy has developed the cyclical rhythms of expansion and stagnation as a result of the imbalance between world effective demand and world supply of goods. When world supply outstrips world demand, when there are too many goods on the market without enough consumers to buy them, factories have to be closed and workers have to be laid off. The world economy then moves into the B-phase of economic stagnation. During this downward phase, the core weakens its control over the periphery, giving the periphery a chance to promote autonomous development and to catch up with the core. The downward phase, therefore, serves as a period of redistribution of world surplus from the core to the periphery. However, after a fairly long period of recession, core production revives as the result of increased demand from the developing periphery and technological breakthrough. When world demand begins to outstrip world supply, this starts another upward A-phase of economic expansion. During an economic boom, the core tries to regain its power and to tighten its control over the periphery in order to dominate the world market. This economic boom, however, cannot last forever and will finally lead to overproduction. At every occurrence of these upward and downward turns in the world-economy, there is ample opportunity for the periphery to catch up and for the core to fall behind. This is a dynamic model, since the nation-states are always put on trial, and are always in the process of transforming to either the core or the periphery at each stage of the cyclical development.

Third, unlike the dependency school, the world-system school has a unique *theoretical structure*. Instead of a simplistic core-periphery model, Wallerstein's capitalist world-economy has three layers: the core, the periphery, and the semiperiphery, which stands between the core and the periphery and exhibits characteristics of both.

The formulation of the semiperiphery concept is a theoretical breakthrough because it enables researchers to examine the complexity and the changing nature of the capitalist world-economy. This three-tiered model allows Wallerstein to entertain the possibilities of upward mobility (a periphery moving into the semi-periphery or a semiperiphery moving into the core) as well as downward mobility (a core moving into the semiperiphery or a semiperiphery moving into the periphery). With this intermediate layer of semiperiphery in the model, the world-system perspective is thus capable of studying the changing locations of the state in relation to the contradictions and crises that are built into the working of the capitalist world-system.

Fourth, with respect to the *direction of development*, Wallerstein's three-tiered model avoids the deterministic statement of the dependency school, namely, that a periphery is bound to have under-development or dependent development because the core always exploits the periphery. With the semiperiphery concept, the world-system perspective no longer needs to explain away the problem of the path of autonomous, independent development in Third World peripheries. Instead, the concept enables researchers to ask such interesting questions as why a few East Asian states are able to transcend their peripheral statuses in the late twentieth century.

Finally, unlike the dependency school, which concentrates on the study of the periphery, the world-system perspective has a much broader *research focus*. The world-system perspective studies not only the backward Third World peripheries but also the advanced capitalist cores, the new socialist states, and the rise, development (the secular trends and the cyclical rhythms), and future demise of the capitalist world-economy.

In sum, the world-system school is different from the dependency school in that it treats the whole world as its unit of analysis, adopts a historical methodology that perceives reality as a state of flux, develops a trimodal theoretical structure, abandons the deterministic point of view on the direction of development, and has a much broader research focus. As will be discussed in the next chapter, these new orientations have led to a series of world-system studies at the global level.

CHAPTER 9

World-System Studies at the Global Level

Among the three dominant schools of development, the world-system perspective is the only one that insists on taking the whole world as the unit of analysis. Therefore, the world-system perspective contributes by offering a distinctive approach to the examination of the global dynamics that are generally neglected by the modernization and dependency perspectives. In this chapter, three world-system empirical studies at the global level are discussed: Wallerstein on the downward phase of the capitalist world-economy during the crisis of the seventeenth century, Bergesen and Schoenberg on the long waves of colonialism, and the Research Working Group of the Fernand Braudel Center on the global patterns of labor movements. These three studies illustrate how the basic assumptions of the world-system perspective shape the research agenda, methodology, data bases, and findings of world-system researchers.

WALLERSTEIN: THE DOWNWARD PHASE OF THE CAPITALIST WORLD-ECONOMY

Based upon the premise that economic processes in the modern world take place within the framework of the capitalist world-economy, Wallerstein (1979d, p. 73) contends that "neither 'the development' nor the 'underdevelopment' of any specific territorial unit can be analyzed or interpreted without fitting it onto the cyclical rhythms and secular trends of the world-economy as a whole." How then can researchers examine the cyclical rhythms of the capitalist world-economy? Wallerstein points out that there are in fact two different sets of cyclical rhythms: Kondratieff cycles, with an expansion A-phase and a contraction B-phase, each cycle presumably lasting 40-55 years; and the longer "logistics" cycles, which presumably last 150-300 years. The latter are so called because they take the shape of statistical logistics curves, in that although the A-phase is an expansion, the B-phase is not a contraction but a stagnation.

Wallerstein (1979d) has examined the impact of the logistics cycle from 1450 to 1750. This particular cyclical rhythm is important because it provides the evidence for the existence of a capitalist world-economy. Therefore, unlike the previous cycle in the late Middle Ages (1100-1450), the expansions and contractions of which took place more or less uniformly throughout Europe, this cycle (1450-1750) exhibited an asymmetrical pattern of development in different zones of Europe. For example, political apparatuses were strengthened in western Europe and weakened in eastern Europe, and "feudal" obligations were strengthened in eastern Europe (the second serfdom) but weakened still further in northwestern Europe.

What explains this asymmetrical pattern of development in Europe? Focusing on the B-phase during the crisis of the seventeenth century, Wallerstein's research task was to investigate how the same B-phase had led to vastly different consequences in the three spatial zones (the core, the periphery, and the semiperiphery) of the capitalist world-economy.

The Core

A downturn in the world-economy poses the same problem for all its zones. Demand is sluggish and profits decline. To maintain the same level of profit, one must perform the following two activities: (1) Reduce cost by increasing efficiency or by extracting a higher rate of surplus value from the labor force; and (2) increase one's share of the total market by underselling, monopolizing, or being the beneficiary of the failures of competitors. While everyone tries to do these things, only a few can succeed. Therefore, downturns in the capitalist world-economy are always moments of *increased concentration* of capital. Wallerstein notes that this concentration is seen not only at the level of the firm, but also at the level of the world-economy as a whole.

In the case of the B-phase during the crisis of the seventeenth century, the core countries (the United Provinces, England, and France) tried to reduce costs by improving the techniques of cereal and textile production. With rising productivity, the production of the core countries in western Europe effectively displaced production from eastern and southern Europe. Through capturing a larger share of the key products in the world market, the core experienced an increase in the concentration of capital at the expense of the periphery.

Another means of concentration of capital in the core is colonization. The economic downturn in the world-economy led the core powers of northeastern Europe in the early seventeenth century to explore the economic advantages of creating new areas of primary production under their direct control. This led to a competitive scramble for sugar colonies in the Caribbean. In addition, there was a second wave of colonization in the Americas, aiming to create protected markets for the core-country manufacturers.

The core countries not only competed for colonial territories, they also struggled among themselves for the hegemonic domination of the capitalist world-economy. At the onset of the long economic downturn, there was Dutch hegemony. The United Provinces, with a strong state, enjoyed triple superiority in the spheres of agroindustrial, commercial, and financial activities. In opposition to this Dutch hegemony, England and France put forward a *mercantilist policy*. In a tight economy, England and France needed to protect their internal markets in order to maintain their level of profitability. Through this mercantilist policy and an increase in the efficiency of their production, England and France finally unseated the Dutch from their hegemonic position in 1672.

The Periphery

How could the periphery, which specialized in export staples, maneuver in the face of the onset of a decline in world prices and a weakened world market for its products? According to Wallerstein, the periphery could react like everyone else, by seeking to lower costs and to gain an increased share of the market.

In the periphery of eastern Europe, the large owner-producers lowered costs primarily by using their combined political and economic power over the rural laborers to obtain an increase in the amount of corvée labor, by ending quit-rent tenancies, and by forcing the former tenants into the role of serfs or wage laborers.

With respect to the expansion of the share of the market, the large owner-producers in eastern Europe accomplished this goal by increasing corvée labor. The decline of small owner-producers and/or tenant-producers meant, on the one hand, that the serfs then had less time for independent production for the market and thus could no longer produce products to compete with those of the large owner-producers; on the other hand, there was an increased market in the peripheral areas for the products of the large owner-producers in order to meet the daily necessities of the serfs. The market now, however, was no longer the world market, but a regional one.

Because regional markets were less profitable than the previous world markets, the large owner-producers in eastern Europe sought to supplement their income by recreating local industrial production for the regional markets. Thus there was the revival of local nonluxury textile and metalware production in eastern Europe. Wallerstein (1979d, p. 80) argues that this "increased concentration of capital in the hands of the large owner-producers went hand in hand with the increase of their political rights and legal jurisdiction. The strength of the state either steadily declined (as in Poland) or became entirely subordinate to foreign states (as in Hungary, Livonia, Naples, etc.)."

The Semiperiphery

What happened to the semiperipheral areas in this B-phase? Did they share the relative advantages of the cores or the relative decline of the peripheries? On this subject, Wallerstein distinguishes two kinds of semiperipheries—areas that were semiperipheries as part of a decline, and areas that were semiperipheries as part of a rise.

Semiperipheral areas in decline (Spain, Portugal) looked more like peripheral zones. They experienced a decline in population as well as in the power of the state. They were, therefore, prey to the core powers, and the core powers felt free to intervene in the internal affairs of these declining semiperipheral states. Wallerstein (1979d, p. 81) observes that "Portugal became economically a satellite of, and transmission belt for, first Dutch, then English interests, while Spain played this role for France." This was also the era of the relative deindustrialization of central Spain, which involved the transfer of capital investment from industry to agriculture, and the growth of the seigniorial domain at the expense of the peasant economy.

The rising semiperipheral areas (Sweden, Prussia), however, shared some of the advantages of the core areas. There was the creation of a strong tax base, a strong military force, and a strong state, which made possible the implementation of the mercantilist measures. These rising semiperipheral areas, through alternating alliances and economic sweeteners (for example, opening their protected economies at crucial junctures to core-country investment), sought to manipulate the core-power rivalries to aid their advance in the capitalist world-economy.

The External Arena

Already in the sixteenth century, many nations (e.g., Russia, India, and West Africa) were externally linked by trade to the European world-economy. In the B-phase, when the core states were primarily concerned with their struggles against one another, they did not have the time and energy to undermine the state apparatuses of these external arenas sufficiently. Thus Wallerstein argues that these states remained outside of the capitalist world-economy at the onset of the crisis of the seventeenth century.

In sum, Wallerstein (1979d, p. 82) concludes that the allocation of roles in the capitalist world-economy is not static. This was particularly so in the B-phase, when large positional movements took place. Thus the B-phase "represents stagnation over all to be sure, but stagnation as the sum of increased concentration of capital and therefore of increased polarization and differentiation. It does *not* slow down the workings of capitalism; it is rather an integral part of them."

Wallerstein's focus on the cyclical rhythm of the capitalist world-economy started a new direction in research among his followers. The next section offers a discussion of the study of the long waves of colonial expansion and contraction.

BERGESEN AND SCHOENBERG: LONG WAVES OF COLONIALISM

According to Bergesen and Schoenberg (1980), most studies of colonialism are carried out from the viewpoint of the core or from the viewpoint of the periphery. Rarely has colonialism been examined from the points of view of both the core and the periphery. As a structural linkage between core and periphery, colonialism can be seen as a property of the capitalist world-economy as a whole. The aim of Bergesen and Schoenberg's study, therefore, is to specify colonialism as a distinctive collective dynamic of the capitalist world-economy and to anchor analysis of colonialism at a level higher than that of discrete national societies.

Measuring Colonial Activities

Measurement of colonialism at the world-system level requires a design of some form of constant metric system to capture the long waves of colonialism from their inception in the sixteenth century to the present era. Relying upon Henige's (1970) study, Bergesen and Schoenberg used "the presence of a colonial government" as a measure of colonialism. This measure enabled them to record (1) the total number of colonies established each year between 1415 and 1969, (2) the total number of colonies terminated each year, and (3) the cumulative net number of colonies in existence each year.

The Findings

With respect to the establishment of colonies, the largest spurt of colonialism came toward the end of the nineteenth century, but there were also outbursts of colonial activity during the seventeenth century, the second half of the eighteenth century, and the middle of the nineteenth century.

The termination of colonies took place in two very distinct and well-defined spurts: in the first quarter of the nineteenth century (centering on the collapse of the Spanish empire in Latin America), and in the post-1945 decolonization of Africa, India, and Asia.

As for the cumulative net number of colonies, there were again two distinctive waves of colonialism: The first cycle began in 1415, reached its peak in 1770 at 147 colonies, then declined in 1825 to 81 colonies; the second cycle began in 1826, reached its peak in 1921 with 168 colonies, then declined to 58 colonies in 1969 (the year in which Henige completed his study).

Comparing these two long waves of colonialism, Bergesen and Schoenberg note an increasing amplitude and frequency of global cycles. The first cycle lasted 410 years—colonies were established at a rate of .530 colonies per year during the upswing (1415-1770) and were terminated at a rate of 1.900 per year during the downswing (1775-1825). The second cycle lasted only 143 years—colonies were established at a much faster rate of 1.452 per year during the upswing (1826-1921) and were also terminated at a much faster rate of 2.953 during the downswing (1926-1969). Bergesen and Schoenberg assert that this increase in amplitude and frequency reflects the property of the world-system itself. It is only through the examination of the aggregation of all colonial links and the tracing of virtually the entire historical development of colonialism (1415-1969) that researchers can identify the collective properties of the world-system. How do they explain this changing nature of the world-system as reflected in the long waves of colonialism?

The Theoretical Model

Bergesen and Schoenberg's theoretical model focuses on three factors: the distribution of power within the core, core stability, and systemic responses in the form of colonialism and mercantilism. When there is a dispersion of power within the core (a multicentric core), a plurality of rival powers compete with one another for domination in the world-system. In the midst of this instability and conflict within the core, the world-system "pulls itself together and reaffirms its fundamental social relationships. Colonialism, then, is an extra-economic mechanism for resetting the basic core-periphery division of labor in times of disorder and stress" (Bergesen and Schoenberg 1980, p. 239). Corresponding to the same period of core instability and colonialism, there is also a period of more pronounced political regulation of trade relations between the core and the periphery, such as mercantilism, rising tariffs, import restrictions, and protectionism. In short, a multicentric core leads to core instability, expanding colonialism, and mercantilism.

However, when there is a concentration of power within the core (a unicentric core), the hegemonic state provides the mechanisms through which the collective interests of the core can be realized. With such core stability, there is less need for explicit political regulation of core-periphery relations. Thus a unicentric core and core stability are associated with decolonization and the collapse of mercantilism. The integration of the world-system then depends more on economic linkages than on political linkages.

Over the long history of the world-system, the core has moved back and forth along this unicentric-multicentric continuum, leading to global cycles of colonization and decolonization. Bergesen and Schoenberg apply this theoretical model to an interpretation of the long-term historical movement of colonialism from 1815 to the present.

The Long Waves of Colonialism

Bergesen and Schoenberg have distinguished five phases of the historical movement of colonialism. First, the period between 1500 and 1815 was marked by core instability. After the collapse of feudalism, the plurality of states representing the emerging European state system constituted an unstable molecular structure, since no single state was in a position to exercise enough hegemony to give the system any long-term stability. This multicentric core structure led to endless warfare and conflicts. During this period, the first wave of colonial expansion, led by Spain and Portugal, was centered in the Americas. The economic relations between core and periphery were also highly structured and politically regulated. The mercantile control of colonial trade was carried out through such regulations as the exclusion of foreign ships from colonial ports, the manufacturing of certain limited products in the colonies, and the shipment of colonial imports and exports through the ports of the core country.

Second, during the period between 1815 and 1870 there was core stability. After Britain emerged as a hegemonic world power, the core as a whole took on more of a corporate existence—a Pax Britannica. The endless conflicts of the earlier centuries ceased, and there was a period of peace among the major core powers.

With this core stability, the explicit political domination of the periphery temporarily receded. Colonialism contracted with the decolonization of the Americas, the mercantile regulations of the remaining colonial trade largely disappeared, and the era of the free trade began.

Third, in the period between 1870 and 1945, the core as a whole became increasingly unstable. Britain's hegemony declined, and Germany and the United States emerged as powerful core states. There was international rivalry, leading to frictions, crises, and finally the overt conflict of the "Second Thirty Years War" of 1914-1945. This instability in the core generated a systemic response: a second wave of colonialism, centered this time in Africa, India, and Asia; and highly politically regulated core-periphery economic relationships, with rising tariffs and neomercantile protectionism.

Fourth, the period between 1945 and 1973 was again marked by core stability. The core was dominated by a hegemonic power (the United States), and there was peace among the core powers (with the Pax Americana replacing the earlier Pax Britannica). With this core stability, there was once again a movement toward decolonization in Africa, India, and Asia, as well as a shift toward a liberal, free-trading world-economy.

Since 1973, according to Bergesen and Schoenberg, "we appear to be entering yet another global cycle of the third wave of colonialism." Although acknowledging the disappearance of formal colonialism, Bergesen and Schoenberg describe the following traits as indicators of the expansion of colonialism in the 1970s:

(1) decline in the hegemonic power of the United States, leading to an instability among the core states; Japan, Germany, and the Soviet Union challenge the economic and military power of the United States

(2) reemergence for a third time of a more politically regulated trade policy in the form of protectionism and import restrictions

(3) reimposition of more explicit political controls over the peripheral areas through arms sales, and decline of the "nonaligned" status of the Third World as it becomes increasingly divided into spheres of influence of the major core powers

Long-Term Trends

Upon comparing the three long waves of colonialism, Bergesen and Schoenberg observe that the waves of colonialism have been changing, becoming less disruptive, shorter, and more widespread. Each of these changes is discussed in turn below.

The first wave of colonialism, which is often characterized as "settler colonies," was the most disruptive. The term *settler* refers not only to the transport of corelike societies to the peripheral areas, but also to the uprooting of local peoples, their virtual annihilation through enslavement, and the total destruction of local social arrangements. When the second wave emerged, since its scale and amount of disruption were less, it was more a matter of "occupation" than the replacement of one people and social arrangement with another. The third wave was more a matter of "dependence" and "influence." Control by the core has become less overt and more indirect in its effect upon peripheral peoples and social arrangements.

As they have become less disruptive, the waves have also become shorter. The first wave lasted some 300 years, while the second lasted a little over 100 years. If this trend continues, Bergesen and Schoenberg note that the third wave should be even shorter than the second.

With respect to the scope of colonialism, with each wave more of the world has been included and brought within the web of the world-economy. The first wave reached a peak of 147 colonies in 1770, and the second climbed to a peak of 168 in 1921. Bergesen and Schoenberg argue that the third wave seems to be even more extensive than the second—with arms sales including even the former independent states of Latin America.

What explains this secular trend of core domination that becomes less disruptive, shorter, and more widespread? Bergesen and Schoenberg argue that this secular trend actually reflects the long-term extensive and intensive development of the capitalist world-economy. The first wave was the most disruptive and lasted the longest because it represented the initial phase of destroying and reconstituting unincorporated areas in the process of assigning them peripheral positions in the world division of labor. This reconstitution of local production into functioning components of a worldwide division of labor required a tremendous exertion of energy and force. Conquest, plunder, slavery, and the annihilation of indigenous peoples therefore all played a part in linking the various territories together into an integrated world-system.

As the infrastructures of the peripheral regions became more and more in line with their roles in the world division of labor, economic relations such as economic exchange could grow, expand, and assume increasingly greater responsibility for overall system integration. Consequently, Bergesen and Schoenberg (1980, p. 269) conclude:

> The stronger the world-economy grows, the more it carries the collective reality of a world-system, and the less extra-economic linkages are required, so that these waves of colonialism and politically regulated trade have become progressively milder, and shorter in length. Their growing extensiveness also reflects the overall expansion of the system as a whole.

However, when the world-economy experienced difficulties, there was a tendency to revert to the extraeconomic linkages of colonialism. The task of system integration then was passed on to the more explicit political ties of the second wave of colonialism. Nevertheless, the world-economy did not return to its original state, since it was stronger than before and thus required less extraeconomic effort to perpetuate its normal operation. This may explain why the second wave was less disruptive and lasted for a shorter time than the first wave.

Following this line of argument, it seems that the waves of colonialism could eventually become so short and mild that they would virtually disappear. However, Bergesen and Schoenberg (1980, p. 272) speculate that "the periodic crises of capitalism may continue to require some sort of 'primitive accumulation' to put the system back on its feet. . . . In this case whenever we have a major downturn in the world-economy, political regulation will reappear to reset the mechanisms and restart the system."

Based upon their insights derived from the concept of the world-system, Bergesen and Schoenberg have contributed by reinterpreting the history of colonialism from 1415 to the present. Other researchers in the world-system school also have applied the world-system concept to the study of such neglected topics as the labor movement.

THE RESEARCH WORKING GROUP:
GLOBAL PATTERNS OF LABOR MOVEMENTS

According to the Research Working Group on World Labor (RWG; 1986) of the Fernand Braudel Center, the two classical theories of labor movement behavior have been called into question. On the one hand, the Marxist paradigm has failed to explain the most salient developments of the past 50 years, when the trajectory of worker movements in the advanced capitalist world diverged sharply from its projection. On the other hand, the Wisconsin model seemed to be too restrictive in its economism to encompass the multifaceted dimension of working-class culture and behavior.

According to the RWG, a major part of the problem with classical theories of labor movement stems from their unit of analysis. The classical studies are based largely on histories of national and local labor movements that usually cover relatively short periods of time and narrow parts of the world. The studies that have offered comparative analyses of national situations have stopped short of elaborating on world-level implications.

From a world-system perspective, in their preliminary findings the RWG (1986, p. 141)

> discovered distinct waves of labor militancy that can be identified at the world level over the course of the modern industrial era (1870s to the present). The peaks of these waves are to be found at the end of the First World War, the end of the Second World War, and the late 1960s/early 1970s. These heightened levels of conflict were widespread: they were not limited to advanced industrial nations, but also erupted in areas marked by low or middle levels of industrialization.

The existence of such worldwide cyclical outbreaks of labor militancy suggests that labor movements of various national origins share a common set of social processes.

For heuristic reasons, the RWG distinguishes two types of labor movements—the political labor movement (PLM) and the social labor movement (SLM). The PLM "primarily pursues the objective of increasing the power of its representative organizations within a political system." The RWG argues that the PLM reached its peak in the global clash between labor and capital following World War I. The epicenter of the clash at the time of its peak was in Europe. After the PLM declined as a world phenomenon, its epicenter shifted from Europe toward the periphery of the world-economy.

The decline of the PLM, however, has been accompanied by the rise of the SLM. Instead of aiming to obtain state power, the SLM "is characterized by relative autonomy from political parties and established trade union structures, and by its orientation to the workplace rather than the political arena as the main locus of labor conflicts." Instead of shifting its epicenter toward the periphery, the SLM is clearly manifested in western Europe and in other semiperipheral areas of the world-economy.

The aim of the RWG is to explain the changing worldwide pattern, the extent, and the form of the struggle of the labor movement during the twentieth century (1870 to the present). Focusing on the structure of production/labor process and the structure of the labor force, the RWG has developed two hypotheses to explain how these two structures have affected the nature of the waves of the PLM and the SLM.

- *Hypothesis 1:* "The rise and peaking of the political labor movement on a world-scale was associated with a period during which the two processes mentioned above combined to weaken labor's bargaining power vis-à-vis capital. Politicization of the movement was aimed at counteracting this weakness" (RWG 1986, p. 143).

According to the RWG, the peaking of the PLM in the early twentieth century occurred during a period in which transformations in the structure of the production/labor process weakened labor on three simultaneous fronts: (1) As capitalism advanced to the monopoly phase, price competition was undermined, and the real buying power of the workers could no longer be enhanced by the continuous cheapening of commodities resulting from falling prices; (2) the increasing organic composition of capital, together with the elimination of the nonwage sector, increased the competitive pressures on the active labor force due to unemployment; and (3) the transformation in the labor process (mechanization and automation) progressively deskilled the laborers and reduced their bargaining power in the labor market. Under these conditions, workers became less able to protect themselves through their bargaining power in the labor market. As such, political power through the labor movement strengthened the power of the workers vis-à-vis the capitalists.

The RWG also takes note of the relatively small size of the working class within the national social structure as a factor contributing to the weakening of labor. With such small size, the strength of labor came to depend in large part on the movement's ability to make alliances with other strata, and such a strategy required the existence of the labor movement as a politically organized presence. In contemporary peripheral countries, since the size of the working class remains small, labor movements continue to take the form of the political labor movement.

- *Hypothesis 2:* "The rise of the social labor movement was associated with a period during which the same two processes have combined to strengthen labor's bargaining power" (RWG 1986, p. 143).

Just as transformations in the structure of the production/labor process and the labor force partly explain the rise and peripheralization of the PLM, so the RWG hypothesizes that further transformations in the two spheres explain the rise of the SLM. The new production techniques introduced in the twentieth century, such as continuous-flow assembly lines, which connected the activities of each worker to other workers on the line, have increased the vulnerability of capital to localized interruptions in the flow of production. Consequently, the SLM emerged to capture this new source of "workplace bargaining power." The strength of the movement then no longer depended primarily on political organization (as with the PLM), but was derived instead from the very organization of production in which the workers were embedded.

Changes in the labor force structure have also facilitated the rise of the SLM. The progressive exhaustion of nonwage and semi-proletarianized strata and the expansion of the size of the working class have served to undermine two tendencies associated with politicization of the labor movement: the need to form alliances, and the need to protect the established labor force from underselling in the labor market.

In addition to changes in the structure of production/labor process and the labor force, the RWG mentions the role of the state in the management of labor-capital relations. In the core countries where the SLM has grown predominant, the state has become less repressive in its policies toward labor. On the other hand, where the state has been repressive in its response to labor movements (as in most peripheral areas), the PLM has not been submerged by the SLM.

The Need for World-Level Data

The hypotheses listed above were developed on the basis of the RWG's preliminary analysis of two sets of data set: national statistics on strike activity and national case studies of the labor movement. However, the RWG asserts that these national data sets have shortcomings. First, reliable statistical data on strike activity are available only for recent periods and for a limited number of countries. In addition, the comparability of national data is limited because of the different ways in which they were recorded. It is therefore impossible simply to aggregate the raw national data into supranational or world-level indices. This means that national statistics on strike activity and national case studies are incapable of invalidating the above-described hypotheses concerning the world-economy. If this is true, what are the appropriate research procedures for the collection of world-level data?

Research Procedures

The RWG suggests four research steps in studying global patterns of labor movements. The first step is to carry out a content analysis of a select group of weekly magazines, indexed daily newspapers, and almanacs from 1870 to the present. Specifically, the RWG has proposed examining *The Economist* (United Kingdom), *Economiste Francais* (France, 1880s to World War II), *Le Monde* (France, post-World War II), the *New York Times*, the London *Times*, *Keesings Contemporary Archives* (United Kingdom), *Whitakers Almanac* (United Kingdom), and the *World Almanac* (United States). The RWG recommends a combination of the above sources because as a whole the sources used should balance out the tendency of any one source toward reporting on events in the regions that are within its sphere of interest.

According to the RWG (1986, p. 147), the content analysis should overcome the limitations of quantitative national statistics in two ways: "(1) by the qualitative information provided in the report of the strike, and (2) by the fact that the extent of coverage that a strike receives in the international press can in itself be seen as a qualitative indication of the strike's wider impact." Through the content analysis, the RWG records information on the extent of the labor movement (as measured by the number of times strikes are reported by country and by the reported size and duration of the strike). The RWG also assesses the degree of politicization of the movement (as measured by the number of general strikes reported, whether the strikes received union or labor party support, the demands of the strikes, and so on).

In the second research step, the RWG constructs a number of indices on the basis of the data collected in the content analysis. It then aggregates the data into world-level indices, and disaggregates them by the three zones of the world-economy (core, periphery, semiperiphery). The world-level and zone-level indices will include the extent and the politicization of the labor movement.

In the third research step, the RWG compares and contrasts the world-level patterns of the labor movement derived from indices constructed on the basis of the content analysis with indices constructed from other sources of information.

There are many national statistics collections, such as the *Historical Statistics of the United States* and the *ILO Yearbook of Labor Statistics*, that contain information on strike activities. These statistical data banks will provide another index on the extent of the labor movement. With respect to the variable of politicization of the labor movement, Arthur Banks's *Cross Polity Time Series Data* (1973) provides another index on general strikes; Walter Kendall's *The Labor Movement in Europe* (1975) provides information on labor voting patterns; and the Inter-University Consortium for Political and Social Research provides data on union membership as a percentage of the wage labor force. The RWG then attempts to explain any anomalies that may arise from a comparison of the pictures that are compiled from the different types of indices on the extent and politicization of the labor movement.

The final research step is to explain the worldwide pattern of labor movements as it emerges out of the above research findings. The focus is on (1) the points of time and epicenters of heightened labor unrest, and (2) the degree of politicization of labor unrest in these places and times.

The RWG (1986, p. 139) suggests that "an analysis of the trajectory of labor-capital conflict at a world level can assist in reinterpreting the studies of labor movement at the national and local levels. If global processes of accumulation and of struggle have shaped the pattern of conflict in all locales . . . then the insights from world-level analysis should be brought to bear on these conflicts." However, although the RWG has hypothesized an association between world structural factors and the labor movement, it also makes clear that it is not postulating a unidirectional line of causation from structure to human action. Instead, in assessing its case studies in the light of global and zonal patterns, the RWG also wants to highlight the extent to which divergent national patterns of the labor movement are rooted in historical contingency and diverse national traditions. Thus the RWG (1986, p. 152) expects that the national and local cases "will reveal that divergent patterns of individual and collective human action (e.g. labor militancy) have been responsible for pushing these social structural transformations forward at different speeds and in diverging directions at least as much as human action itself has been constrained and shaped by these social-structural factors."

In sum, the RWG has outlined a new approach to the study of the familiar capital-labor conflict. It has raised new questions and is collecting a new set of world-level data. Since the RWG has just started its research process, it will take a few years for its research product to come out. Only then can we judge whether this proposed world-level analysis has added anything new to our understanding of the history of the labor movement.

POWERS OF THE WORLD-SYSTEM PERSPECTIVE AT THE GLOBAL LEVEL

Unlike other schools of development, the world-system perspective insists that the unit of analysis should be the world-system. Thus world-system researchers are interested in examining the global dynamics that have transcended the confines of national boundaries. In its pursuit of the examination of global dynamics, the world-system perspective has adopted a unique historical methodology for studying long-term cyclical rhythms. It also needs to search for a new data set that will reveal the dynamics of the capitalist world-economy. These innovative world-system orientations have guided the research processes of the three empirical studies discussed above.

The Research Agenda. The world-system perspective directs researchers to examine global dynamics. Thus Wallerstein has addressed the research problem of how the downward phase of the capitalist world-economy in the seventeenth century affected the development of core, the periphery, and the semiperiphery. Bergesen and Schoenberg have examined how the properties of the capitalist world-economy (such as distribution of power within the core and core stability) have affected systemic responses in the form of colonization and decolonization. And the RWG has studied changing patterns in labor militancy at the world level. These kinds of global research questions have seldom been raised by modernization and dependency researchers.

The Methodology. The world-system perspective has adopted a long-term historical approach to the study of research problems. Instead of focusing on a time span of a decade or two, world-system researchers tend to analyze long-term secular trends and cyclical rhythms that have lasted more than a century. For example, Wallerstein has studied the downward phase of the cycle of 1450-1750. Bergesen and Schoenberg not only trace the three different waves of colonialism from 1415 to the present, they also distinguish a secular trend of colonialism moving toward less disruption and shorter duration. And the RWG has attempted to locate different waves of labor militancy over the course of industrialization from 1870 to the present.

The Data Base. Current data sets, most of which have been collected at the national level, are insufficient to answer the global research questions posed by world-system researchers. Consequently, these researchers have begun a quest for new, world-level data sets. Henige's (1970) study has provided helpful information on the long waves of colonialism because it lists the total number of colonies established and terminated each year between 1415 and 1969. And the RWG is engaging in content analysis of magazines, newspapers, and almanacs from 1870 to the present in order to extract information on global labor movements.

In sum, the world-system school has made a significant contribution by starting a new direction of research toward the study of cyclical movements of the world-economy, the long waves of colonialism, and world labor movements. Nevertheless, as will be discussed in the next section, the world-system perspective is not without its critics.

CRITICISMS OF THE WORLD-SYSTEM PERSPECTIVE

Since the mid-1970s, critics have charged the world-system perspective with presenting a reified concept of the world-system, with neglecting historically specific development at the national level, and with highlighting stratification analysis at the expense of class analysis (see Brenner 1977; Chirot 1981; Fagen 1983; Fitzgerald 1981; Gulalp 1981; Howe and Sica 1980; Kaplan 1980; Koo 1984; Petras 1978; Skocpol 1977; Smith 1982; Trimberger 1979; Worsley 1982; Zeitlin 1984). The following discussion draws heavily upon Zeitlin's (1984, p. 222-237) incisive criticisms of the world-system perspective.

Reification of the Concept of the World-System

The concept of the world-system is just a concept, no matter how useful it is in drawing the attention of researchers to the study of global dynamics. So when it is hardened to the extent that it becomes a reality of its own, the concept of the world-system becomes counterproductive, serving to distract researchers from raising fruitful questions. Thus Zeitlin (1984, p. 227) points out that Wallerstein

> reifies the so-called capitalist world economy and inverts the real historical process in which these global relations were created. The world economy itself, so it is said, apparently "assigned specific economic roles" within itself to its own "zones," and these "zones" then "used different modes of labor control" and so forth. What has happened here, unfortunately, is that the theory's atemporal categories have imperceptibly been given *a life of their own* and have imposed [whatever their author's intentions] on the social reality that

was meant to be understood by them, so now the categories make that reality fit their own a priori selves. (emphasis added)

We can see that this reification process is at work in the study of colonialism. Bergesen and Schoenberg (1980, p. 239) contend that there is a "distinctly organic quality to the world-system, such that when internal difficulties arise . . . the system pulls itself together and reaffirms its fundamental social relationships." This organic quality of the world-system is then used to explain the nature of colonialism: "When trouble appears, colonialism reappears, as a means of more explicitly—and forcefully—realigning and resetting the hierarchal structure of the world-system."

In addition, Zeitlin accuses Wallerstein of providing an "unwitting historical teleology"—historical events are used to explain the origins of the world-economy, but these historical events had to happen because the world-economy required them to happen. For example, Zeitlin (1984, p. 228) quotes Wallerstein, saying:

The world economy was based precisely on the assumption [whose?] that there were in fact these three zones and that they did in fact have different modes of labor control. *Were this not so*, it would not have been possible to assure the kind of *flow* of the surplus which *enabled the capitalist system to come into existence*. (emphasis added by Zeitlin)

Zeitlin says that this formulation is teleological because "the world economy *originated* because of its *consequences*, because its inner purpose was realized in the birth of capitalism."

Neglect of Historically Specific Development

Due to reification and teleology, world-system analysis is criticized for neglecting the study of historically specific development. According to Zeitlin (1984, p. 234, 225), Wallerstein's focus on the totality prevents him from engaging "in the concrete analysis of historically specific interrelations in particular societies." By insisting that only the world-system itself is "real," the world-system perspective "obscures rather than reveals the concrete internal social relations that underlie that so-called 'capitalist world economy' and propel its contradictory historical development."

Within the parameters of the world-system perspective, Zeitlin (1984, p. 225) argues that world-system researchers can neither raise nor answer the following critical questions:

> How does the specific historical configuration of class relations in a given social formation affect its internal development? How did this class configuration originate historically, why did class relations take this determinate form, and what were its developmental consequences? What are the specific internal dynamics of accumulation peculiar to these class relations and how do they determine the impact of the world market on the society's development? What is the relative effect of the world market versus specific types of penetration and expansion by various units of capital, themselves affected by their internal relations with labor, on the pattern of development?

Zeitlin believes that the world-system perspective is unable to probe into the above issues because it provides "stratification analysis" rather than "class analysis."

Stratification Analysis

According to its critics, the world-system perspective has focused on exchange relations and the distribution of rewards in the market rather than on classes and class conflict in the production sphere. Consequently, Wallerstein is often labeled a "circulationist." According to Zeitlin, when Wallerstein talks about "classes," he is actually referring to "strata" differentiated by their place along the hierarchy of occupational tasks in the capitalist world-economy. The strata would receive unequal rewards in accordance with their productive tasks, levels of skill, and contributions to the self-maintenance of the world-economy. Thus different positions in the world division of labor have led to different patterns of stratification and politics. To illustrate this point, Zeitlin (1984, p. 228, 233) again quotes Wallerstein:

> The division of a world economy involves a hierarchy of occupational tasks, in which tasks requiring higher levels of skill and greater capitalization are reserved [how? by whom or what?] for higher ranking areas. Since a capitalist world economy essentially rewards accumulated capital, including human capital, at a higher rate than "raw" labor power, the geographical maldistribution of these occupational skills involves a strong trend toward self-maintenance. . . the different roles [in the division of labor] led to different class structures which led to different politics.

However, this stratification model has problems. Zeitlin (1984, p. 228-229) points out that it

> conceals the real nature of class relations and mystifies their historical origins, and thereby also turns the real connection between the division of labor and class relations topsyturvy. Within this abstract model, there are no relations of compulsion, coercion, and exploitation, no relationship between producers and appropriators, oppressors and oppressed, dominant and subordinate classes. Slaves, serfs, tenant farmers, yeomen, artisans, and workers become mere technical "occupational categories."

In addition, Zeitlin (1984, p. 233) notes that "in this abstract, ahistorical model, the 'capitalist world market' (or 'international division of labor') thus appears upside down; it appears as the cause of class relations in particular societies rather than as, in reality, their refracted historical *products*." Consequently, Zeitlin charges that the world-system perspective seldom examines the historically specific "*class relations within nations that shape the global relations between them* and that determine how these global relations will affect their internal development."

In sum, the world-system perspective has been criticized for reification, for neglect of historically specific development, and for stratification analysis. Although the critics would like to see the demise of the world-system school, many students of the world-system perspective have found Wallerstein's studies insightful. The next chapter shows how students of the world-system perspective have responded to these criticisms.

CHAPTER 10

World-System Studies at the National Level

RESPONSES TO THE CRITICS

Except on one occasion, Wallerstein has not directly answered the charges of his critics (see Wallerstein 1977a). However, other researchers interested in world-system analysis point out that Wallerstein has incorporated the criticisms in his later work, or they argue that Wallerstein's framework is more sophisticated than the vulgarized version presented by his critics (for example, see Chase-Dunn 1981, 1982a; Garst 1985; So 1981, 1986a; Palat 1988).

On Reification

The critics charge that Wallerstein, following in the footsteps of Parsons, has reified the "world-system" to such an extent that it has a real life of its own. For example, the world-system is said to have the capacity of assigning different tasks to various zones and of rewarding them accordingly. Responding to this criticism, Palat (1988, p. 150) points out that the world-system is not a reified concept: "A world-systems perspective insists that units of analysis be constructed *in the course of research*" (emphasis added). Similarly, in discussing the history of the capitalist world-economy,

Wallerstein (1987, p. 318) makes it clear that he presents merely "a set of *hypotheses* within world-system analysis, open to debate, refinement, rejection. The crucial issue is that defining and explicating the units of analysis—the historical systems—becomes a central object of the scientific enterprise" (emphasis added).

If the "world-system" is seen merely as a concept rather than as a reified reality, then it can become a very useful tool for research. It directs our attention to the study of the impact of "extrasocietal" forces, and it corrects the deficiencies of class theorists' studies that see global dynamics as playing only a minor role in national transformation (see, e.g., Moore 1966; Lippit 1978). This is because global dynamics are very important in the shaping of the path of national development, although they are not the sole determining factor. Very often, global dynamics start the chain of social change, influence the contour of class struggle, and set the limits and bounds within which national development takes place. In this respect, Wallerstein (1984, p. 12) correctly points out that "we will not be able to analyze intelligently any social phenomenon, however 'micro' it may seem, without placing it as an element constrained by the real system in which it finds itself."

On the Lack of Historically Specific Studies

The critics contend that there is an absence of historical specification in the world-system perspective. In studying global dynamics, world-system analysts are said to have neglected the analysis of historically specific concrete cases. Although the general focus of the world-system school has been on global dynamics, this focus nevertheless should not preclude researchers from applying the global perspective to the study of historical developments at the national or local level. So's (1986a) study of the South China silk district, for instance, examines how the historical processes of global dynamics—such as incorporation, commercialization of agriculture, industrialization, proletarianization, and the cyclical rhythms of the capitalist world-system—have penetrated into the local society, triggered multiple forms of class struggle, and opened up new opportunities for local development. In fact, the adoption of world-system analysis for the study of local regions may even throw new light on old issues that anthropologists have taken for granted, because anthropologists have too often "developed a defensive blindness to the macrostructures that shaped the societies they studied" (Nash 1981, p. 409).

On Stratification Analysis

The critics further contend that Wallerstein has provided only a stratification analysis, and therefore he is unable to explain how class conflict has shaped the history of national development.

In response to this charge, Wallerstein (1977a, p. 105) asserts, "Not only do I think the class struggle is central to the dynamics of capitalism, but I personally regard as the most cogent part of my book chapter V, which is intended to be, as the title indicates, an analysis of why the class struggle took sometimes similar, sometimes divergent, forms." Recently, Wallerstein has further underscored the need for a world-level class struggle movement by means of which the producers would attack the flow of surplus at the point of production.

However, what separates Wallerstein from his class critics is that they have different conceptions of social class. Wallerstein's historical method has prompted him to conceptualize social class as a dynamic process of perpetual re-creation and hence of constant change of form and composition. Wallerstein (1979a, p. 224) contends that "classes do not have some permanent reality. Rather, they are formed, they consolidate themselves, they disintegrate or disaggregate, and they are re-formed. It is a process of constant movement, and the greatest barrier to understanding their action is reification."

Consequently, for Wallerstein, social class is not an attribute but a set of changing relations with other classes in a particular historical context, and it cannot be defined narrowly in the production sphere. On this subject, Wallerstein (1979a, p. 222) notes: "It is probably most useful if we use it [social class] as historically specific to this kind of world-system. Class analysis loses its power of explanation whenever it moves towards formal models and away from dialectical dynamics. Thus, we wish to analyze here classes as evolving and changing structures, wearing ever-changing ideological clothing, in order to see to whose advantage it is at specific points of time to define class memberships in particular conceptual terms." This dynamic and historical conceptualization of social class is, of course, quite different from the approach of Wallerstein's critics, who tend to focus on the political economy and define social classes at the production level.

Although Wallerstein's class analysis is described as "unorthodox" by some American researchers, it is quite close to the analysis adopted by British historians (So and Hikam, forthcoming). E. P. Thompson (1984, p. 114), one of the most well-known of the British class theorists, also emphasizes the historical and dynamic aspects of class relations: "The notion of class entails the notion of historical relationship, it is a fluency which evades analysis if we attempt to stop it dead at any given moment and anatomize its structure." Similar to Wallerstein, Thompson (1984, p. 116) sees class as more than an economic relationship: "We cannot understand class unless we see it as a social and cultural formation, arising from processes which can only be studied as they work themselves out over a considerable historical period." Adopting such an approach, class relationships are defined very "loosely," as Thompson (1984, p. 115, 116) contends that "class happens when some men, as a result of common experiences (inherited or shared), feel and articulate the identity of their interests as between themselves, and as against other men whose interests are different from (and usually opposed to) theirs. . . . Class is defined by men as they live their own history, and, in the end, this is its only definition" (see also Kaye 1983; Roy 1984; Thompson 1978).

The merit of Thompson's argument lies in his extension of the concept of class from the economic level to social and cultural levels. But Wallerstein goes even further than Thompson in stressing not just social class but also status group and the constant interaction between social class and status group. In a coauthored article, Wallerstein and his colleagues argue that "the whole line between classes as they are constructed and status-groups of every variety is far more fluid and blurred than the classic presumption of an antinomy between class and status-group has indicated" (Arrighi et al. 1983, p. 302). Wallerstein (1979a, p. 200) cites an example indicating that the "anti-imperialist nationalist struggle" between the majority of the population in a periphery and the core capitalists and their local allies is "a mode of *expression* of class interest." Accordingly, Wallerstein argues that status groups (ethnic/national/religious groups) and social class are two sets of clothing for the same basic reality, and that the history of construction of classes, nations, and ethnic groups is a history of the constant rise and fall of the intensity of these political claims in cultural clothing.

Wallerstein's insights are expressed in his theoretical explanation of why, in the history of the capitalist world-system, the bourgeoisies and proletariats have often defined their class interests in status-group terms and expressed their class consciousness in national/ethnic/religious forms. Wallerstein (1979a, p. 196) asserts that this is the case because

> class represents an antinomy, as a dialectical concept should. On the one hand, class is defined as relationship to the means of production, and hence position in the economic system which is a *world*-economy. On the other hand a class is a real actor only to the extent that it becomes class-*conscious*, which means to the extent that it is organized as a *political* actor. But political actors are located primarily in particular national *states*. Class is not the one or the other. It is both, and class analysis is only meaningful to the extent that it is placed within a given historical context.

It is a consequence of this antinomy of class—*an sich* in a world-economy, but *fur sich* in the states—that most expressions of consciousness take a status group form within a state.

Thus in Wallerstein's work "class" is seen as a group of political actors who consciously attempt to promote their own interests in the capitalist world-economy. Although classes often struggle in status group terms, Wallerstein maintains that various forms of class struggle have shaped the history of the capitalist world-economy since the sixteenth century (Arrighi et al. 1986).

In sum, in response to the critics, students of the world-system perspective have conceded that the concept of "world-system" is merely a research tool, that the world-system perspective can be used to study local historical developments, and that social class should be conceptualized as a dynamic historical process.

Drawing upon So's (1986b, n.d.; So and Cho 1988) empirical studies, the following discussion examines how these modifications in the world-system perspective have shed new light on the study of the economic success of Hong Kong, the changing class structure in socialist China, and the deindustrialization and reindustrialization of the United States. Unlike the dependency school, which has specialized in the study of the periphery, the world-system perspective has a much broader research focus. It examines not only the periphery, but also the semiperiphery and the core countries.

THE PERIPHERY:
THE ECONOMIC SUCCESS OF HONG KONG

The economic success of Hong Kong is well known. From a fishing village in the nineteenth century, it has grown to be one the most promising industrial states of the world. Hong Kong's gross national product increased at a rate of around 10% per year in the late 1970s. Hong Kong exports more commodities than the entire nation of India and is the third largest financial center of the world. These impressive figures raise the following questions: What are the factors that led to the economic success of Hong Kong? In what ways do development theories shed new light on this issue?

In the modernization literature, there is a cultural explanation that asserts that *neo-Confucianism* encourages individual commitment to the work ethic and loyalty to the company, and that its familism aspect helps to pull resources and capital together through kinship networks (Kahn 1984). In addition, there is a *free market* explanation that argues that Hong Kong is a capitalist paradise (Gibson 1984). The capitalists are free to invest, free to create new products, and free to develop their entrepreneurial potential. Surely neo-Confucianism and free market forces are important factors, but by themselves they are insufficient to explain the particular pattern of Hong Kong's development. For example, they do not explain why Hong Kong's industrialization took place only after World War II and why it took the path of export-industrialization. A broader world-system perspective is needed to place the cultural/market forces in the proper context.

The neo-Marxist literature has recently put forward an *authoritarian state* explanation to account for the rapid industrialization of East Asian countries (Koo 1987). It shows that when the state is strong and authoritarian (with military government, one-party rule, and suppression of dissent), and when the state managers are committed to development, the state can quickly build up the infrastructure, impose import-substitution, and promote export-industrialization. However, this explanation is not applicable to Hong Kong, because the state in Hong Kong is liberal—it allows the coexistence of opposing ideologies and it seldom suppresses dissidents. Moreover, instead of actively intervening in the economy, the state in Hong Kong adopts a laissez-faire policy of minimum intervention.

In the development literature, therefore, there is no satisfactory explanation for the economic success of Hong Kong. This is why the world-system perspective may help to shed new light on the Hong Kong case. The following discussion presents first the origins of the industrial revolution in the 1950s and then an examination of the diversification of the economy in the late 1960s; finally, it explores the expansion of the financial sector in the 1970s.

The First Phase: The Industrial Revolution

In order to understand why Hong Kong started to industrialize in the 1950s, one must know the nature of the capitalist world-system in that period. The 1950s were a time of postwar recovery for the core countries, and there was a large demand for consumer goods and cheap raw materials. Moreover, labor costs in the core countries began to rise, resulting in a trend of transfer of some of the labor-intensive production to the periphery. Brown (1973, p. 12) points out that big British buyers of textiles expended considerable effort in assisting Hong Kong factories to develop their production capacity, and overseas producers came to Hong Kong to have their products assembled from the parts they had supplied.

In addition, the interaction between socialist China and the capitalist power bloc also unintentionally promoted Hong Kong's industrialization. After the Chinese Communist Revolution in 1949, many capitalists fled from Shanghai to Hong Kong in order to avoid communist rule. They brought with them technology, managerial skills, and capital. Political uncertainty and flight from the communist mentality at that time also drove many South China urban masses to Hong Kong to seek a living. It was this conjuncture of refugee capital and refugee labor that provided the impetus for Hong Kong's industrialization. It was if the best of socialist China's assets in terms of capital and labor had suddenly been transplanted to Hong Kong to reap the benefits of the economic upswing of the capitalist world-system.

In the midst of the Cold War, U.S. policymakers, in their anticommunist zeal, tried to contain communist expansion by supporting the Taiwan government, by sending troops to Korea, and by economic blockades. Such heightened hostility with the capitalist power bloc explained why socialist China did not take back control of Hong Kong right after the Communist Revolution. Hong Kong was the only port from through China could gain foreign currency to buy necessary foreign equipment. As a result, China was very willing to supply food products, raw materials, and even drinking water to Hong Kong in exchange for that much-needed foreign currency. This "unequal exchange" between cheap Chinese products and Hong Kong currency subsidized the Hong Kong economy, lowered the cost of living, and strengthened Hong Kong's competitiveness in the world market.

The intense conflict between socialist China and the capitalist power bloc also explains the political stability of Hong Kong. As refugees who had fled from communist rule, the Chinese capitalists tolerated the British monopoly of the Hong Kong state machinery so as not to rock the boat. The Chinese working class was also fairly satisfied with the existing situation. Although critics claimed to have observed terrible working conditions in Hong Kong, the refugee laborers themselves perceived marked improvement of their condition compared to their previous working conditions in China. Of course, there were unions and there were strikes, but the unions tended to be small and ideologically divided between prosocialist and pronationalist factions, and China was reported to have held back the radical demands of the prosocialist trade unions so as not to risk any disturbance of its substantial foreign exchange earnings. This absence of intensive class struggle further enhanced the industrialization process, with economic output, employment, and export figures in the 1950s doubling within a short span of a few years.

This favorable world-market situation and the lack of domestic class struggle help to explain the liberal and nonintervention policies of the Hong Kong state. Unlike the Taiwan state, the Hong Kong state did not need to militarize in order to stop the spread of communism or to strengthen its police force to suppress local opposition. The Hong Kong state also did not have to involve itself with the promotion of export-industrialization, because the Chinese capitalists were already performing so well in the world-market.

Furthermore, the senior state managers of Hong Kong were mostly British expatriates, and the central organs of the Hong Kong government (Exco and Legco) were controlled by British businesspeople who monopolized the colony's banking and public utilities sectors. Since the British business interests were in the financial sector, they did not want state interference in the financial world that would limit their freedom. Subsequently, the Hong Kong government continued to carry out its old colonial laissez-faire policy even after Hong Kong had entered a new phase of export-industrialization in the 1950s.

The Second Phase: Toward Diversification

Beginning in the late 1960s, the U.S. hegemonic domination of the capitalist world-system came to an end. The United States was challenged in the Vietnam War, and there were new industrial states—such as Japan and West Germany—competing for industrial supremacy. Just as in other periods of declining hegemonic power, the ideology of free trade was replaced by the ideology of protectionism. Import restrictions were tightened and trade quotas were quickly set up. This new wave of protectionism posed a threat to the expanding export economy of Hong Kong.

Another threat to the Hong Kong economy was peripheral competition. The 1960s saw the rise of other industrial peripheries such as Taiwan and South Korea, which also engaged in export-industrialization. These latecomers were keen competitors in Hong Kong's export markets.

One more threat to the Hong Kong economy came from the Chinese socialist state. After stabilization of its political power, socialist China stopped the influx of refugee labor to Hong Kong. Lacking further external labor supply, the Hong Kong economy in the 1960s frequently ran into labor shortages, with job vacancies of often more than 4% of the labor force. Thus housewives were attracted to become factory workers and the "putting-out system" was revived so that the home labor of the elderly and children could be utilized. This intense competition for labor among the factories drove up the wages of the Hong Kong workers, with real wages doubling between 1973 and 1980. Since the 1970s, Hong Kong labor has no longer been cheap compared to that of other peripheral areas.

Facing the triple threat of protectionism, peripheral competition, and rising labor costs, the capitalists in Hong Kong responded with dynamic adaptation to the ever-changing market and diversification of their products. For instance, when there was a cut in quotas on low-quality clothing and plastic flowers, the Hong Kong capitalists diversified their factories to produce high-class garments and silk flowers. Through constant innovation in technology, design, and advertisement, the Hong Kong garment industry rid itself of its bad reputation for being "cheap but rather nasty." There was also diversification into other kinds of industry, such as electronics and watchmaking, as well as diversification into other economic sectors, such as the tourist industry, the shipping industry, and the entrepot trade.

The dynamic nature of the Hong Kong capitalists was a result of the nature of the Hong Kong firms. Over 90% of Hong Kong firms employed fewer than 50 workers. Being small, these firms were obstructed less by bureaucratic red tape, were more adaptable to new markets and to rush orders, were better able to try new methods of production, and required only a small amount of capital to get started. Thus the economic success of Hong Kong was the direct result of the efforts of Hong Kong capitalists. The government of Hong Kong took some initiative in building up the infrastructure (such as freeways), but it undertook a much less active role in the promotion of technological research and international marketing.

Without the backing of the state, the small firms were always being put on trial by the changing world market. Although as a whole the Hong Kong economy has prospered, there were fluctuations and casualties during the downward swing of the capitalist world-economy. The oil crisis in the early 1970s, for instance, caused a sharp drop in the stock market, closed numerous small firms, and produced an unexpectedly high unemployment rate of 9%. Seen in this light, the Hong Kong economy should be conceptualized as in a state of flux, of constantly rising and falling small firms.

The Third Phase: Becoming a World Financial Center

In the late 1970s there was rapid expansion of the financial sector in Hong Kong. Every giant bank of the leading core countries had a branch set up in Hong Kong, and it became the financial capital of Asia and the third largest financial center of the world.

The rise to world financial centrality can again be traced back to the changing nature of the capitalist world-system. In the late 1970s, Latin America had incurred too much debt, Africa was too remote, and the Middle East was too politically unstable; Asia thereby became the best investment locale for the financial giants of Japan and the United States. Furthermore, the lowering of profit rates in the core and the relocation of industries in the periphery also called for a new financial center outside of New York and London.

This climb to world financial dominance was also related to the incorporation of socialist China into the capitalist world-system. In the late 1970s, China abandoned its practice self-reliance to establish an open-door policy. The goal was to attract active introduction of foreign capital and foreign technology in order to achieve "the Four Modernizations" (So, 1988). China's special economic zones and joint-ventured oil field explorations were typical examples of investment opportunities that lured foreign investment. These new developments in China enhanced the possibility of establishing a new financial center close to its territory.

But why was Hong Kong chosen as a world center rather than Taiwan or Japan? This may be related to the liberal state policy of Hong Kong. As Chung (1983, p. 181) explains: "Hong Kong is the only place in Asia where there is absolutely no control on the international flow of money and no discrimination against foreign operators. Taxes in Hong Kong are few and simple . . . and there is no withholding tax for foreign currency deposits."

When investment capital started to flow into Hong Kong, it was mostly invested in stocks and real estate, causing a sudden real estate boom at the end of the 1970s. Hong Kong land prices doubled and tripled within a few years. Having too much idle capital floating around, the banks in Hong Kong lent fuel to this boom by offering easy credit on loans. The result was land speculation.

The government of Hong Kong did nothing to halt the land speculation; rather, the government speeded it up by rapidly putting the best crown land in the colony up for auction. The government reaped huge profits from this sale. The revenue from the land sale, which accounted for one-third of the state's total revenue, strengthened the finances of the state and enabled it to carry out construction of massive infrastructure projects without even raising taxes higher than 15%.

The state of Hong Kong tried to "walk on two legs" in the 1970s. On one hand, it promoted export industrialization by building the necessary infrastructure; on the other, it strove to set up Hong Kong as a world financial center by promoting its laissez-faire policies. From the state's viewpoint, this policy appeared to work in the late 1970s. Transforming Hong Kong into a financial center attracted foreign capital investments, escalated land values, increased revenue to the state through public land auctions, and provided the funds necessary to promote export-industrialization.

However, this "two legs" policy also created problems of development. The financial sector was developed at the expense of the industrial sector. Rising land prices caused a chain reaction of rising prices in services, food, and transportation, leading to a high rate of inflation and high cost of living. Moreover, rising land prices also meant higher rent and more expensive industrial sites. This led to rising costs of production for industrialists, as well as a decrease in their profits and their competitiveness in the world export market.

This conflict between industrialists and financiers was often intermixed with conflict between Chinese capital and British capital. Due to three decades of economic success, many Chinese businesspeople in Hong Kong had accumulated enough capital to challenge the British corporations. After exerting power in the market, the Chinese capitalists made their influence felt in the Hong Kong state. The early 1980s observed a growing proportion of Chinese members in Exco and Legco, leading Hook (1983, p. 508) to remark that "the European hongs have been to some extent eclipsed by the growth of their Chinese competitors." This increase in the number of Chinese legislators explains why the state gradually changed its nonintervention industrial policy in the late 1970s. The Hong Kong state had proposed the acceleration of technological education, the building of new industrial towns, and the exploration of overseas markets. However, without the support of British financiers, the state of Hong Kong was reluctant to change its nonintervention policy on interest rates and bank regulations.

In addition, the "two legs" policy of the Hong Kong state had linked the Hong Kong economy to two kinds of fluctuations in the world-economy: an economic one relating to world supply and demand, and a financial one that is usually politically cultivated. These double linkages increased Hong Kong's vulnerability to cyclical trends in the capitalist world-economy. For instance, the economic recession in 1980 reduced Hong Kong's exports, while the political prospect of being taken over by socialist China in 1997 resulted in a plunge of the real estate market, a sharp drop in the value of Hong Kong currency, the bankruptcy of a few giant financial companies and banks, and the sudden outflow of capital to the United States.

If world-system analysis is helpful in explaining the origins of peripheral industrialization, can it be equally helpful in examining the changing economic structure in the core? The next section will discuss this issue.

THE CORE: THE DEINDUSTRIALIZATION AND REINDUSTRIALIZATION OF THE UNITED STATES

Deindustrialization

When a new wave of industrialization swept East Asia, many newly industrializing states celebrated their gains in industrial employment. However, it seems that the joys of Third World workers were developed at the expense of American workers. In the early 1980s, many American workers were in distress as a result of plant closings in midwestern and northeastern cities. The term *deindustrialization* refers to the loss of industrial employment as the result of a massive relocation of U.S. manufacturing plants to about 200 export processing zones in the periphery. Bluestone (1984, p. 41) observes that "a field visit to Detroit, Buffalo, Youngstown, or Akron, would seem to leave little doubt that capital investment has been insufficient to maintain basic industry or mitigate the apparent abandonment of entire communities." In addition, Harris (1984) points to the following patterns of deindustrialization:

(1) *sectorial deindustrialization:* Plant closings occur in the manufacturing sector, but most new jobs are created in the service sector.
(2) *regional deindustrialization:* Regions that have experienced job losses are the Northeast, Northwest, and Midwest, but new jobs are mostly created in the South, the West, and the Southwest.

(3) *mismatch between job characteristics:* High-paying jobs are replaced by low-paying jobs. Bluestone (1984, p. 50) estimates that "it takes two department store jobs or three restaurant jobs to make up for the earnings loss of just one average manufacturing position."

(4) *TNC plant closings:* Large subsidiaries of transnational corporations are closing, rather than independent firms in the small business sector, as has been the case in the past.

In sum, the deindustrialization of the U.S. economy is shown by the loss of high-paying manufacturing jobs among the subsidiaries of the transnational corporations located in the Northeast and the Midwest. This deindustrialization process received national attention during the recession in the early 1980s. By the mid-1980s, however, the deindustrialization process seemed to have slowed down. Researchers began to focus on another trend generally called *reindustrialization*.

Reindustrialization

In the United States, although many manufacturing jobs were lost, numerous new jobs have been created in the so-called ascending and descending industries. Unlike the knowledge-intensive "ascending" high-tech industries (e.g., the electronic industry), the "descending" industries were labor-intensive and restricted by technological obsolescence (e.g., the garment industry). No researcher had predicted the sudden revival of the descending industries in the United States in the late twentieth century.

Surprisingly, despite their differences, the ascending and descending industries share the following job characteristics: Their small firms tend to offer unstable, low-skilled, low-paying jobs; their working conditions are very poor; and their factories are in run-down buildings in the inner cities. There is neither overtime work compensation nor unemployment insurance; minimum-wage and standard labor regulations are frequently not observed; and the workers are allowed to carry the parts home and assemble them with their children at the kitchen table (Fernandez-Kelly and Garcia 1985).

In addition, the workers in the ascending and descending industries share the following characteristics. Many of their workers are illegal immigrants from Mexico and Central America, recent arrivals who can barely speak any English, and a large majority of them are women. Employers prefer to hire women because of their good eyesight, manual dexterity, ability to perform minute handiwork, docility, and little incentive to join unions.

To summarize, the 1980s have seen changes in job and worker characteristics in the U.S. economy. Deindustrialization has eliminated semiskilled, high-paying, secure, and unionized jobs in the manufacturing sector, while reindustrialization has created unskilled, low-paying, insecure, and nonunionized jobs in the ascending and descending industries. For the most part, these jobs have not been filled by the native-born white male workers displaced by deindustrialization, but by female workers, many of whom are illegal aliens.

What were the causes of the deindustrialization and reindustrialization processes? What impacts have these two processes had on U.S. society? To what extent has the world-system perspective helped researchers to explain this structural transformation of the core economy?

Why Deindustrialization?

In order to trace the origins of the deindustrialization process, researchers need to study production conditions in both the United States and the periphery. In the United States, transnational corporations were not pleased with the existing production conditions. Due to labor union pressures, the TNCs constantly had to enter into collective bargaining over wage rates, job classifications, job security, and fringe benefits. The U.S. government also imposed high taxes, social security payments, antitrust laws, and regulations concerning minimum wages and hazardous working conditions. U.S. TNCs, however, did not have to accept the constraints imposed by labor unions and the state, because in this age of computers and efficient transportation, geographical distance is no longer a hindrance to worldwide production. Thus the transnational corporations could subdivide the manufacture of a product into distinct phases, relocate them to Third World countries, and still monitor the output, plan manufacturing, and exert efficient inventory supervision of their subsidiaries located in distant geographical areas.

Morales (1983, p. 585) reports a case in which a TNC moved its plant to Mexico in order to avoid union controls:

> With the move, wages dropped to approximately $1.60 per hour compared with $6.50 in L.A. In Mexico, they no longer had to pay workers' compensation (which had previously come to 7 percent of the wage bill), social security, or state disability. Rental space came to 9 cents per square foot (or $50 per month) as opposed to the 26 cents per square foot they paid in the United States. The plant in Mexico operates in a special industrial zone from which they export duty-free to Canada. Imports to the United States are taxed only for the value added to the header in the manufacturing process which consists of the cost of low-wage labor.

Consequently, transnational corporations became attracted to the production conditions in Third World countries. Third World workers were known to be docile, and they worked with high intensity and were willing to work long hours for low wages. Third World states cooperated with the TNCs, granting them many concessions, including low taxation, tax holidays, no regulations on health standards, cheap rent, and free import to the export processing zones.

Another reason the deindustrialization process took place was that many TNCs found it more profitable to invest in stocks than to undertake the costly structural changes required by technological innovation. Thus instead of upgrading their aging plants in the United States, many just let their plants run down. Buying up other corporations meant immediate huge profits for the TNCs, while technological renovation of aging plants would require tremendous outlays of capital, investments that would take too long to recoup. Thus U.S. Steel decided to buy Marathon Oil in the early 1980s rather than to invest its capital in upgrading its steel plants.

In addition, the transnational corporations were attracted to capital investment in high-tech industries. It seemed that high-tech industries had enormous potential for expansion because microprocessors could be used in designing machinery, building cars, creating robots, and speeding up banking transactions. In this computer age, TNCs prefer to invest in high-tech industries, through which they can easily monitor the production, marketing, and financial networks of their subsidiaries and their competitors in the capitalist world-economy. From a world-system analysis, the rise of high-tech industries signals a new era in the international division of labor. Capital-intensive and labor-intensive industries could be relocated to the periphery (Frobel et al. 1979; Portes and Walton 1982), while knowledge-intensive industries could remain in the core. From a national viewpoint, however, this new international division of labor was condemned by core workers as deindustrialization.

Why Reindustrialization?

If the above factors explain the deindustrialization process in the early 1980s, what then were the causes of reindustrialization in the mid-1980s? Again, researchers need to go beyond nation-state boundaries to examine the supply side and the demand side of the reindustrialization process. Let us start with the supply side: Why were Third World countries sending laborers off to the United States? Since most of the undocumented workers came from Mexico, some background on the political economy of Mexico may shed some light on the causes of this emigration.

The Mexican economy has been in deep trouble since the late 1970s. As explained in Chapter 6, Mexico has experienced an acute balance-of-payments problem, serious debt difficulties, drastic devaluation of the peso, and rampant inflation. In order to make interest payments on foreign debts, the Mexican state cut spending on social programs and industrial projects, causing more hardship for the poor and intensifying an already serious unemployment problem.

If the Mexican cities were in trouble, the Mexican countryside was in bankruptcy. The Mexican peasants owned little land, had few employment opportunities, and received no help from the state in making ends meet. They peasants were forced to leave their native villages in search of food and jobs. Once this rural population was uprooted, it kept on migrating—from one village to another, from village to city, from one city to another—until it could find a decent living. This explains the massive emigration out of Mexico, as the Mexican people did not hesitate to go wherever they could find employment opportunities (Cockcroft 1982).

Why did the Mexicans go to the United States instead of to other countries? To answer this question, we need to study the demand side of reindustrialization, that is, why the U.S. economy needed cheap immigrant labor. For the United States to maintain its superior economic position, its products must be able to compete in the world market. Deindustrialization—the relocation of U.S. manufacturing industries to Third World countries—was certainly a good strategy to cut production costs and to make the U.S. products competitive. However, this global option was becoming less available in the 1980s than before. In many prosperous Third World states such as Hong Kong, labor was no longer cheap, and the governments had imposed stricter regulations on the transnational corporations than before. In the poor Third World countries, such as the Philippines, anti-American sentiment was on the rise, making foreign investment highly insecure. The declining hegemony of the United States, moreover, decreased its ability to protect the overseas investments of its transnational corporations (Lembcke and Hart-Landsberg 1985). As a result, instead of adopting a deindustrialization strategy, the TNCs reconsidered the strategy of shoring up their American economic base, especially after they discovered the merits of subcontracting.

For the transnational corporations, subcontracting was not the same as hiring workers or forming a subsidiary. To do either of these, the TNCs had to deal with the labor unions and their rules, and thus could not discharge workers easily. The plant closings that took place during the deindustrialization process, for instance, frequently led to worker resentment and public protest.

With subcontracting, however, the TNCs had little obligation to the labor force, did not need to confront labor unions, and could dispense with workers simply by not renewing their contracts with the small firms. Subcontracting thus carried less political risk, adapted better to the fluctuating market demands, and gave the TNCs greater flexibility in altering their models and outputs than they would have had if they hired workers directly (Fernandez-Kelly 1987). Consequently, instead of relocating manufacturing industries to Third World countries, the TNCs subcontracted with small firms in the United States to process unskilled and low-paying tasks.

And where do the transnational corporations get their supply of cheap labor? The answer lies in the recruitment of illegal immigrants. U.S. capitalists justified their demand for cheap immigrant labor by using such political slogans as "to reinvigorate the national economy of the United States" and "the U.S. industry needs to remain competitive in the world market." In passing, it should be noted that this immigrant labor strategy was not new at all; it has been used many times during the past century. Whenever U.S. capitalists have found it necessary to cut domestic worker wages and curb union power, they have speeded up new waves of immigration, hoping that the cheap, docile, immigrant labor can be used to divide the American working class.

The U.S. government has also been very active in promoting the reindustrialization process. Instead of taking a strong stand against illegal immigration, the Reagan administration tolerated it and neither sent more patrols to the U.S. border nor imposed more sanctions against undocumented workers. In the mid-1980s, the Reagan administration actually promoted illegal immigration by granting amnesty to all undocumented workers who could prove illegal residence in the United States for a period of more than five years. Furthermore, the Reagan administration promoted the investment climate in the United States by relaxing environmental and occupational regulations, lowering corporate taxes, reducing various social programs, undermining the strength of the labor movement, and boosting defense spending.

To promote reindustrialization, many municipal governments have also established "inner-city enterprise zones," where investor corporations enjoy tax privileges and exemptions from environmental protection laws and where workers have waived the right to form labor unions (Lembcke and Hart-Landsberg 1985). If "urban enterprise zones" become a reality, Fernandez-Kelly (1985, p. 214) predicts that Chicanos and other minority teenagers will perform low-paying, high-intensity sweatshop jobs similar to those held by young women in export processing zones in Asia and Latin America. These new American workers could earn half of the current minimum wage for temporary, menial jobs.

Impacts of Deindustrialization
and Reindustrialization

Reindustrialization has probably slowed down the deindustrialization process, since more jobs have remained within the United States. Possibility due to this wave of reindustrialization, the recession of the early 1980s proved to be short-lived. The outlook for the U.S. economy in the mid-1980s seemed pretty hopeful. Economic growth has continued, with a new wave of capital accumulation in key cities, such as New York and Los Angeles, helping municipal governments to recover from their budget deficits in the 1970s.

Politically, however, it was a different picture. Not only did workers in the manufacturing sector experience plant shutdowns, but their union power was weakened considerably by layoffs and the shrinking size of the American work force in that sector. As reported in *Time* (July 13, 1987, p. 48), U.S. organized labor faced a crisis of declining union membership from 20.1 million in 1980 to 17 million in 1986.

The labor unions, however, were fighting a losing battle with the deindustrialization process. In the 1980s, unions failed to influence the U.S. government to develop programs to help laid-off workers and to require that companies give 60 days' notice to workers in the event of a plant closing. This failure to articulate the interests of the working class at the state level, Burris (1985, p. 109) explains, was "mainly because labor has not been able to mount a sufficient economic or political threat to force concessions and compromise from the side of business. To pose such a threat would require a mass mobilization of the rank-and-file—something of which the current leadership is either incapable or wants to avoid out of a concern that it might be captured by those to their left."

In passing, it should be noted that from a world-system perspective, the transnational corporations generally have had an edge over national unions. Labor is less mobile than capital (since labor is tied to a particular community or region), and can protest only within the boundaries of a nation-state. But capital is highly mobile because it can move from one nation to another in search of labor, raw materials, credit, and markets. Each move across national boundaries, therefore, strengthens transnational capital at the expense of the national labor unions, local communities, and the nation-state, leading to loss of jobs, decrease in tax revenues, and dislocation of the national economy.

Unable to exert its influence on state policy through labor unions, the white working class has reacted to its declining class interests by reasserting its "superior" ethnic status. In Southern California, for example, this has taken the form of an "English as the official language" movement, showing the hostility of many in the white community toward the multilingual abilities of new immigrants. If this sentiment continues, there may be an intensification of racism and ethnic conflict in the 1990s. Reindustrialization, therefore, has served to intensify ethnic divisions in the working class. It has created conflicts within the working class instead of between the working class and the transnational corporations (Cockcroft 1982).

THE SEMIPERIPHERY: THE CHANGING CLASS STRUCTURE IN SOCIALIST CHINA

In the twentieth century, many socialist states have been transformed from peripheral status to semiperipheral status. World-system analysis can help us to understand the changing path of socialist development.

During the Cold War era of the 1950s, conservative scholars tended to characterize socialist states as "evil empires" with features such as one-person dictatorship, one-party monopolization of power, and the frequent use of terror to suppress dissent. On the other hand, many Marxist researchers, dissatisfied by what had happened in the Soviet Union, postulated that although the Soviet Union had instituted public ownership, the Soviet state had become parasitic and had developed interests that were in opposition to those of the working class.

The problem with both of these approaches is that the researchers incorrectly assume that socialist states have a lot of autonomy to formulate and implement their own policies. In other words, socialist states are seen to be so independent that their political economy can be examined in isolation from other states. Taking socialist states as a unit of analysis and focusing on their internal dynamics, conservative researchers therefore tended to exaggerate the unlimited authority of the socialist dictators, while the Marxists tended to expect too many miracles from socialist development.

From a world-system perspective (Chase-Dunn 1982b; Chirot 1986; Dixon 1979; Kraus 1979), however, the research mentioned above has a one-sided focus. This is because a socialist state is still a unit within the capitalist world-economy, and its activities are very much constrained by the interstate system of the capitalist world-economy. Thus understanding the interaction between socialist states and the capitalist world-economy is crucial to an understanding of the internal dynamics of the socialist states. Drawing upon the insightful analysis found in Kraus's (1979) work, the following discussion shows that China's withdrawal from and reintegration into the capitalist world-economy have led to a change of class structure in socialist China.

The First Phase:
Withdrawal from the Capitalist World-Economy

The immediate reaction of the capitalist core states to the 1949 Chinese Communist Revolution was to suppress it through military intervention. The capitalist states were concerned that the winds of revolution would spread quickly to other states in East

Asia. As a result, the United States took an active role in attempting to destroy the new socialist state in China, sending naval ships to protect the Nationalist party in Taiwan, fighting a war with the Chinese in Korea, preventing socialist China from becoming a member of the United Nations, and starting an international embargo against China.

Facing such hostilities from the capitalist core states, socialist China had no choice but to withdraw from the capitalist world-economy. After the 1949 Communist Revolution, the Chinese Communist Party (the CCP) was forced to sever diplomatic relations with the West due to core hostilities. Political isolation was then followed by economic isolation. Socialist China's foreign trade with the West came almost to a halt due to the U.S. embargo, and it could not rely on foreign capital investment, as most foreign capitalists had already left by the time of the Korean War in the early 1950s. This forced withdrawal from the capitalist world-economy produced an interesting contradiction. It seems that the more the United States heightened its hostilities toward China, the more the CCP was determined to move rapidly into socialism.

The CCP carried out some radical programs in this withdrawal phase. In order to withstand foreign aggression, the CCP needed to consolidate its external and internal bases of support. Externally, socialist China turned to the Soviet Union for help in spite of their policy differences in the 1930s (because the Soviet Union did not support a guerrilla warfare strategy). Internally, the CCP wanted to ensure the loyalty of its key supporters. Thus at the height of the Korean War, the CCP carried out land reform at full speed in order to consolidate support from the peasantry. Through violent confrontations with the landlords, the poor peasants gradually asserted themselves, acquired the political capacity to protect their class interests, and took land ownership away from the landlords. In this respect, the land reform program was proclaimed to be a great success. Not only did it satisfy the land hunger of the poor peasants, it also politically mobilized the peasantry at the grassroots level and consolidated the power of the CCP in the countryside.

However, giving land to the peasantry was not a sufficient means to bring social equality to the countryside. Large peasant families, because they possessed more labor power, were allocated more farmland, more farm implements, and more farm animals than were small peasant families. Consequently, shortly after the completion of land reform, rapid social differentiation in the Chinese countryside was seen. Large peasant families were getting richer, while small peasant families were falling further behind in their socioeconomic status. In response to this social differentiation, the CCP put forward collectivization and communization policies. Farmland and other resources became collectively owned, and peasants, from large and small families alike, worked collectively in production teams for the commune. Rewards were distributed according to labor contributions to a production team. This collectivization policy was aimed at stopping social differentiation in the countryside, eliminating the rich peasant stratum, and exercising state control over the individual. After the formation of communes, the CCP not only received further support from the poor peasants but could easily mobilize them to withstand foreign aggression.

Meanwhile, in the cities, socialist China began to nationalize its industries. Although nationalization was aimed at eliminating the capitalists as a class, the CCP wanted to minimize the dissatisfaction of the "national capitalists" because it needed their expertise and organization skills to run the urban economy. As a result, the CCP not only paid compensation to the capitalists for their industrial assets, it also hired them as directors to manage the factories. After nationalization, the state dominated the urban economy and central planning was made possible. The two important targets of the Chinese central planning were to avoid inflation and to guarantee full employment, thus helping the CCP to gain the support of the urban working class.

Once the capitalist class was eliminated, the next target of the CCP was the new middle class. In the mid-1950s, Western-trained Chinese intellectuals, who believed in the ideals of democracy and individualism, became more and more critical of the new policies of the socialist state. They conveyed negative feelings toward the CCP and wanted to form a second political party during the Hundred Flowers Campaign in 1957. In the withdrawal phase, the CCP could not afford the luxury of tolerating an internal dissent group, for this would weaken national unity and give core countries an excuse to intensify their hostilities toward China. Hence the CCP quickly cracked down on the dissenting intellectuals—they were labeled "rightists," were not allowed to publish their work or to make public appearances, and many were banished to remote regions to carry out "thought reform." Through this ideological hegemony, the CCP successfully mobilized the Chinese people to speak with one voice.

At the peak of core hostility during the Vietnam War in the mid-1960s, socialist China further radicalized its policy of mobilizing support from the masses. By that time, however, almost all the old classes (foreign capitalists, landlords, rich peasants, bourgeoisie, and the new middle class) had been weakened or eliminated. So which class would become the new target of attack in order to sustain mass mobilization? The Maoists in the Cultural Revolution found that the state bureaucrats had emerged as a new exploiting class in China. This new class enjoyed privileges such as high salaries, special housing, recreation homes, frequent vacation trips, and access to Western consumer goods. Furthermore, this new class was in the process of passing these advantages to their offspring. In order to expose these bureaucratic privileges and abuses, the Maoists mobilized the masses through a series of violent class struggles during the Cultural Revolution. There was also a destratification experiment, and the masses were encouraged to promote their class interests at the expense of those of the bureaucrats. As a result, large numbers of bureaucrats were sent to the countryside to be "reeducated" through farm labor. Recruitment into the Communist party, into the universities, and into the top management stratum of the factories was based on social class origins and political commitment rather than on technical expertise and credentials.

In sum, core hostilities and withdrawal from the capitalist world-economy led China to pursue a radical mobilization policy. In order to arouse uninterrupted enthusiasm from the masses, socialist China put forward an egalitarian destratification policy, eliminating the interests of all classes except those of the peasants and workers (see Table 10.1). But this mass mobilization policy

Table 10.1 China's Class Structure and the Capitalist World-Economy

Withdrawal Phase	Policy	Target Class (to eliminate/weaken)
	Core hostilities	foreign capitalist
	Land reforms	landlord
	Collectivization and communes	rich peasant
	Nationalization of industry	bourgeoisie
	Hundred Flowers Campaign	new middle class
	The Cultural Revolution	bureaucrat
Reintegration Phase	Policy	Target Class (to create/strengthen)
	Open door policy— special economic zones, joint ventures	foreign capitalist
	Decollectivization, self-responsibility system	rich peasant
	Urban reforms— reintroduction of the market, company responsibility system	bourgeoisie
	Elite education, intellectuals as workers	new middle class
	Separation of party and state, professionalization	bureaucrat

could not be continued indefinitely. After a few decades of socialist rule, China dropped its radical policies and began the second phase of socialist development to reenter the capitalist world-economy.

The Second Phase:
Reintegration into the Capitalist World-Economy

What explains China's reentry into the capitalist world-economy? By the late 1970s, the capitalist core states had gradually lowered their hostilities toward socialist China because they realized that it was futile to overthrow the socialist regime by military means. Moreover, it was to the advantage of the core states to lure China back into the capitalist world-economy. Since the late 1960s, the world-economy had reached a downward phase, and many core states found it difficult to maintain a growing GNP. For these reasons the core states had turned to China, as well as to other socialist states, for a stimulus to their economic growth. The core states could make use of China's cheap labor force, abundant raw materials, rich mineral resources, and huge consumer market.

It was also to China's advantage to be reintegrated into the capitalist world-economy. During the first decade of socialist rule, land reform and collectivization programs stimulated mass enthusiasm, leading to higher productivity and a larger output. But the techniques of mass mobilization had their economic limit. After several decades of withdrawal from the capitalist world-economy, mass enthusiasm gradually died down, work discipline relaxed, and productivity became stagnant. The Chinese economy had finally reached a plateau and could not be raised further except through technological investment. This situation necessitated greater contact with the more technologically advanced capitalist cores. Before China would be able to buy Western technology, it first needed either to borrow money from the World Bank or to sell products to the world-economy to earn the necessary foreign currency. This means that if China wanted to overcome its economic stagnation, it must reenter the capitalist world-economy.

This reentry process was facilitated by the passing away of the first generation of peasant revolutionaries. In the previous withdrawal phase, these peasant revolutionaries had pushed for radical mass mobilization policies. They were replaced by a whole new generation of career-minded bureaucrats who saw no necessity to be an enemy of the capitalist core states; they generally accepted the capitalist order and gave up the revolutionary aspirations of the Maoists. This new generation of bureaucrats has been labeled "economic reformers" by the core states.

Beginning in the late 1970s, socialist China adopted a new open-door policy to encourage the establishment of Sino-foreign joint ventures and wholly foreign-owned businesses in China. As Premier Zhao (1987, p. x) points out:

> In future we should enter the world economic arena more boldly, decide on correct strategies for export and import and for the use of foreign funds, and expand trade and our economic and technological cooperation with other countries, . . . we should make vigorous efforts to develop export-oriented industries and products that are competitive and can bring back quick and high economic returns. . . . Priority should be given to the import of advanced technology and key equipment, . . . it is necessary to consolidate and develop the pattern of opening to the outside world that has begun to take shape, with the open policy extending progressively from the special economic zones to coastal cities, then to coastal economic regions and finally to interior areas.

Through this open-door policy, the interests of foreign capitalists gradually reemerged in the Chinese economy.

In the 1980s, despite import restrictions, Western goods (e.g., television sets, refrigerators, bicycles) entered China on a massive scale to compete with Chinese products. Chinese enterprises were forced to produce cheaper and higher-quality goods in order to capture the domestic market. In addition, since China wanted to earn needed foreign currency through exports, its export products also had to be competitive in the capitalist world-economy. In order to make Chinese products competitive, the following restructuring of the Chinese economy was necessary.

In the countryside, the policy of communes was abandoned, and there are no more collectively owned farms. Instead, there is a new self-responsibility system by which each peasant family is given a plot of land to cultivate. The peasants are now responsible for their own gains and losses. If a peasant has a good harvest, it means a higher family income for the coming year. If the harvest is bad, the collective or the state will not subsidize or provide welfare for the peasant family. As a means of decollectivization, the self-responsibility policy is aimed at restoring the peasant family as a unit of production and at forcing the peasants to respond to market demands and prices so as to enhance farm productivity. Under this policy, rich peasants, who have large families, good political connections, and abundant resources, will get richer; poor peasants, who have small families, narrow social networks, and few resources, could fall even farther behind in socioeconomic status. Consequently, in the 1980s, we have begun to observe rapid social differentiation in the Chinese countryside.

In the cities, the economic reformers wanted to invigorate the inefficient industrial enterprises. They called for a reduction of central planning, a gradual expansion of the scope of market forces, and the setting up of collective and individual enterprises to replace some of the state enterprises. In addition, even in the state sector, party officials were warned not to interfere with the activities of the enterprise directors. Self-responsibility enterprise reform includes changes aimed at giving real management power to enterprise directors, who now have the authority to go to the market sector to buy the cheapest raw materials, to go to the bank to get the most favorable interest loan, to go the big cities to recruit the most qualified professional managers, to work with the labor unions to hire and fire workers, to enforce scientific management, and to set wages and bonuses. As such, even though the enterprises are still owned by the state, they have become independent units of production and are responsible for their own profits and losses. It is hoped that this new freedom for enterprise directors to make economic decisions will provide a new dynamism to transform aging, inefficient state enterprises into modern, profit-oriented corporations. The urban economic reforms mentioned above have, therefore, created a "bourgeois" class of enterprise directors whose sole function is to attain profit maximization in the market.

Side by side with these enterprise reforms is a policy to upgrade scientific and technocratic education in the universities. During this reintegration phase, college education has expanded very rapidly; there is a national competitive examination to recruit the brightest students to the elite universities. The new middle class (college professors, technicians, managers, lawyers, doctors) is now classified as a part of the working class by the CCP. Members of this new middle class have high status, good income, decent working conditions, and good foreign connections; some have even become important party officials and state administrators. Since the new middle class is allowed to form professional organizations, develop class consciousness, and participate in democratic movements, it has played an increasingly active role in China's politics. In fact, this new middle class almost succeeded in forcing the CCP to yield to its demands for democracy, freedom, and liberty in 1989.

All these economic and educational reforms naturally have required reforms in the political structure to facilitate implementation. The latest political reform, during the reintegration phase, was the separation of the CCP from the government. The previous practice of party officials concurrently holding many government posts is strongly discouraged, and party officials are warned not to interfere with state administration. Aging cadres of peasant/worker origins, who were not trained for this new Four Modernization era, have been replaced by young college-educated cadres. The economic reformers want the state administrators to have a command of professional expertise so that they can do their work competently.

The two social classes that were neglected by the economic reformers were the poor peasants and the unskilled workers. In the withdrawal phase, these two classes were recruited to be the main supporters of the radical socialist policies, and they were mobilized to attack other classes. However, in the reintegration phase, since the socialist state no longer needed to mobilize workers and peasants, they have been depoliticized. The state encouraged the masses to pursue private life-styles (romance, dancing, sports) and to strive for individual upward mobility (entering college, making profits).

The above discussion shows that reintegration into the capitalist world-economy has produced a new set of class relations in socialist China. Instead of egalitarianism and mass mobilization, the consequences of recent reforms are restratification and demobilization of the masses. On the one hand, the old social classes—such as foreign capitalists, rich peasants, capitalists, the new middle class, and bureaucrats—have reemerged and strengthened their class power. On the other hand, the peasants and workers are encouraged to pursue their individual mobility and family interests instead of articulating their interests through class action. During the reintegration phase, socialist China clearly wants to shift its social bases of support from a peasant-worker alliance to an alliance of foreign capitalist-rich peasantry-capitalist-new middle class in order to stimulate economic development and to compete with core states in the capitalist world-economy (see Table 10.1).

POWERS OF THE WORLD-SYSTEM PERSPECTIVE AT THE NATIONAL LEVEL

The world-system perspective is distinguished by its insistence on taking the whole world as the unit of analysis. Chapter 9 illustrated how this approach has contributed to an original line of research on the cyclical rhythms of global dynamics. However, the world-system perspective has been criticized for reification, and for its ahistorical and stratification analyses. In response to these criticisms, world-system researchers started a new line of empirical studies at the national level. Following the spirit of the world-system perspective, this new line of research still insists on an examination of the cyclical rhythms of the world-economy, but these national-level studies pay more attention to the intricate connections between global dynamics and national forces. In this chapter, the discussion of three empirical studies of Hong Kong, the United States, and socialist China have illustrated how this "national-level" world-system analysis works.

The Nature of the World-System

World-system analysis starts with an examination of the changing nature of the capitalist world-economy throughout the period under study. For example, the discussion on the Hong Kong case started with an examination of the changing nature of the world-economy in explaining the origins and the transformation of the Hong Kong industrialization process. In the 1950s, the postwar economic boom laid the foundation for the rise of Hong Kong industry. In the 1960s, the spread of protectionism and peripheral competition stimulated Hong Kong's economy to undergo diversification and technological innovation. And in the 1970s, the core's turning to Asia for financial investments prompted Hong Kong to become a world financial center.

In the case of the United States, the world-system perspective has shed new light on the structural transformation of the core economy. In order to remain competitive in the world market, the U.S. transnational corporations had to cut production costs and maximize productivity through deindustrialization (the relocation of labor-intensive industries to the periphery), reindustrialization (the recruitment of cheap immigrant labor from the periphery), or both. Before the 1980s, when the United States was still a hegemonic superpower, deindustrialization was the most effective way for TNCs to cut production costs. But by the early 1980s, after the United States had lost its hegemonic control of the world, and after the debt crisis had led to anti-Americanism, reindustrialization seemed to be a viable option.

In the case of socialist China, the world-system perspective has drawn the researcher's attention to an examination of the changing response of the core states to socialist China. In the early 1950s, there were intense core hostilities toward China. American soldiers were fighting the Chinese in Korea, and the United States had imposed a trade embargo against China. In the late 1970s, however, the core countries not only lowered their hostilities, they were willing to develop trade, investment, and diplomatic and military relationships with the CCP.

The Study of Cyclical Rhythms

Another typical approach of the world-system perspective is to trace the pattern of cyclical rhythms throughout the period under study. This cyclical approach led researchers to study Hong Kong's development in terms of a process of transformation from one phase to another, from an industrial state specializing in the export of cheap clothing to one producing high-quality goods and services, and then to a world financial center. In the case of the United States, deindustrialization speeded up during the recession in the early 1980s, and there was a massive laying-off of workers in the manufacturing sector in the Frostbelt. However, during the expansionary period in the mid-1980s, when there was a demand for low-cost, easily releasable workers, reindustrialization began with the recruitment of undocumented female workers in the Sunbelt. Through this cyclical trend of deindustrialization and reindustrialization, American workers were dislocated from unionized manufacturing industries to nonunionized ascending and descending industries, a change that strengthened the power of the transnational corporations at the expense of the American working class. Socialist China also went through a cyclical pattern from the withdrawal phase to the reintegration phase, as a result of an intensification and then a lowering of core hostilities toward that country.

Global Dynamics and National Forces

Unlike global-level studies, national-level studies are inclined to highlight the intricate interactions between global dynamics and national forces such as classes, ethnic tensions, and state policies. In stressing the need to follow the historical process of how global dynamics affected the Hong Kong economy, the world-system perspective leads the researcher to explore the shaping of Hong Kong class and ethnic relations by global dynamics. For instance, the mentality of fleeing from communism explains the lack of capital versus labor conflict and the absence of Chinese capitalist versus British ruling class struggle in the 1950s. The intrusion of foreign financial capitalists into the Hong Kong economy in the late 1970s helps to explain the rise of intraclass struggle between the British financial capitalists and the Chinese industrial capitalists for control over Hong Kong state policy.

In the case of the United States, it has been pointed out that global dynamics have strongly affected class relations, state policy, and ethnic relations. Deindustrialization and reindustrialization have restructured the contour of class struggle in the United States, leading to the weakening of organized labor in the manufacturing industries and the revival of sweatshop production through the practice of subcontracting. To assist reindustrialization, some municipal and state governments have established inner-city enterprise zones to attract business investment. National and ethnic relations, too, have been affected. Nationalism was on the rise in the 1980s because U.S. workers blamed foreign imports for their depressed economic situation, and racism was also intensified because many white workers accused immigrants of taking away their jobs.

In the case of socialist China, the researchers argued that it went through a phase of withdrawal from the capitalist world-economy, and that it pursued a radical destratification policy in order to mobilize the masses to withstand foreign invasion. However, after the core hostilities had subsided, socialist China reentered the capitalist world-economy, restratified the society, and shifted its social basis of support from a peasant-worker alliance to an alliance of foreign capitalist-rich peasantry-capitalist-new middle class in order to stimulate economic development and to compete with the core states in the capitalist world-economy.

In summary, it may be helpful to point out similarities and differences between the new dependency studies and world-system studies at the national-level. These two kinds of studies are similar with respect to their focus on the interaction between external and internal dynamics. However, they are different with respect to the scope of their research and their treatment of the direction of development. Compared to the new dependency studies, which focus mostly on the peripheries, the world-system studies have a much wider scope of research—they examine the peripheries as well as the cores and the semiperipheries. And unlike the new dependency studies, which assume that Third World countries cannot completely break out of the situation of dependency, the world-system studies postulate that under certain conditions it is possible to have mobility in the world-economy. Thus they explain that Hong Kong and China could escape peripheral status, while the United States could lose its hegemonic status in the capitalist world-economy.

CHAPTER 11

Conclusion

Over the past four decades, the field of development has been dominated by the three different schools of research discussed in this volume: the modernization school, the dependency school, and the world-system school. These three schools rose up under different historical contexts and were influenced by different theoretical traditions; their empirical studies have been informed by different theoretical assumptions. Thus these schools have offered different solutions to the problems attached to Third World development. However, as I have argued in this book, the three schools themselves have had a common pattern of development—after each came under attack by other schools, it modified its basic assumptions and initiated a new research agenda in response to the arguments of its critics.

The modernization school emerged in the 1950s, when the United States became the superpower of the world. American social scientists were called upon to develop a program for the promotion of modernization in the newly independent Third World countries. Heavily influenced by the evolutionary theory, American social scientists conceptualized modernization as a phased, irreversible, progressive, lengthy process that moves in the direction of the American model. Strongly influenced by Parsons's functionalist theory, they looked upon modernity as incompatible with tradition. Subsequently, American social scientists proposed that Third World countries should copy American values, rely on

U.S. loans and aid, and transform their traditional institutions. However, when the modernization school came under attack in the late 1960s, its researchers modified their basic assumptions. The latest theme of the modernization school is that tradition can play a beneficial role in development and Third World countries can pursue their own paths of development. These recent modifications of the modernization school have started a new direction of research referred to here as the "new modernization studies."

Although the modernization school was an American product, the dependency school had its roots in the Third World. Specifically, it arose as a response to the failure of the ECLA program and the crisis of orthodox Marxism in Latin American countries in the early 1960s. Drawing heavily upon radical ECLA and neo-Marxist theories, the dependency school conceptualized the linkages between Western and Third World countries as a set of externally imposed, exploitative, dependent, economic relationships incompatible with development. Thus the dependency school advocated that Third World countries should sever their linkages with Western countries in order to promote an autonomous, independent path of development. However, when the dependency school came under attack in the early 1970s, its researchers modified their basic assumptions. The latest assertions of the dependency school are as follows: Dependency is not just an economic but also a sociopolitical process; dependency is not just an external relationship but also a historically specific internal relationship; and development can occur side by side with dependency. These recent modifications in the dependency school started a new direction of research referred to in this volume as the "new dependency studies."

The world-system perspective is the latest school to emerge in the field of development. It offered a new orientation to the interpretation of major events in the 1970s, such as East Asian industrialization, the crisis of the socialist states, and the decline of the capitalist world-economy. Influenced first by the dependency school and then by the French Annales school, world-system researchers emphasized the need to examine the totality and the *longue duree*. The unit of analysis thus should be the world-economy, a historical system composed of three strata: the core, the semiperiphery, and the periphery. The world-system school contended that by the late twentieth century, the capitalist world-economy would reach a transitional stage at which real choices might be made to change the path of human history. However, when the world-system school came under attack in the late 1970s, its researchers modified some of their basic assumptions. In the modified version, the concept of the world-system is taken merely as a research tool rather than as a reified reality; studies are now conducted on both the world level and the national level; and class analysis is brought back in to supplement stratification analysis and the like. These modifications started a research trend referred to here as "world-system studies at the national level."

Although in this book I have reviewed the rise, development, and transformation of the three dominant schools of development, the volume should not be taken as a work on metatheory (see Skocpol's 1987 critique of Alford and Friedland, 1985). I do not profess to categorize all works in the development literature into three pigeonholes and to label each as a modernization, dependency, or world-system study. I am not interested in creating typologies and classifications about other people's theories on development. Instead, this book should be taken as an attempt to link development theories with substantive research. My goal is to show how the changes in the theoretical assumptions of the three dominant schools of development have led to a corresponding shift in research orientations in the development literature from the 1950s to the 1980s.

KUHN'S SCIENTIFIC REVOLUTION

What explains the changes in theoretical perspectives and research orientations that have taken place in development over the past four decades? Drawing upon his study of the history of natural sciences, Kuhn (1962) presents a model of scientific revolution that explains how a scientific discipline comes into existence and how it may change. According to Kuhn's model, a scientific

discipline grows through a process of revolutionary transformation rather than through a linear accumulation of verified hypotheses.

Kuhn asserts that a scientific discipline begins with the setting
up of a *paradigm*—a common frame of reference, a definition of the
situation, or a shared worldview that provides a basic focus of
orientation. The consolidation of the paradigm occurs as the discipline acquires a recognized place in the scientific community and
curriculum, develops its own journals, writes its own textbooks,
and informs a set of classical studies. The classical studies serve the
function of shaping a discipline's sense of where its problems lie,
what its appropriate tools and methods are, and the kinds of
solution for which it might settle (Friedrichs 1970). A discipline
usually expands rapidly after the establishment of a paradigm
because its researchers can easily follow the research direction of
the classical studies.

Anomalies of major dimensions that cannot be explained by the
paradigm then begin to appear. When the burden of the anomalies
grows too great, a *scientific revolution* occurs. A new paradigm
eventually emerges, offering a competing gestalt that redefines
crucial problems, introduces new methods, rewrites textbooks,
and establishes unique new standards for solutions. At the height
of the "paradigm war," advocates of alternative paradigms talk
past one another, because there is no fully institutionalized framework of basic assumptions that both can accept. Since science
cannot proceed without a paradigm (for by Kuhn's definition it
represents a scientist's fundamental frame of reference), the destruction of the old paradigm must await the birth of the new
paradigm, and the two activities must occur simultaneously
(Friedrichs 1970).

To a certain extent, Kuhn's model can be applied to the shift of
theoretical perspectives in the literature of development. In the
1950s, the modernization school emerged as the paradigm for the
study of Third World development. The classical studies by Levy,
McClelland, Inkeless, Rostow, and Bellah set the agenda for researchers in the field of development, namely, how tradition can
be displaced in order to help Third World countries to follow the
U.S. path of modernization. In the 1960s, when the modernization

school failed to explain what had happened in Latin America, a new dependency school rose to offer a totally different perspective. The classical studies by Dos Santos, Frank, Baran, and the *Monthly Review* researchers formulated a completely new research agenda to examine the harmful impact of foreign domination. No doubt the "paradigm war" in the late 1960s was intense. With persistent onslaught of criticism and outright demolition, researchers from the modernization and dependency schools frequently talked past one another.

However, Kuhn's model fails to explain other activities in the field of development. First, it overlooks the tenacity of the early paradigm. Although the modernization school, sensing a loss of persuasiveness, retreated in the late 1960s, although the dependency school was popular among radical graduate students and young professors in the late 1960s, and although the world-system school attracted a new generation of researchers in the mid-1970s, these changes were insufficient to bring about the demise of the modernization perspective. In the American academic community, tenured professors could not be fired, research projects would not be denied funding, and professional journals would not be closed down just because their paradigm was unpopular among radical researchers. Of course, the modernization school no longer served as a paradigm for the field of development after the late 1960s, but the dependency school and the world-system school have also failed to provide a convincing paradigm to take the place of the modernization school.

In addition, Kuhn's model underestimates the degree to which a paradigm can modify itself. For Kuhn, normal science is rigid—it does not readily countenance threats to its foundation, and provides only ad hoc modifications to cover the anomalies that it cannot explain. Kuhn's characterization of the rigidity of normal science is quite correct during the initial encounter between a new challenging paradigm and the old paradigm. At the height of the "paradigm wars," researchers talk past one another and are unwilling to accept the arguments of their critics. Nevertheless, after the emotional debates have died down, researchers do accept criticism, drop simplistic basic assumptions, modify their old theoretical frameworks, and carry out new research agendas. For ex-

ample, although the classical modernization studies explored how
modernity can displace tradition, the new modernization studies
center upon the theme of how tradition has promoted modernization. Although the classical dependency studies stressed underdevelopment and Third World bankruptcy, the new dependency
studies address how development can occur despite the dependency situation. And although world-system studies have contributed by providing a world-level analysis of cyclical trends and
long waves, recent world-system research has shown that the
world-system perspective is quite useful for "micro" national,
regional, and local analyses.

Furthermore, Kuhn's model ignores the possibility of a *pluralistic* academic discipline. Kuhn assumes that the new paradigm
must replace the old one, otherwise the scientists will not have a
fundamental frame of reference. This assertion may be true for
disciplines in the physical sciences, but it is not totally appropriate
for the field of development in social science. Since the mid-1970s,
the field of development has been characterized by the coexistence
of the modernization, dependency, and world-system perspectives. However, none of these perspectives has been able to turn
itself into a paradigm by completely eliminating the other perspectives. On the contrary, the coexistence of several competing perspectives has furnished a fertile intellectual environment for
substantive research in the field of development in the 1980s.

DEVELOPMENT THEORIES IN THE 1990s

Given the current pluralism in the development literature, what
does the future hold for theories of development? Many researchers observe that the field of development is moving in the direction
of synthesis. For example, Evans and Stephens (1988, p. 759) have
dubbed this synthesis the "new comparative political economy."
Portes (1980, p. 224) notes that there is a possible convergence
between the "culturalist" modernization perspective and the
"structuralist" dependency and world-system perspectives. And
Hermassi (1978, p. 255) suggests that "disciplined eclecticism" is a

better guide than overreliance on paradigmatic thinking by the "liberal, managerial, neo-Marxist" approaches to development.

The chapters of this volume also point in the direction of convergence. It seems that the three dominant schools of development have shared the following traits in the 1980s. First, each has seen a call to bring history back in. Instead of focusing on the ideal types of modernity and tradition, instead of outlining the universal pattern of dependency, and instead of constructing the totality of the world-system, researchers are now more interested in understanding historically specific concrete cases. They probe into research problems that require detailed historical analyses, such as why the Islam Revolution occurred in Iran, how the triple alliance broke down in Brazil in the 1980s, and what caused the economic miracle of Hong Kong over the past four decades.

Second, the new studies attempt to provide a *multi-institutional* analysis. Instead of just relying on one variable such as achievement motivation, instead of treating dependency merely as an economic process, and instead of stressing the overwhelming constraints of the world-system, researchers are now examining the complex interplay among different institutions, that is, how the family, religion, ethnic groups, classes, the state, social movements, transnational corporations, the interstate system, and the world-economy interact to shape the historical development of Third World countries. Subsequently, the new studies have become more sophisticated than the old ones, and they have moved beyond the simplistic argument of whether external factors are more important than internal factors.

Third, the question of whether development is beneficial or harmful is left open. Instead of portraying modernization as a progressive process, and instead of emphasizing the damaging effects of dependency, recent studies indicate that development has *both* beneficial and harmful effects. Researchers now need to examine each concrete case against its own historical conjuncture before deciding whether development has a positive or negative effect and on which segment of the population. For example, when Japan modernized its economy, Japanese workers turned to folk religion for refuge. When China withdrew from the capitalist world-economy, the interests of the Chinese peasants and workers were developed at the expense of the interests of the Chinese capitalists and bureaucrats.

In sum, there appears to be a trend toward convergence in the literature of development. The new studies should be more satisfactory than their predecessors because they generally do less violence to historical realities. They also seem to provide a more sophisticated, multi-institutional analysis to explain the major historical events that took place in the capitalist world-economy in the 1980s.

However, the trend toward convergence is far from complete. The literature seems to be moving toward a kind of selective convergence rather than toward a wholesale convergence. Despite sharing a few similar traits, the three dominant schools of development still maintain their individual features and "trademarks," as indicated by their names. The modernization school still focuses on the relationship between modernity and tradition, although now more on the positive role of tradition than before. The dependency school still analyzes the linkages between dependency and development, although now more on the positive side of development than before. And the world-system school still examines the secular and the cyclical trends of the world-economy and their impact, although now it is more concerned with microregions than before. It seems clear that the modernization, dependency, and world-system schools will not disappear; rather, they will all be very active in generating a variety of fruitful research products in the 1990s.

References

Alford, Robert R. and Roger Friedland. 1985. *Powers of Theory: Capitalism, the State, and Democracy*. Cambridge: Cambridge University Press.

Almond, Gabriel. 1987. "The Development of Political Development." Pp. 437-490 in Myron Weiner and Samuel Huntington (eds.) *Understanding Political Development*. Boston: Little, Brown.

Amin, Samir. 1971. *L'Afrique de l'Quest bloqueé*. Paris: de Minuit.

———. 1976. *Unequal Development: An Essay on the Social Formation of Peripheral Capitalism*. New York: Monthly Review Press.

Apter, David. 1987. *Rethinking Development: Modernization, Dependency, and Postmodern Politics*. Newbury Park, CA: Sage.

Arrighi, G., Terence Hopkins, and Immanuel Wallerstein. 1983. "Rethinking the Concepts of Class and Status-Group in a World-System Perspective." *Review* 6: 283-304.

———. 1986. "Dilemmas of Antisystemic Movements." *Social Research* 53: 185-206.

Bach, Robert L. 1982. "On the Holism of a World-System Perspective." Pp. 159-180 in Terence Hopkins and Immanuel Wallerstein (eds.) *World-System Analysis*. Beverly Hills, CA: Sage.

Banks, Arthur. 1973. *Cross Polity Time Series Data*. Binghamton, NY: Center for Comparative Political Research.

Banuazizi, Ali. 1987. "Social-Psychological Approach to Political Development." Pp. 281-316 in Myron Weiner and Samuel Huntington (eds.) *Understanding Political Development*. Boston: Little, Brown.

Baran, Paul. 1957. *The Political Economy of Growth*. New York: Monthly Review Press.

Barrett, Richard E. and Martin K. Whyte. 1982. "Dependency Theory and Taiwan: Analysis of a Deviant Case." *American Journal of Sociology* 87: 1064-1089.

Bellah, Robert N. 1957. *Tokugawa Religion*. Boston: Beacon.

Bendix, Reinhard. 1967. "Tradition and Modernity Reconsidered." *Comparative Studies in Society and History* 9: 292-346.

Bergesen, Albert. 1983. *The Crises of the Capitalist World-Economy*. Beverly Hills, CA: Sage.

Bergesen, Albert and Ronald Schoenberg. 1980. "Long Waves of Colonial Expansion and Contraction, 1415-1969." Pp. 231-277 in Albert Bergesen (ed.) *Studies of the Modern World-System*. New York: Academic Press.

Bergquist, Charles. 1984. *Labor in the Capitalist World-Economy*. Beverly Hills, CA: Sage.

Binder, Leonard et al. 1971. *Crises and Sequences in Political Development*. Princeton, NJ: Princeton University Press.

Blomstrom, Magnus and Bjorn Hettne. 1984. *Development Theory in Transition: The Dependency Debate and Beyond—Third World Responses*. London: Zed.

Bluestone, Barry. 1984. "Is Deindustrialization a Myth? Capital Mobility Versus Absorption Capacity in the U.S. Economy." *Annals of American Academy of Political and Social Science* 475: 39-51.

Bodenheimer, S. 1970a. "Dependency and Imperialism: The Roots of Latin American Underdevelopment." *North American Congress in Latin America (NACLA) Newsletter* 4 (3): 18-27.

———. 1970b. "The Ideology of Developmentalism." *Berkeley Journal of Sociology* 15: 95-137.

Brenner, Robert. 1977. "The Origins of Capitalist Development: A Critique of Neo-Smithian Marxism." *New Left Review* 104: 25-92.

Brown, E.H. Phelps. 1973. "The Hong Kong Economy: Achievements and Prospects." Pp. 1-20 in Keith Hopkins (ed.) *Hong Kong: The Industrial Colony*. Hong Kong: Oxford University Press.

Burris, Val. 1985. "Reindustrialization: Myth or Reality." *Insurgent Sociologist* 13: 105-112.

Cardoso, Fernando H. 1973. "Associated-Dependent Development: Theoretical and Practical Implications." Pp. 142-176 in Alfred Stephen (ed.) *Authoritarian Brazil*. New Haven, CT: Yale University Press.

———. 1977. "The Consumption of Dependency Theory in the United States." *Latin American Research Review* 12: 7-24.

Cardoso, Fernando H. and Enzo Faletto. 1979. *Dependency and Development in Latin America*. Berkeley: University of California Press.

Chase-Dunn, Christopher. 1981. "Interstate System and Capitalist World- Economy: One Logic or Two?" *International Studies Quarterly* 25: 19-42.

———. 1982a. "A World-System Perspective on Dependency and Development in Latin America." *Latin American Research Review* 17: 166-171.

———. 1982b. *Socialist States in the World-System*. Beverly Hills, CA: Sage.

Chilcote, Ronald, ed. 1982. *Dependency and Marxism: Toward a Resolution of the Debate*. Boulder, CO: Westview.

Chilcote, Ronald and Joel Edelstein. 1974. *Latin America: The Struggle with Dependency and Beyond*. New York: John Wiley.

Chinweizu. 1985. "Debt Trap Peonage." *Monthly Review* 37 (November): 21-35.

Chirot, Daniel. 1976. *Social Change in a Peripheral Society: The Creation of a Balkan Colony*. New York: Academic Press.

———. 1981. "Changing Fashions in the Study of the Social Causes of Economic and Political Change." Pp. 259-282 in James Short (ed.) *The State of Sociology*. Beverly Hills, CA: Sage.

———. 1986. *Social Change in the Modern Era*. Orlando, FL: Harcourt Brace Jovanovich.

Chirot, Daniel and Thomas D. Hall. 1982. "World-System Theory." *Annual Review of Sociology* 8: 81-106.

Chung, S. Y. 1983. "Hong Kong: A Springboard into Asia." *Hong Kong Manager* 19: 17-21.

Cockcroft, James. 1982. "Mexican Migration, Crisis, and the Internationalization of Labor Struggle." *Contemporary Marxism* 5: 48-61.

Coleman, James S. 1965. *Education and Political Development.* Princeton, NJ: Princeton University Press.

———. 1968. "Modernization: Political Aspects." Pp. 395-402 in David L. Sills (ed.) *International Encyclopedia of the Social Sciences* (Vol. 10). New York: Macmillan.

Comte, A. 1964. "The Progress of Civilization Through Three States." Pp. 14-19 in Amitai Etzioni and Eva Etzioni (eds.) *Social Change.* New York: Basic Books.

Davis, Winston. 1987. "Religion and Development: Weber and East Asia Experience." Pp. 221-279 in Myron Weiner and Samuel Huntington (eds.) *Understanding Political Development.* Boston: Little, Brown.

Dixon, Marlene. 1979. "The Transition to Socialism as a World Process." *Synthesis* 3: 28-30.

Dos Santos, Theotonio. 1971. "The Structure of Dependence." Pp. 225-236 in K. T. Kan and Donald C. Hodges (eds.) *Readings in the U.S. Imperialism.* Boston: Extending Horizons.

———. 1973. "The Crisis of Development Theory and the Problem of Dependence in Latin America." Pp. 57-80 in H. Bernstein (ed.) *Underdevelopment and Development.* Harmondsworth: Penguin.

Dutt, Romesh. 1901. *The Economic History of India.* London.

Eisenstadt, S. N. 1974. "Studies of Modernization and Sociological Theory." *History and Theory* 13: 225-252.

Evans, Peter B. 1983. "State, Local and Multinational Capital in Brazil: Prospects for the Stability of the 'Triple Alliance' in the Eighties." Pp. 139-168 in Diana Tussie (ed.) *Latin America in the World-Economy: New Perspectives.* New York: St. Martin's.

Evans, Peter, Dietrich Rueschemeyer, and Evelyne H. Stephens. 1985. *State Versus Markets in the World-System.* Beverly Hills, CA: Sage.

Evans, Peter and John D. Stephens. 1988. "Development and the World Economy." Pp. 739-773 in Neil Smelser (ed.) *Handbook of Sociology.* Newbury Park, CA: Sage.

Fagen, Richard R. 1983. "Theories of Development: The Question of Class Struggle." *Monthly Review* 35: 13-24.

Fernandez-Kelly, M. Patricia. 1987. "Economic Restructuring in the United States: The Case of Hispanic Women in Garment and Electronic Industries in Southern California." Paper presented at the annual meeting of the American Sociological Association, Chicago.

Fernandez-Kelly, M. Patricia and Anna M. Garcia. 1985. "The Making of an Underground Economy: Hispanic Women, Home Work, and the Advanced Capitalist State." *Urban Anthropology* 14: 59-85.

Fitzgerald, Frank T. 1981. "Sociologies of Development." *Journal of Contemporary Asia* 11: 5-18.

Foster-Carter, Aiden. 1973. "Neo-Marxist Approaches to Development and Underdevelopment." *Journal of Contemporary Asia* 3: 7-33.

Frank, Andre Gunder. 1967. *Capitalism and Underdevelopment in Latin America.* New York: Monthly Review Press.

———. 1969. *Latin America: Underdevelopment or Revolution.* New York: Monthly Review Press.

Friedman, Edward. 1982. *Ascent and Decline in the World-System.* Beverly Hills, CA: Sage.

Friedrichs, Robert W. 1970. *A Sociology of Sociology.* New York: Free Press.

Frobel, F., J. Heinrichs, and O. Kreyo. 1979. *The New International Division of Labor.* New York: Cambridge University Press.

Furtado, Celso, ed. 1968. *Brasil: Temtos Modernos.* Rio de Janeiro: Editora Paz e Terra.

Garst, Daniel. 1985. "Wallerstein and His Critics." *Theory and Society* 14: 445-468.

Gibson, R. W. 1984. "Asia's Little Dragon Spews Economic Life." *Los Angeles Times* (July 15): Part V.

Gold, Thomas B. 1986. *State and Society in the Taiwan Miracle.* New York: M. E. Sharpe.

Goldfrank, Walter L., ed. 1979. *The World-System of Capitalism: Past and Present.* Beverly Hills, CA: Sage.

Gulalp, Haldun. 1981. "Frank and Wallerstein Revisited: A Contribution to Brenner's Critique." *Journal of Contemporary Asia* 11: 169-188.

Gusfield, Joseph R. 1967. "Tradition and Modernity: Misplaced Polarities in the Study of Social Change." *American Journal of Sociology* 72: 351-362.

Harris, Candee. 1984. "The Magnitude of Job Loss from Plant Closings and the Generation of Replacement Jobs." *Annals of the American Academy of Political and Social Science* 475: 15-27.

Hechter, Michael. 1975. *Internal Colonialism: The Celtic Fringe in British National Development 1536-1966.* London: Routledge & Kegan Paul.

Henderson, Jeffrey and Manuel Castells. 1987. *Global Restructuring and Territorial Development.* Newbury Park, CA: Sage.

Henige, D. 1970. *Colonial Governors.* Madison: University of Wisconsin Press.

Hermassi, Elbaki. 1978. "Changing Patterns in Research on the Third World." *Annual Review of Sociology* 4: 239-257.

Hettne, B. and P. Wallensteen, eds. 1978. "Emerging Trends in Development Theory." SAREC Report R3.

Hook, Brian. 1983. "The Government of Hong Kong: Change Within Tradition." *China Quarterly* 95: 491-512.

Hopkins, Terence and Immanuel Wallerstein. 1980. *Process of the World-System.* Beverly Hills, CA: Sage.

———. 1982. *World-System Analysis.* Beverly Hills, CA: Sage.

Howe, Gary N. and Alan M. Sica. 1980. "Political Economy, Imperialism, and the Problem of World-System Theory." *Current Perspectives in Social Theory* 1: 235-286.

Huntington, Samuel. 1976. "The Change to Change: Modernization, Development, and Politics." Pp. 25-61 in Cyril E. Black (ed.) *Comparative Modernization: A Reader.* New York: Free Press.

———. 1984. "Will More Countries Become Democratic?" *Political Science Quarterly* 99: 193-218.

Inkeless, Alex. 1964. "Making Men Modern: On the Causes and Consequences of Individual Change in Six Developing Countries." Pp. 342-361 in Amitai Etzioni and Eva Etzioni (eds.) *Social Change.* New York: Basic Books.

Kahn, Herman. 1984. "The Confucian Ethic and Economic Growth." Pp. 78-80 in Mitchell A. Seligson (ed.) *The Gap Between Rich and Poor: Contending Perspectives on the Political Economy of Development.* Boulder, CO: Westview.

Kaplan, Barbara H. 1978. *Social Change in the Capitalist World-Economy.* Beverly Hills, CA: Sage.

———. 1980. "On World Systems Theory." *Current Perspectives in Social Theory* 1: 3-5.

Kaye, Harvey J. 1979. "Totality: Its Application to Historical and Social Analysis by Wallerstein and Genovese." *Historical Reflections* 6: 405-419.

———. 1983. "History and Social Theory: Notes on the Contribution of British Marxist Historiography to Our Understanding of Class." *Canadian Review of Sociology and Anthropology* 20: 167-192.

Kendall, Walter. 1975. *The Labor Movement in Europe*. London: A. Lane.

Koo, Hagen. 1984. "World Systems, Class, and State in Third World Development." *Sociological Perspectives* 27: 33-52.

———. 1987. "The Interplay of State, Social Class, and World System in East Asian Development: The Cases of South Korea and Taiwan." Pp. 165-180 in Frederic C. Deyo (ed.) *The Political Economy of the East Asian Industrialization*. Ithaca, NY: Cornell University Press.

Kraus, R. C. 1979. "Withdrawing from the World-System: Self-Reliance and Class Structure in China." Pp. 237-59 in Walter L. Goldfrank (ed.) *The World-System of Capitalism: Past and Present*. Beverly Hills, CA: Sage.

Kuhn, Thomas. 1962. *The Structure of Scientific Revolutions*. Chicago: University of Chicago Press.

Laclau, Ernesto. 1977. *Politics and Ideology in Marxist Theory*. London: New Left.

Landsberg, Martin. 1979. "Export-Led Industrialization in the Third World: Manufacturing Imperialism." *Review of Radical Political Economics* 11: 50-63.

LaPalombara, Joseph. 1963. *Bureaucracy and Political Development*. Princeton, NJ: Princeton University Press.

LaPalombara, Joseph and Myron Weiner, eds. 1966. *Political Parties and Political Development*. Princeton, NJ: Princeton University Press.

Lauer, Robert H. 1971. "The Scientific Legitimation of Fallacy: Neutralizing Social Change Theory." *American Sociological Review* 36: 881-889.

Lembcke, Jerry and Martin Hart-Landsberg. 1985. "Reindustrialization and the Logic of Class Politics in the Late Twentieth Century America." *Insurgent Sociologist* 33: 7-22.

Levy, Marion J., Jr. 1967. "Social Patterns (Structures) and Problems of Modernization." Pp. 189-208 in Wilbert Moore and Robert M. Cook (eds.) *Readings on Social Change*. Englewood Cliffs, NJ: Prentice-Hall.

Lippit, Victor. 1978. "The Development of Underdevelopment of China." *Modern China* 4: 251-328.

Lipset, S. M. 1963. "Economic Development and Democracy." Pp. 27-63 in S. M. Lipset, *Political Man*. Garden City, NY: Anchor.

MacEwan, Arthur. 1986. "Latin America: Why Not Default." *Monthly Review* 38 (September): 1-13.

Magdoff, Harry. 1986. "Third World Debt: Past and Present." *Monthly Review* 37 (February): 1-10.

McClelland, David. 1964. "Business Drive and National Achievement." Pp. 165-178 in Amitai Etzioni and Eva Etzioni (eds.) *Social Change*. New York: Basic Books.

Moore, Barrington. 1966. *The Social Origins of Dictatorship and Democracy*. Harmondsworth: Penguin.

Moore, Wilbert. 1979. *World Modernization: The Limit of Convergence*. New York: Elsevier.

Morales, Rebecca. 1983. "Transitional Labor: Undocumented Workers in the Los Angeles Automobile Industry." *International Migration Review* 17: 570-596.

Morishima, Michio. 1982. *Why Has Japan Succeeded? Western Technology and the Japanese Ethos.* Cambridge: Cambridge University Press.

Moulder, Frances V. 1977. *Japan, China, and the Modern World Economy.* Cambridge: Cambridge University Press.

Nash, June. 1981. "Ethnographic Aspects of the World Capitalist System." *Annual Review of Anthropology* 10: 393-423.

Nisbet, Robert. 1969. *Social Change and History: Aspects of the Western Theory of Development.* New York: Oxford University Press.

O'Brien, Philip. 1975. "A Critique of Latin American Theories of Dependency." Pp. 7-27 in Ivar Oxaal et al. (eds.) *Beyond the Sociology of Development: Economy and Society in Latin America and Africa.* London: Routledge & Kegan Paul.

O'Donnell, Guillermo. 1978. "Reflections on the Pattern of Change in the Bureaucratic-Authoritarian State." *Latin American Review* 8: 3-38.

Palat, Ravi. 1988. "A Rejoinder to Subrahmanyam." *Review* 12: 149-154.

Palma, Gabriel. 1978. "Dependency: A Formal Theory of Underdevelopment or a Methodology for the Analysis of Concrete Situations of Underdevelopment." *World Development* 6: 881-894.

Parsons, Talcott. 1951. *The Social System.* Glencoe, IL: Free Press.

Parsons, Talcott and Edward Shils. 1951. *Toward a General Theory of Action.* Cambridge, MA: Harvard University Press.

Petras, James. 1978. *Critical Perspectives on Imperialism and Social Class in the Third World.* New York: Monthly Review Press.

———. 1982. "Dependency and World-System Theory: A Critique and New Directions." Pp. 148-155 in Ronald H. Chilcote (ed.) *Dependency and Marxism: Toward a Resolution of the Debate.* Boulder, CO: Westview.

Polanyi, Karl. 1944. *The Great Transformation.* Boston: Beacon.

Pool, John C. and Stephen C. Stamos. 1985. "The Uneasy Calm: Third World Debt—The Case of Mexico." *Monthly Review* 36: 7-19.

Portes, Alejandro. 1976. "On the Sociology of National Development: Theories and Issues." *American Journal of Sociology* 82: 55-85.

———. 1980. "Convergencies Between Conflicting Theoretical Perspectives in National Development." Pp. 220-227 in Herbert Blalock (ed.) *Sociological Theory and Research.* New York: Free Press.

Portes, A. and J. Walton. 1982. *Labor, Class, and the International System.* New York: Aberdeen.

Pratt, Raymond B. 1973. "The Underdeveloped Political Science of Development." *Studies in Comparative International Development* 8: 88-112.

Prebisch, R. 1950. *The Economic Development of Latin America and Its Principal Problems.* New York: United Nations.

Pye, Lucien W., ed. 1963. *Communications and Political Development.* Princeton, NJ: Princeton University Press.

Pye, Lucien W. and Sidney Verba, eds. 1965. *Political Culture and Political Development.* Princeton, NJ: Princeton University Press.

Ragin, Charles and Daniel Chirot. 1984. "The World System of Immanuel Wallerstein: Sociology and Politics as History." Pp. 276-312 in Theda Skocpol (ed.) *Vision and Method in Historical Sociology.* Cambridge: Cambridge University Press.

Redfield, Robert. 1965. *Peasant Society and Culture.* Chicago: University of Chicago Press.

Research Working Group on World Labor (RWG). 1986. "Global Patterns of Labor Movements in Historical Perspectives." *Review* 10: 137-155.

Rhodes, Robert I. 1968. "The Disguised Conservatism in Evolutionary Development Theory." *Science and Society* 32: 383-412.

Rostow, W. W. 1964. "The Takeoff into Self-Sustained Growth." Pp. 285-300 in Amitai Etzioni and Eva Etzioni (eds.) *Social Change*. New York: Basic Books.

Roy, William G. 1984. "Class Conflict and Social Change in Historical Perspective." *Annual Review of Sociology* 10: 483-506.

Rubinson, Richard. 1981. *Dynamics of World Development*. Beverly Hills, CA: Sage.

Seers, Dudley. 1981. *Dependency Theory: A Critical Reassessment*. London: Frances Printer.

Skocpol, Theda. 1977. "Wallerstein's World Capitalist System: A Theoretical and Historical Critique." *American Journal of Sociology* 82: 1075-1090.

————. 1987. "The Dead End of Metatheory." *Contemporary Sociology* 16: 10-12.

Smelser, Neil. 1964. "Toward a Theory of Modernization." Pp. 268-284 in Amitai Etzioni and Eva Etzioni (eds.) *Social Change*. New York: Basic Books.

Smith, Sheila. 1982. "Class Analysis Versus World-Systems: Critique of Samir Amin's Typology of Under-development." *Journal of Contemporary Asia* 12: 7-18.

So, Alvin Y. 1981. "Developing Inside the Capitalist World-Economy: A Study of the Japanese and Chinese Silk Industry." *Journal of Asian Culture* 5: 33-56.

————. 1986a. *The South China Silk District*. Albany: SUNY Press.

————. 1986b. "The Economic Success of Hong Kong: Insights from a World-System Perspective." *Sociological Perspectives* 29: 241-258.

————. 1988. "Shenzhen Special Economic Zone: China's Struggle for Independent Development." *Canadian Journal of Development Studies* 9: 313-323.

————. n.d. "The Deindustrialization and the Reindustrialization of the U.S." Unpublished manuscript, University of Hawaii, Department of Sociology.

So, Alvin Y. and Sungnam Cho. 1988. "China's Class Structure and the Capitalist World-System: The Impact of Withdrawal and Reintegration." Paper presented at the annual meeting of the American Sociological Association, Atlanta, August.

So, Alvin Y. and Muhammad Hikam. Forthcoming. " 'Class' in the Writings of Wallerstein and Thompson: Toward a Class Struggle Analysis." *Sociological Perspectives*.

Sweezy, Paul and Harry Magdoff. 1984. "The Two Faces of Third World Debt: A Fragile Financial Environment and Debt Enslavement." *Monthly Review* 35 (January): 1-10.

Thompson, E. P. 1978. "Eighteenth-Century English Society: Class Struggle Without Class?" *Social History* 3: 133-165.

————. 1984. "Class Consciousness." Pp. 114-142 in R. S. Neale (ed.) *History and Class*. New York: Blackwell.

Thompson, William R. 1983. *Contending Approaches to World-System Analysis*. Beverly Hills, CA: Sage.

Tipps, Dean C. 1976. "Modernization Theory and the Comparative Study of Societies: A Critical Perspective." Pp. 62-88 in Cyril E. Black (ed.) *Comparative Modernization: A Reader*. New York: Free Press.

Trimberger, Ellen Kay. 1979. "World Systems Analysis: The Problem of Unequal Development." *Theory and Society* 8: 101-126.

Wallerstein, Immanuel. 1964. *The Road to Independence: Ghana and the Ivory Coast*. The Hague: Mouton.

————. 1967. *Africa: The Politics of Unity*. New York: Random House.

————. 1976. *The Modern World System: Capitalist Agriculture and the Origins of the European World Economy in the Sixteenth Century*. New York: Academic Press.

————. 1977a. "How Do We Know Class Struggle When We See It?" *Insurgent Sociologist* 7: 104-106.

————. 1977b. "The Tasks of Historical Social Science." *Review* 1: 3-7.

————. 1978. "The Annales as Resistance." *Review* 1 (3/4): 5-7.

————. 1979a. *The Capitalist World-Economy*. New York: Cambridge University Press.

————. 1979b. "Dependence in an Interdependent World: The Limited Possibilities of Transformation Within the Capitalist World-Economy." Pp. 66-94 in Immanuel Wallerstein, *The Capitalist World-Economy*. New York: Cambridge University Press.

————. 1979c. "Fernand Braudel." Pp. 69-72 in *International Encyclopedia of the Social Sciences* (Vol. 18, Biographical Supplement). New York: Free Press.

————. 1979d. "Underdevelopment Phase-B: Effect of the Seventeenth-Century Stagnation on Core and Periphery of the European World-Economy." Pp. 73-84 in Walter L. Goldfrank (ed.) *The World-System of Capitalism: Past and Present*. Beverly Hills, CA: Sage.

————. 1982. "Fernand Braudel, Historian." *Radical History Review* 26: 105-119.

————. 1984. *The Politics of the Capitalist World-Economy*. Cambridge: Cambridge University Press.

————. 1986. "Braudel on Capitalism and the Market." *Monthly Review* 37 (February): 11-19.

————. 1987. "World-System Analysis." Pp. 309-324 in Anthony Giddens and Jonathan H. Turner (eds.) *Social Theory Today*. Stanford: Stanford University Press.

————. 1988a. "The Reception of Fernand Braudel in the United States." Grant proposal submitted to NEH.

————. 1988b. "Development: Lodestar or Illusion." *Economic and Political Weekly* 23 (39): 2017-2023.

Warren, Bill. 1973. "Imperialism and Capitalist Industrialization." *New Left Review* 81: 3-44.

Weaver, James and Marguerite Berger. 1984. "The Marxist Critique of Dependency Theory: An Introduction." Pp. 45-64 in Charles K. Wilber (ed.) *The Political Economy of Development and Underdevelopment*. New York: Random House.

Weber, Max. 1958. *The Protestant Ethic and the Spirit of Capitalism*. New York: Scribner.

Wong Siu-Lun. 1988. "The Applicability of Asian Family Values to Other Sociocultural Settings." Pp. 134-154 in Peter L. Berger and Hsin-Huang Michael Hsiao (eds.) *In Search of an East Asian Development Model*. New Brunswick, NJ: Transaction.

Worsley, Peter. 1982. "One World or Three? A Critique of the World-System Theory of Immanuel Wallerstein." Pp. 504-525 in David Held (ed.) *State and Societies*. New York: New York University Press.

Zeitlin, Maurice. 1984. *The Civil Wars in Chile (Or the Bourgeois Revolutions That Never Were)*. Princeton, NJ: Princeton University Press.

Zhao Ziyang. 1987. "Advance Along the Road of Socialism with Chinese Characteristics." *Beijing Review* 45: 1-27.

Index

About the Author

Alvin Y. So was born and raised in Hong Kong, and received his B.A. degree from the Chinese University of Hong Kong. He studied sociology at the University of California, Los Angeles, where he received his M.A. and Ph.D. degrees. From 1983 to 1984, he taught at the University of Hong Kong. He is now an Associate Professor at the University of Hawaii at Manoa, where he has taught a variety of courses, including Social Change and Development, Contemporary Sociological Theory, Theory of Social Conflict, People and Institutions of China, Seminar in Modern China, and Introduction to Sociology. He received a Regents' Medal for Excellence in Teaching from the University of Hawaii in 1989. His primary research interests are in the areas of Third World development, class theory, ethnic relation, China, and Hong Kong. He is the author of *The South China Silk District: Local Historical Transformation and World-System Theory* (SUNY Press, 1986) and has contributed articles to such journals as the *Annual Review of Sociology, The Insurgent Sociologist, Sociology and Social Research, Scandinavian Journal of Development Alternatives, Review, Journal of Ethnic Studies, Urban Education, National Journal of Bilingual Education, International Journal of Social Psychiatry,* and *Asian Profile.*

NOTES

NOTES

NOTES

NOTES

NOTES